D0287889

CURRENT TRENDS IN THEOLOGY

CURRENT TRENDS IN THEOLOGY

Edited by

DONALD J. WOLF, S.J.

and

JAMES V. SCHALL, S.J.

Garden City, New York

DOUBLEDAY & COMPANY, INC.

1965

Imprimi potest: Rev. John F. X. Connolly, S.J.

Nihil obstat: Rev. John R. Post, S.J.

Imprimatur: ✠ Most Rev. Vincent J. Hines, D.D.
Bishop of Norwich
November 17, 1964

Library of Congress Catalog Card Number 65–12362

Printed in the United States of America
First Edition

CONTENTS

INTRODUCTION

This book is intended for two types of people—those who have a commitment to the Catholic faith and those not of the Catholic faith who wish to understand better the meaning of the Catholic's commitment in today's world. We hope that what it contains and represents will make clearer to both groups the relevance of Catholicism to the many problems of our age.

No Catholic or non-Catholic today can be unaware of the spirit of life and growth of the Church, especially since the beginning of the Second Vatican Council. We can see new interest in the importance of Scripture and liturgy, and in the relation of Christian teaching to the intellectual and social problems of our day. It should be obvious that no Catholic can claim to have a mature faith if he ignores these developments. No non-Catholic can properly understand the Church in America and the world if he ignores these developments.

Yet it is difficult to reach these developments in accessible form. The wealth of theological research and exposition is too often unknown outside Catholic seminaries. The articles in this book are an attempt to bridge that gap. They form the material for a course—"Catholic Theology Confronts the Sixties"—presented Wednesday evenings during the fall semester, 1962, at the Newman Center of the University of California, Berkeley. Father Daniel O'Hanlon, S.J., professor of Fundamental Theology at the Jesuit Theologate, Alma College, in Los Gatos, arranged for the series in cooperation with Father Joseph Quinn, C.S.P., Director of Newman Hall.

All in all, the program has been successful. The response of the students was encouraging and the seminary professors expressed appreciation for the chance to describe their special fields to a wider audience. Three other series of lectures have been given—"The Bible: Salvation History," "The Meaning of Christ Today," and "The Church in the Modern World"—over a two-year period. We expect that this two-year sequence will be repeated in the future, to form a continuing and growing opportunity for Catholics and non-Catholics on the Berkeley campus to gain a contemporary context for an informed and educated understanding of the Catholic outlook.

This book then is for people who seek to know more about the Catholic faith. We hope that the material and bibliographies here can provide an incentive and a basis for study and discussion at other secular colleges and among all Catholics and non-Catholics of good will.

THOMAS BANCHOFF
Academic Chairman
Newman Hall
Berkeley, California

CURRENT TRENDS IN THEOLOGY

Chapter I

CATHOLIC THEOLOGY: A BRIEF HISTORY

by

Daniel J. O'Hanlon

What we hope to accomplish in this book is to give some idea of what is happening in Catholic theological work. For that reason its chapters will be mostly descriptive. They are not a series of disguised sermons. They are not even directly theological essays in the sense that their immediate purpose is to achieve an understanding of the realities grasped by Christian faith. Their purpose is something a step removed from actual theological work; they are meant to stand back and describe what is happening among Catholic theologians, to give an account of how their thoughts are moving, an account of the developments which are taking place among them. This means that the book can be read with profit by those who are far from being Catholic theologians; by those, in fact, who are not Catholics; even by those who are not Christians, or by those who do not believe in God at all. The story is told of the conversation between the theologian and the metaphysician. The theologian was the first to speak, and he had very little use for the metaphysician. "As far as I can make out," he told him, "the work of the metaphysician amounts to this: he spends his time in a dark basement at midnight looking for a black cat which isn't there." The metaphysician smiled blandly and said, "We metaphysicians may be mad enough to search in a dark cellar at midnight for a black cat which isn't there, but you theologians go us one better. You find it."

Perhaps even those who think the theologians are finding a black cat which is not there at all may be interested in seeing how they go about their work. Catholics, naturally, will have a greater interest than others in the understanding of the faith by which they live, but some knowledge and understanding of the faith by which these Catholics live should be of interest to every educated man. Current developments in the understanding of the religious beliefs of one out of six people who inhabit this planet, of one out of four citizens of the country in which we live, should stir the interest of anyone who has even a minimum of human curiosity.

The purpose of this book, then, is primarily descriptive; it aims at giving some kind of an understanding of what is going on in Catholic theological work in our day.

How Christian Theology Began

If there is any science which can be understood apart from its history, Christian theology is unquestionably not such a science. So if we expect to come to any understanding of what Catholic theologians are doing now, we must begin by some kind of a survey of the course which theology has followed from the beginning up to the present. We begin by asking ourselves how it all began, this science which we call theology.

It did not begin with a book. It did not begin with any writing at all. It began in an obscure corner of the world through the life, through the deeds, through the preaching of a man called Jesus of Nazareth. It began through the growth and the spread of the community who believed in Him as God and Saviour, who spread the good news of His Resurrection from the dead and who invited all men to enter into this joyous community of believers. In this initial stage, as one would expect, there was a minimum of conscious theological reflection. Christians were absorbed above all simply in living the Christian life and faith, preaching the Gospel, sharing in common worship. However, as time went on, being intelligent and impelled by the inevitable human drive toward understanding, these Christians began to reflect on this new life to which they had committed themselves. Since, however, objections were raised by those with whom they lived, it was natural for them to rise to the defense of their new way of life. Attempts were made to synthesize Christianity with all the human values which surrounded them; yet at the same time everything they said or wrote was totally based upon the Sacred Scriptures which documented these primary events of which we have spoken.

From St. Augustine to the Carolingian Revival

This kind of work went on and, after passing through many developments which we are unable to describe in this short sketch, culminated in the work of St. Augustine. For Augustine, theology was a very personal thing, something growing out of his own devout absorption in the Christian mysteries, out of his personal meditation on the Word of God. Yet at the same time Augustine was trying to use all of the legitimate human values of the classical world; they were all incorporated in principle into the work of theology. St. Augustine died in 430 when the lights were going out all over Europe, and a period of barbarism and darkness had begun. Yet even during those centuries of darkness, as history moved through the seventh, eighth, and following centuries, the torch of Christian tradition was kept alight by the devoted work of the monastery scribes, faithfully transcribing the books of the Scriptures and the commentaries of the Fathers of the Church, waiting and patiently preparing for the dawn. By the end of the eighth century, a revival was under way in the life of learning in the West. At the instigation of Charlemagne, Alcuin had begun a renewal of scholarship. This Carolingian renaissance may seem very insignificant to us but, compared to the Dark Ages which went before it, it was something of great importance and pregnant with meaning for the future of theology.

In the study of theology, which was the almost exclusive concern of men who pursued learning during these centuries, the principal auxiliary discipline was simply grammar. That may sound very primitive; and compared to what happened later it was indeed primitive. The works of Aristotle which were available to scholars of that period were few, practically nothing more than the very simple, logical works which were really not much else but aids to grammar, to the study of the structure of words. We must keep in mind that the context in which this study was carried on was not the university as we know it. It was a study carried on in the context of the monastery and the cathedral schools. Those who taught were not professors in the sense in which we think of professors; rather they were ecclesiastics for whom the Word of God was the bread of life, the source of their instruction. The moral lessons which were to be drawn from Scripture were their main preoccupation.

The Three "Entrances" of Aristotle

There were three stages of this revival of learning culminating in the thirteenth century. These three stages are tied to three different entrances of the works of Aristotle into Europe. The first one we have already considered, the period in which only the very simple works of Aristotle, which had been translated in the sixth century by Boethius, were available to scholars. Perhaps it would be less misleading if we did not even call them scholars; they were religious men who spent their lives reading, contemplating, and meditating upon the Scriptures. As we move along farther into the eleventh and twelfth century renaissance, we find that more of Aristotle's works were being translated—more of the *Organon,* the collection of his books on logic. These more advanced logical books deal not merely with the relationship of words but also with the structure of argumentation, with logic and dialectic, and so at this stage logic and dialectic were brought to bear upon the Word of God, which always remained the solid substance upon which theologians reflected. Naturally, as one might expect, when this began, those who were unfamiliar with this new approach were disturbed. Thus began the controversy between the dialecticians and the anti-dialecticians; between such men as Abelard, one of the dialecticians, and Bernard, who thought that dialectics was a work of the devil. Bernard, more pious than Abelard, felt that to introduce this kind of human dialectic and argumentation was to falsify and destroy the purity of the Word of God. And so a long struggle began, a struggle which, as we shall see, had very complex results. Up to this time the work of the theologian had been almost exclusively a commentary on the scriptural text with the aid of those grammatical writings of Aristotle which have already been mentioned, a commentary on the Biblical text, taking it verse by verse, and drawing from it the moral lessons for one's life which one could find there. Now something new began. The application of dialectic to the study of the sacred text gave rise to what came to be known as the *quaestio*, the question. The raising of questions was not restricted to asking what this particular text of Scripture might mean, but began to include other questions which were less directly raised by the scriptural text. This meant that in the study of theology something new had entered in besides the traditional bare, simple, repetitive commentary. This commentary had for the most part simply made use of the writings of the Church Fathers which were available, and a good deal of the theologian's work was mere memory. Now, instead of confining his activity to such unimaginative plodding, the inquiring mind began to go to work. It began to ask all sorts of questions, with the consequence that two different departments of theological work came into existence: commentary on the Scripture, and disputation on the raising of questions. Naturally, as more and more of these questions began to be raised, as more and more of them were disputed, the tendency arose to group the questions together into some kind of a system. This meant that some kind of a systematic approach to theology began to develop, in contrast to the moralizing commentary, the more straightforward, positive exposition of the Word of God.

At the same time, during this period, the eleventh and twelfth centuries, schools began to appear, schools in the sense of centers which gathered together eminent scholars to make it more convenient for interested students to come and hear them. This was the second of the two stages, the use of dialectic, of logical argumentation, a further step beyond the earlier first stage, when grammar provided the student of Scripture with his principal human instrument of work.

The Third "Entrance" of Aristotle

The third stage was something of even greater significance for theological work. At the beginning of the thirteenth century, more of Aristotle's works were translated. Remember that books were rare and precious possessions in those times, and although Aristotle was *the* philosopher, so much so that if you talked about philosophy you were talking about Aristotle, only a selection of his writings were available in the West. It was an important event, then, when the slim shelf of Aristotle's writings in translation was augmented. The principal works were the *Ethics* and the addition of his writings on the nature of man, on metaphysics, on ethics, and on political philosophy.

These new works of Aristotle were not merely explaining the structure of the relationship of words. They were not merely telling people how an argument could be logically put together. In these works of Aristotle there was a definite view of the nature of man and the nature of reality. This meant that something new and something important had happened. The theologians of this period, of whom Thomas Aquinas was certainly the most outstanding, went about their work not merely by drawing out of the Scripture text itself what it explicitly said; they now brought to their work a concept of the nature of man, a concept of the nature of reality, and were convinced that something could be known about nature, about man and all of reality, even before the reading of the Word of God. Reason was not just a tool, not just an instrument. Reason could know something about the nature of things.

To the theologian of the twentieth century, to the Catholic theologian, at least, this may seem a very simple and obvious idea. But at that time it was a revolutionary idea, and it met very severe opposition. The meaning of this new development was that the structure of theological work was amplified. Not merely Scripture and the commentary on Scripture, but other aspects of reality as well were incorporated into a new theological synthesis. Remember that the raising of questions had become important in the earlier period. It was the collection of these questions which eventually became the *Summa Theologica*. The *Summa* of St. Thomas is simply a large, well-ordered collection of questions arising from disputations, accompanied by a series of objections, and the answers which were given to both the questions and the objections.

Traditionalists vs. Philosopher-Theologians

This new development gave rise to a very bitter controversy between the traditionalists and these new philosopher-theologians. There was a very important difference in their approach to the work of theology. The more traditional theologians, representing the dominant approach of Augustinianism, felt that this was a dangerous intrusion. They felt that true knowledge in theology came only from the very personal reality of love and union with God, not from simple knowledge of things in themselves, nor from the work of philosophers. St. Bonaventure is a good example of this Augustinian approach, although in his case, as in the case of St. Thomas, controversy was never bitter. Although these two saints differed radically, they were always very good friends. However, for Bonaventure, nothing had meaning at all except inasmuch as it was referred directly to God who is our final end to whom we can reach out in love. It is impossible, as far as he is concerned, to give any meaning to anything independently of its relationship to God. Now for Thomas, and for those in this new philosopher-theologian group, if I may so name them, things had in themselves a nature, a nature which was not merely their relationship to God. This does not mean that St. Thomas considered the relationship of all things to God to be in any way insignificant. But it does mean that he considered that all reality, all the things which we see, have an intelligibility, a meaning, and a value in themselves. This value, then, must be related to God as its final end; but at the same time the things can be understood in themselves. As a consequence of this intrinsic value given to the nature of things in themselves, theology incorporates an understanding of these natures, the nature of man, for instance, and the nature of the visible world, into its total synthesis.

A Precarious Synthesis

The synthesis which Thomas structured, the greatest of all the medieval *summae*, was in many ways a very precarious construct, as future events would make clear. There were elements in this synthesis which in the hands of those of lesser ability could be dangerous, and in actual fact did lead to dangerous and undesirable developments in the history of theology. By bringing Aristotle on this large scale into the work of theology, St. Thomas in a certain sense gave reason an independent existence and a value of its own, apart from theology. St. Thomas and those of his time were steeped in the Word of God and spent their lives meditating on it and trying to understand it more deeply. But it was possible for those who did not have this kind of solid grounding in Scripture to make merely human reflection the primary point of departure and impose upon the Word of God meanings which did not belong there at all. There was the risk of subordinating the mysteries of faith to merely human categories. As time went on this danger was frequently not avoided. Now this was precisely the kind of development which had worried those who opposed this move at the beginning. They felt that the unique character of Christianity would be swallowed up in some general system of human values. St. Bonaventure, for example, taught a system which was aimed more at reaching God than it was at knowing and reconstructing in a scientific way the order of God's work. For Bonaventure these creatures, these things which we see about us, do not really give us knowledge of God; they are only symbols which remind us of Him. It is fairly easy to see that Bonaventure and the Augustinian tradition is much more closely allied to the philosophical system of Plato than it is to that of Aristotle.

Disintegration and the Breakdown of Unity

In this survey of the centuries, we have to telescope many of these developments and perhaps, in a certain sense, even caricature them—not with any desire to distort but rather to set the main lines in bold relief. Many of the nuanced distinctions and qualifications which would be in place in a larger study have necessarily been left out.

Let us move on at the same pace, then, into the fourteenth century. So far we have been noticing a gradual trend to incorporate more and more elements into some kind of a synthesis. We know that this trend toward synthesis was paralleled in other aspects of life and culture. Now we are about to see an opposite movement toward disintegration and a breakdown of unity. The disintegration of the theological synthesis has begun, a disintegration whose seeds were already present even at the high point of unity.

One instance of this movement toward a breakdown of integral unity was the insistence of Duns Scotus, a fourteenth-century theologian, that human reason cannot make any valid statement at all about the reality of God. There is, he maintained, a discontinuity between philosophy and theology. Each of the two may have a value of its own, but they cannot be put together. This was a further development of the line of thought we saw in Bonaventure and the Augustinian school.

A further and more extreme development was nominalism, exemplified by William of Occam. For the nominalists, faith and reason, religion and philosophy, were further divorced. Faith for Occam, and for the nominalists in general, gave some kind of an approach, some kind of a grasp upon the all-powerful and sovereignly free God who does what He wills with us and the universe, but it left all of this enveloped in impenetrable mystery. For Occam, reason as opposed to faith could give us nothing more than concepts; not reality, but simply a set of concepts or names. That, of course, is where the term "nominalism" came from; the Latin word *nomen* means name. So the nominalists held that human reason was incapable of doing anything more than assembling a group of concepts or names. What was the result of this development?

Anti-rational Faith and Barren Dialectic

The result was that there were two streams which moved apart from one another. On the one side there was a purely personal religious faith of a semi-mystical and often of an anti-rational character, and on the other side there was a purely formal and increasingly barren dialectical structure. The kind of split which now began to develop had its beginning at least as far back as the eleventh century. Elements which were then held in dynamic tension now began to get out of hand and produce serious difficulties.

The *quaestio* whose beginnings we saw back in the eleventh century had taken up more and more of the theologian's time and energy, leading to the excessive domination of a too exclusively rational and logical method. The work of theology had been cut off from its sources. This was one of the great tragedies of the fourteenth and succeeding centuries, a large-scale and especially disastrous instance of what frequently happens in many spheres of knowledge. After a certain period of time, during which a structure of explanation has been built on the basis of solid reality, men become so preoccupied with these structures that the source, the basic living reality out of which these structures grow, is forgotten and men spend all their time exploring and rearranging or even merely memorizing and repeating these structures, these dialectical categories. Meanwhile the primary reality which all these structures were intended to explain gets lost in the shuffle.

What were the safeguards which in an earlier period had been set up against this kind of a development? In the thirteenth century and, although decreasingly so, even in succeeding centuries Biblical instruction had been vigorously maintained together with the *quaestiones* and disputations. By insisting on a solid, complete, and thorough study of the Word of God, by insisting that a proportionate amount of time be given to Bible reading and commentary, a counterbalance had been preserved. But then, little by little, dialectical discussions began to encroach more and more on the time given to directly Biblical studies, with the resulting degeneration of which we have spoken. By the fifteenth century, then, practically all of the theological work in the schools was little more than the piling together of very complicated syllogisms.

Another weakness (which was not something altogether new) was a lack of a proper historical sense, a failure to read these texts (if they read them at all) in the context of the time and place in which they had been written. The men of these centuries were inclined to take all texts—whether from the first, third, fifth, or twelfth century—as though they could be read only one way. All of them were homogeneous quarries for abstract generalizations. Another result of this overemphasis on disputation and logic was an excessive subtlety. Everything can be made a question if the mind is set to it, and empty curiosity can easily mislead one into forgetting what is central in Christianity. It may be that a number of these questions are interesting, legitimate questions, but there is such a thing as a proper sense of proportion and balance. If one spends all one's time asking questions in such a way that the central realities are obscured, serious damage has been done even if no single answer is erroneous. It is not enough for a theologian to refrain from saying things which are untrue; it is also necessary that in what he says the proper balance and structure and proportion of Christian reality is conveyed at all times. During this period, a properly proportioned view of the whole was lost. The result was the crystallization of frozen systems. Since most of these systems were tied to religious families—Dominicans, Franciscans, Augustinians, and others—a many-sided competition emerged, with each group defending its system against the system of another group. Instead of trying to understand real problems, men lost contact with the basic Christian realities and wore themselves out wrangling about the superstructures.

Search for Remedies

As the fourteenth century melted into the fifteenth and the fifteenth into the sixteenth, it began to be obvious to more and more people that there were very serious needs which had to be met. New needs were crying out to be satisfied. One of the most important and basic needs was a deep and unsatisfied religious hunger. Men yearned for food for their souls which were famishing on this diet of dry syllogisms. They hungered for some direct contact with Christ and God, for more elemental, basic religious realities. New texts of earlier Christian and classical sources were also becoming available and demanded exploration.

What were some of the answers given to these needs? One of them was Renaissance humanism. This was to a great extent a reaction against the decadent Scholasticism of which we have spoken, a reaction against the barbarous Latin, the interminable disputations, and the barren dialectic. It was an appeal for a return to the pure and simple text in its original language. It was a cultivated, literary, anti-speculative, anti-Scholastic movement. It was the forerunner, in some ways, of modern religion without dogmas and antagonistic to any kind of dogmatic formulation, a forerunner of the general human religion of deism, and eventually of atheistic humanism.

Martin Luther

A second way of responding to these new needs, as the fifteenth century moved into the sixteenth, was the answer given by Martin Luther. Seeing the desperate dryness, the lack of basic religion in the lives of so many people, his reaction was what might have been expected from a monk formed in the Augustinian tradition. He insisted that Christianity should concern itself with only one thing: with salvation, which is found in Christ and in each man's personal conversion to Him. This, Luther proclaimed, is the only reason why He has given us His Word in the Scripture, and the preaching of that Word in the Church. Therefore, Scripture and Christian doctrine are not to give us any speculative knowledge, not to increase our information. They are intended exclusively to bring about our conversion to Christ. So none of our natural knowledge is of any value in theology. This is an attitude with which we can deeply sympathize. Here is a man who sees the religious need of his time and tries desperately to find some answer to that need. Luther goes on further to declare the impossibility of our using our reason to any effect in theology because not only was reason not given us for that purpose, but we are in fact sinners in a fallen state in which our mind is blinded. Reason is useful in purely human affairs, but when it is brought to bear on man's relationship to God it is positively misleading.

What then does Luther ask of theology? In place of an intellectually constructed speculative theology, Luther wants a theology which is true piety, based on a study which is mainly an exposition of the sacred text itself. There are further reasons for Luther's insistence on piety, and recent studies suggest that one of the most compelling reasons of all was the desperate state of public worship at the time. If that deficiency had not been there, the kind of approach which Luther took and the further problems it raised might well have been unnecessary. However, given the situation, it is not at all difficult to sympathize with what Luther undertook to accomplish. The tragedy of the sixteenth century is that what began with the pastoral zeal of Martin Luther ended—because of many sins of many people—with Western Christianity divided into Catholic and Protestant, a wound which only recently shows signs of beginning to heal.

Another answer to the needs of this time was the restoration in many places of medieval Scholasticism cleansed of the grosser aberrations of the fourteenth and fifteenth centuries, but still not providing sufficiently vital contact with the primary sources of theology.

Theology Breaks Up into Separate Specialties

As theology moved into the sixteenth, seventeenth, and later centuries, the proliferation of new kinds of knowledge brought with it the breakup of the unity of theology into specialized areas of study. Some of the separate, and almost independent, branches of theology which begin to have an existence of their own were Scholastic theology, mystical theology, dogmatic theology, moral theology, and apologetic theology. A much larger list of these separate theological disciplines could be compiled with very little effort because the tendency of this period was to break theology down into smaller pieces. There was surely a good side to such a development because it meant that each one of these areas could be given more attention. However, at the same time, there was the danger of these separate departments not fitting into a single, unified picture. The tendency to fragmentation was increased by the fact that a good deal of theology at this time was simply polemical theology.

Some efforts were made to integrate modern needs into theology. Some scholars, for instance, began to make more careful use of sources. But most of this effort on both sides was poisoned by the tragedy of polemic, of dissension, of hate, of wars, of mutual distrust, and of persecution, all of which so rent Christianity asunder, so poisoned the work of theology, that for centuries the conditions under which theology can develop as it should simply did not exist.

As far as Catholic theology is concerned, the nadir was reached in the eighteenth century. This was the century of the *Aufklärung*, the enlightenment, and the response of most Catholic theologians was an effort to make theology a construct of human reason alone. During the eighteenth century most of the theological work which was done at all, poor as it was, was done in France. With the French Revolution all of the schools completely collapsed, with the result that Catholic theology reached bottom. However, there is some advantage in reaching bottom because then there is only one way to move, and that way is up.

Beginnings and Progress of Movements of Renewal

From the beginning of the nineteenth century, with many hesitations, with many difficulties, movements of renewal started to appear. One of the first of them was the movement centered in the Catholic school of Tübingen. The name of Moehler is the most eminent in this group. The Tübingen school was influenced by the Romantic movement which, since it insisted on wholeness and the unified relation of all realms of reality to one another, was by its very nature not merely confined to literature or philosophy, but reached over into theology as well. When it reached theology and began to bring its influence to bear there, the Romantic movement brought about a re-evaluation of tradition. It is easy to see that much of this was in reaction to the rationalism of the eighteenth century. As the eighteenth century had broken things up into little rational pieces, the Romantic movement wanted to counter this trend and put them together into a great living whole. As the eighteenth century had been coldly rational, so, in contrast, the Romantic movement wanted to insist upon what was more warm and more human. Whereas the eighteenth century was somewhat mathematical, somewhat overinsistent on logic and order, the Romantic movement insisted upon life and the vital energies which well up within man. Naturally, this was an influence for good in the renewal of theology.

During the nineteenth century there were many struggles and confusions among Catholic theologians. The basic difficulty was that after the French Revolution, and the collapse of the schools, the basic resources for theological work had been wiped out; even before the Revolution the resources had been slim enough, or at least the use of them had been modest enough. The scholarly resources which were needed for theological work after the Revolution had to be built up slowly and painfully. During those years of struggle and confusion, the problem was compounded by difficulties on the political level. The century was bedeviled with those Church-State controversies with which a later chapter in this book will deal. Among theologians there was a conflict between the rationalists and the traditionalists, each one insisting too strongly on his own direction. The rationalists wanted to reduce all of theology to something entirely available to human reason without serious difficulty. They wanted to reduce the Trinity and all the other mysteries of Christianity to something which could be proved by a syllogism. On the other side were the traditionalists, in many cases men who were reacting against what they saw in the French Revolution, insisting on the value and importance of tradition. They emphasized the difficulty of arriving at any kind of a sure truth except by what had been handed down from generation to generation and ultimately had been received in faith. It goes without saying that both of these approaches were exaggerations.

Toward the later part of the century things began to look a little brighter. Among other things a beginning toward the renewal of the life of worship of Catholics appeared. A little later on, under the inspiration and direction of Leo XIII, scholars went behind the decadent Scholasticism of the fourteenth and fifteenth centuries and returned to the work of medieval Scholasticism at its best. Perhaps more important than any of these stirrings was the Biblical revival sparked by the extraordinary work of Protestant scholars, especially German Protestant scholars, in critical studies of the Bible. Some of the conclusions they came to were radically opposed to traditional Christianity, and it was not until Catholic scholars had been rather thoroughly shocked by the kind of things that were developing, that they began to settle down to serious work on the new information which was pouring in and making possible Biblical studies of a kind which had previously been unknown. Once we get to the last hundred years all those developments of renewal begin which are the subject of the rest of this book.

The Modernist Crisis

There is one more stage in this development which should at least be mentioned: the so-called Modernist crisis, which arose around the turn of the century. To put it in its simplest terms, the Modernist crisis was caused by a combination of two things: first, the flood of new historical knowledge compounded with some heady philosophical ideas from the German idealists; second, the unpreparedness of Catholic scholars of that time, especially in the area of critical historical studies. By reason of these circumstances many of them became very confused, many were overwhelmed. At the time it seemed that critical historical study had made the divinity of Christ and the traditional understanding of Christian origins incompatible with honest historical scholarship. The Modernists faced this challenge simply by capitulating. An interesting thing about the Modernist crisis (and this is why it became a real crisis) was that these men who were very much influenced by those ideas did not conclude that the only honest thing they could do was to leave the Catholic Church. No, they decided to stay in the Church; they decided to try to express their ideas in language which would be acceptable to those in the Church although the meaning had been altogether transformed. The severe (and it might seem to us oversevere) moves which were taken against the Modernists in the early part of this century can only be understood if the circumstances are taken into account. As the result of this very vigorous action, the movement was terminated as far as the Catholic Church was concerned and had no future among Catholic theologians. At the same time, all the positive results of critical scholarship are now being used by Catholic theologians.

The Present Situation

What then is the present situation of Catholic theology? It is unquestionably moving into a period which has very great hopes. The outcome of these developments is something which only history can tell, but a very good case can be made out for the conviction that we are now moving toward a new and richer theological synthesis. New resources of every kind are now available to us. New developments are taking place which enrich our theological knowledge and make it possible for us to draw from the primary sources a fuller, richer theological sustenance. All this progress gives very great promise for the future, as the following chapters will show. Not only on the level of directly theological work, but in what is an even more important and deeper level, in the life of Christian communities, there are well-founded hopes for overcoming the divisions which have weakened Christian life and theology for so many centuries. The conviction is growing among Christians all over the world that this division among Christians is the root cause of most of these other problems.

Summary and Conclusion

Let us briefly recapitulate the movement of theology down through the centuries. Christian theology did not begin with any kind of theological reflection at all. It began with historical events. It began with the preaching of Christ, with the saving events of His life, death, and Resurrection, with the faith of the early Christian community going out and preaching the Gospel, inviting people into this joyous community centered around the risen Christ who lived in their midst. Gradually, as time went on, they began to reflect upon all this in order to make sense of it for themselves and to defend it against the objections raised by their non-Christian contemporaries. Such a challenge called into play the best efforts of their intelligent reflection. This earlier period rose to a peak with Augustine, and then active theological work leveled off. There was very little activity until the eighth century, when the opening of the schools under Alcuin began to revitalize theological work. In the eleventh and twelfth centuries, as more and more of the works of Aristotle were translated in the West, a new and powerful force began to affect the work of theology. In the thirteenth century, not only grammar and logic but an independent philosophy of the nature of man and of being was incorporated into theological work. Then, because of a failure to preserve the proper balance, a trend began which led many away from the primary sources from which theology must live. Things which should have remained together in the life of the Church were separated. Although men and movements arose to try to cope with a situation in which Christianity and Christian theology steadily lost vitality and influence, still the spiritual vigor of Christian man sank so low that hatred and invective and polemic ruled the scene for centuries.

This spiritual degeneration reached bottom, in the opinion of competent scholars, at the beginning of the nineteenth century. Since that time a whole series of movements of renewal have begun, and we can now look forward confidently to a new and richer synthesis of Catholic theology. The rest of this book will describe these movements of renewal: the return to the Bible, the revitalization of the Church's life of worship, the recovery of a richer understanding of the sacramental life of the Church. We shall see that there is renewed emphasis on the vital energies from the grass roots within the Church; that there is an understanding of authority and hierarchy in the Church, as being intended not to dominate, but to serve the Christian community; that there is a new appreciation of the place of laymen in the Church, not merely as those who go to church, but as those who are the Church; that there is a vision of Christianity not merely as a purely personal and individualistic thing, but as a social reality. There is a recognition that all realities, not only the realities of the future world but those of the here-and-now, have value in themselves. This concern for the realities of this world is what Pope John is talking about in *Mater et Magistra* and *Pacem in Terris.*

Finally, we shall study the efforts toward Christian unity: to begin with, what is obviously important for us in this country, efforts toward unity between Catholic and Protestant Christians; then, unity with orthodox Christians. The impulses which have been set on foot by the extraordinary personality of Pope John, and all of the interest and concern for solving these problems which the work of the Council has stimulated, give us solid grounds for great hope. The dominant trend of our time is toward overcoming these divisions, and all the faults which suffocate the life of the Church.

Since the soil out of which theology grows is the vital life of the Christian Church in faith and love, everything which prepares that soil encourages us to look forward to a bright future for Catholic theology.

Chapter II

MODERN TRENDS IN THEOLOGICAL METHOD

by

John H. Wright

It was my good fortune in the spring of 1959, while on the faculty of the Gregorian University at Rome, to make a "theological tour" of France and Belgium. Visiting and talking with some twenty-five or thirty theologians, connected with a dozen different institutions of learning, we discussed the work they were presently engaged in and what they thought were the principal currents in theological thought today. It was a most rewarding experience, and it left one dominant impression: the extraordinary vitality of theology in the Church today. This impression had already been formed by previous association with theologians in Rome, first as a graduate student, and then as a teacher. This visit to France and Belgium deepened and enriched it. Since 1960 I have been teaching theology in the United States; and everywhere I find the same stirrings of intense interest and new life. There is no question of a revolution in theology that would break with all past achievement. There is rather a development, a growth, building on the past, selecting what is most fruitful and pertinent, discarding all appearance of arid formalism.

It is this new vitality in theology that I want to discuss, particularly as it is shown in theological method, in the *way* theologians go about their work of investigation and teaching. First, I would like to explain how theological method is understood today and then to point out some significant developments that have taken place within the last century.

I. Theological Method

In theology, as in every scholarly undertaking, competence is marked far more by a command of method than by an encyclopedic knowledge of all the facts and conclusions proper to the field. A person may know these facts and conclusions, and be ready to quote them at a moment's notice, and yet lack any real interior grasp of how the facts are established and the conclusions arrived at. And on the other hand, one may not have at his fingertips all the latest opinions and fruits of the latest research, and yet, because he is genuinely able to evaluate these opinions and to appreciate the significance of this research, he is truly competent.

A Parable

I should like to introduce this consideration of the nature and importance of theological method by a parable. This parable concerns four students, who for one reason or another wish to learn theology. Since they are all beginners, they decide that a reasonable first step toward becoming a competent theologian is to master a good textbook in theology.

Student number one proceeds to commit the entire book to memory. He knows it from A to Z. He even knows it from Z to A. He can start from either end and go to the other without difficulty. Is he a budding theologian? Is he taking a significant step toward theological competence? Not necessarily. And if we fill out the description of student number one with a further detail, it will become clear that the answer is, "Not at all." For despite his perfect memorizing of the book, he understands only about 10 per cent of it—and even this he finds pretty confusing.

Student number two is also fairly successful in memorizing the textbook. But in addition, he understands it. He knows the meaning of every sentence, and grasps the structure of divisions and subdivisions within the book. Is student number two safely launched on the way to theological competence? Not necessarily. And again, if we add a further consideration, we must reply that he is not. For though he has understood and memorized the book, he has only the faintest inkling as to whether the book is true or false. He understands; but he has made no real judgments on what the book is talking about, and so possesses neither truth nor falsity.

Everyone recognizes that it is very possible to know clearly what something means, and yet have no idea whether it is true or not. If I say, for example, that it is now raining in Manila, the meaning is perfectly clear. Yet none of us can say whether the statement is true or false. As Plato observed in the *Meno*, true knowledge is not simply right opinion. It is not just saying or thinking something that happens to be true. One must also know that it is true. He must judge on some sufficient basis that the statement is true or false. Hence, student number two, since he has not yet begun to judge in the field of theology, has not yet begun to be a theologian.

Student number three compares favorably with student number two in memory and understanding. He has mastered both the words of the text and the meaning of the words. And in addition, he judges: he accepts as true everything that he finds in the textbook. No questions or misgivings on this point enter his mind. Upon inquiry, we find that he has certain reasons for the judgments he makes. First of all, the author is internationally famous, one universally acknowledged to be a great theologian. Secondly, this author is manifestly sincere and convinced himself. Thirdly, the book is written in a fine, crisp style—a clear sign of true scholarship. And finally, the typography of the book is flawless.

We really need not delay to ask whether this student is a budding theologian. There is really less hope for him than for student number two. For while number two has not yet started down the path of judgment, number three has started down a path that leads nowhere. He has committed the unforgivable sin of scholarship—even where he may be right, he is right for the wrong reason.

Student number four, like student number one, has a thorough verbal command of the book. Like number two, his understanding is clear and complete. And like number three, he is engaged in the activity of judging, *but* with a significant difference. As he reads, he ponders. And sometimes he agrees with the book, occasionally he disagrees, and sometimes he suspends judgment. And he does all this not out of whimsey, following some feeling or hunch he happens to have at the moment. He is not judging on the basis of essentially extrinsic considerations like the author's reputation, sincerity, or style. His assent or dissent or further questioning follows from a consideration of the evidence as he sees it. As he reads, he weighs the statements of the author against the theological evidence adduced for them. He makes up his mind as a consequence of this weighing of evidence. Number four is a budding theologian.

Perhaps we should observe parenthetically that at the beginning of any scholarly endeavor a certain amount of almost blind trust in a teacher is required. But this initial period should be passed through as quickly as possible, since during it no genuine critical ability is being developed. It is the teacher's duty to train his students to recognize a particular kind of evidence for what it is, guiding and correcting them, not by the arbitrary exercise of external authority but by leading them to see what is genuinely worthy of consideration. The educational process has really begun only when one has started to exercise his ability to recognize and evaluate the evidence proper to a field.

The Essential Lesson of the Parable

What we have described in this parable is largely a set of symptoms. We have considered certain manifestations of activity in different persons trying to master a textbook in theology and begin the road to scholarly competence in that field. It is fairly easy to recognize which manifestations were insufficient and undesirable, and which were well directed and desirable. But *of what* were these activities the manifestation? In only one case, the last, were they manifestations of a genuine interest in theological truth. The first three may have had many reasons for wanting to be considered theologians, but the desire to possess the truth of theology was either absent or inoperative. They may have been sincere Christians, truly believing the revelation that God has made; but the impulse that led them to a further study of this revelation had little or nothing to do with the impulse that led them to believe. For student number four, on the other hand, the effort to theologize was rooted in faith, the act of believing. This act is motivated by the evidence of God revealing; it was this same evidence that ultimately regulated all his judgments in studying theology. His love for the truth that God reveals, for the evidence proper to theology, guided all his activity in this field.

Evidence and Methodology

The matter of evidence introduces us to the heart of our consideration. In any intellectual enterprise, the most significant factor for the determination of method is the kind of evidence that is being sought in order to discover the answers to the questions being considered. A *question* is the articulated appetite of the mind for truth. It is the desire to know, raised to the level of conscious expression. *Evidence* is the manifestation of truth, an indication of where this desired object is to be found. The investigation and organization of this evidence leads ideally to the formulation of an *answer*, an expression of the truth that was sought and has been found. In our discussion of theological method, after a brief word about the kind of questions theology asks, we will speak about evidence in theology—how it is acquired and organized in order to lead to the formation of a unified body of truth.

Theological Questions

We can say, by way of a general description, that the questions of theology are the ultimate questions. Theology seeks to answer the questions which human life, the total human situation, imposes on us as fundamental questions. These are the questions about first beginnings and final purposes, questions about the immanent meaning of the world we find ourselves in, questions about a possible transcendental unity in which all things are caught up. More precisely, theology seeks to answer questions about God: Who and what is He? How is He known? What is man's relationship to Him? And theology seeks the answers to these questions from God. As we will explain shortly, just as the desire to reach the ultimate meaning of life leads man to accept by faith God's revelation of that ultimate meaning in Himself, so the very same desire leads him to explore the content of this divine self-revelation. Theology springs from the questioning mind illuminated by faith.

Christian Theological Evidence

Theological evidence is, thus, the manifestation of the truth of God. And it is precisely here, in this matter of evidence, that Christian theology—along with Hebrew theology—is distinguished from every other system of religious thought. All religion is concerned with the truth of God and of man's relationship to Him. Some religious systems seek to discover this truth in a reflection upon the world about us, the orderly sequence of seasons and the process of growth, the splendor of the heavens and the beauty of material structure. Other systems turn inward and seek to find God in the depths of human consciousness, in the internal aspirations of the human heart for goodness and truth and beauty and eternal life. Christianity does not deny all value to these approaches to God, but it affirms that the primary evidence of divine truth is historical: God's own word, spoken at definite moments of history, in particular places, reaching a climax in the word spoken through Jesus Christ in Palestine some two thousand years ago. Faith is the total personal acceptance of God revealing Himself in Jesus Christ; theology is the exploration and organization of the truth which has been so revealed.

Faith

Lest faith appear to be something of a blind leap in the dark, an infantile affirmation made to escape the insecurity of doubt and ignorance, and lest theology seem nothing but a massive compounding of this childishness, it seems good to say something here about the relation of the activity of reason to faith. For the same impulse of reason that leads to faith, tends, when it has reached faith, to elaborate a theology.

Since Christian faith is historical in the sense that it is the acceptance of God's word spoken to man at a definite moment in time, the act of believing involves two judgments, one as a necessary prerequisite, the other as the essence of faith itself. The first judgment is an acceptance of the fact that God has indeed spoken. It is admitting the actual personal intervention of the Maker of all things in human history to reveal Himself to man. This is not yet faith. The second act is to accept not merely the *fact* of revelation (*that* God has spoken), but the *content* of this revelation (*what* God has told us of Himself). Concretely, it means accepting God as Saviour through His Son Jesus Christ. Thus, by faith one commits oneself wholly to God, submits mind and will to Him as the source of the meaningful destiny of one's whole existence.

Reason and Faith

A number of observations should be made about these two closely related judgments. Psychologically, it is not really possible for anyone to admit the *fact* of revelation unless he is at that moment prepared also to accept its *content*. However, the evidence for the first judgment is simply historical, within the province of scholarly investigation to explore and affirm. Of itself, it supposes nothing beyond the native competence of reason engaged in historical study. The question of whether or not God has spoken through Jesus Christ can be settled essentially by the same methods which settle whether Caesar crossed the Rubicon or the *Mayflower* landed at Plymouth. It should be noted in all these cases that, even when the evidence is fully sufficient and abundantly convincing, one may choose to deny or ignore it, if for some reason it has consequences one is not prepared to accept. The branch of study which investigates the evidence for the historical fact of divine revelation and its subsequent transmission is called apologetics, or "fundamental" theology (as distinguished from doctrinal or dogmatic theology, theology properly so-called).

The second judgment, the acceptance of the content of God's word, is faith itself. It has for its sole evidence the trustworthiness of God who speaks. To accept the content of revelation is to launch oneself into a world which is totally beyond man's innate powers; it is to allow oneself to be oriented toward a destiny in God that transcends what lies within man's ability to achieve. It is to accept salvation or ultimate well-being as a gift of the divine mercy. The saving truth that God reveals about Himself and His plan of redemption is more than just another piece of information. It is a total reshaping of the meaning of life. To accept this truth, to make this judgment, divine help is required: a light to the mind and an impulse to the will leading one to commit himself to God.

The situation then is this. Believing involves two judgments: one is preliminary and of itself accessible to natural reason alone; the other is substantive and possible only as a divine gift. It is psychologically impossible to make the first without making the second. It is wholly impossible to make the second without the gift of divine grace. Thus, no matter how abundant and satisfying the evidence for the first, without divine grace and the willingness to cooperate with it, one will freely doubt or deny the conclusive value of this evidence. But once one is prepared by God's grace to believe, then at one and the same psychological moment one affirms the truth of both the fact of revelation and the content of revelation. Reason has prepared for faith, but the assent of faith is more than a conclusion of reason; it is the surrender to the light of God. The fact is that if faith in divine revelation did not involve this surrender of one's autonomy, then the acknowledgment that God has spoken would probably be as common as the acknowledgment that Columbus discovered America. If all God wanted to reveal to us were (for some unknown reason) a better way to make peanut butter, or the dimensions of the physical universe, the whole process of investigation and acceptance would involve no special divine help. Truths of this sort, useful and interesting as they may be, require no self-commitment to a transcendent personal engagement; and people generally would have no difficulty in accepting them.

Faith, Reason, and Theology

Just as human reason, confronted by the ultimate questions posed by existence, leads a man under divine grace to the life of faith, so this same impulse of reason, now illumined by faith, continues to wrestle with these ultimate questions. The concern of reason now is not to discover some truth beyond that which God's word has revealed but, in fullest submission to that word, to seek an ever deeper knowledge and understanding of it. It is the development and disciplining of this concern, implicit within the act of faith itself, that leads to theology properly so-called.

Aristotle once observed that all developed human habits are simply the unfolding and stabilizing of inchoative operational tendencies present from the beginning. A rock is not taught to fall upward by throwing it in the air. So theology, as an intellectual habit of the believing mind, is a further evolution of the mind itself, impelled by the desire to know and understand all that has been accepted by faith. Every believer is an incipient theologian, just as everyone who wonders about the phenomena of nature and seeks some explanation for what he sees is an incipient scientist.

Faith and theology are concerned with the same questions; but theology expresses these questions with greater detail and order and, given a partial answer, poses further questions. Faith and theology have the same source of evidence: God's word made known by His revelation in history; but theology is prepared to reason more deeply about the fuller meaning of this evidence. Faith and theology are both in possession of some knowledge and understanding about what God has revealed; but theology seeks a more complete knowledge and a more comprehensive understanding.

The Activity of Theology

The proper activity of theology is twofold: analysis and synthesis, or discovery and understanding. These two processes are continuously going on, and mutually complement each other. In the analytic process, or the way of discovery, the mind is seeking data, amassing additional facts and details about the content of divine revelation. Here the concern is to know as clearly and precisely as possible what individual truths should be affirmed about God and man's relation to

Him. As in every operation of dissection, there is a danger here of dissolving the unity of God's truth into a dusty list of minute propositions. This is offset by the complementary process of synthesis, the way of understanding, wherein an endeavor is made to fit all the parts into a whole, to view as a totality the unified truth of God and His dealings with men. It is by grasping the parts in their relationships to one another and to the whole that the mind understands what it has learned. The mind in its quest for truth may often formulate precise, particular questions; and this moves it along the way of analysis. But it does this in function of a deeper and broader desire to see things in their objective total unity; and this governs the synthetic activity of the mind, ever assimilating and fitting into a perceived totality the details which are newly acquired.

Four Levels of Theological Activity

When analysis and synthesis in theological activity are spelled out more concretely, there emerge four interrelated and mutally interdependent levels of activity. These levels are dictated by what constitutes evidence in theology: God's word spoken at definite times and places. These four levels may be described as (1) textual criticism, (2) exegesis, (3) partial synthesis, and (4) total synthesis. It is because no one in a single lifetime can be an expert in all these fields that theology is essentially a corporate enterprise.

Textual Criticism

Since God's word comes to us through written documents, the first concern of those who would study God's word is for the text of these documents themselves, the chief, of course, being Sacred Scripture. (Even "oral tradition" as a way of transmitting divine revelation is written down for the benefit of those who are not immediate hearers. It differs in its written form from Scripture in that it is not "inspired.") This concern leads to the work of textual criticism. Here there is question both of "lower criticism," which aims at establishing as far as possible the correct text, i.e., what was actually written down in the autograph manuscript, and of "higher criticism," which seeks to discover the origin of the document, its author or authors, its purpose, the precise kind of literary form it represents, and so on. Clearly, both lower and higher criticism are vitally important in finding out what the document means.

Exegesis

The discovery of what the document means is the second level of activity. This is the work of exegesis, or interpretation. It has one supreme guiding objective: to find out what the author meant to say by the words he actually used. This is not always an easy thing to do, given the difference in culture, background, literary forms, and social milieu between the author and the exegete. The great temptation which the exegete must resist is to suppose that the author meant by the words and forms he employed exactly what the exegete himself would mean if he were to use those same words and forms. In fact, this may often be the case; but all available means of archaeology, comparative literature, philology, social anthropology, history, and so on, must be used to find out. Here, in exegesis, the foundation of all theological analysis is laid and the essential lines of development projected.

Exegesis, though essentially it presupposes the work of textual criticism, can itself have an influence on this work. For example, since it is likely that a scribe in copying a manuscript would be inclined to substitute a more easily understood reading for a more difficult one rather than to do the opposite, a modern textual critic will prefer the more difficult reading to the easier when he is trying to establish the original text. And one engaged in higher criticism obviously must take as his starting point the verbal sense of the document, and from this judge whether he is dealing with prose or poetry, narrative or meditation.

Partial Synthesis

Exegesis is almost wholly an analytic work. But if there is to be some deeper penetration into the mind of the author, a synthetic work must also be undertaken. This at first largely takes the form of determining the structure and unified message of each individual document. How, for example, is the Epistle to the Galatians organized, and what is its fundamental teaching? In addition to this sort of study, there is a need to work out the meaning of the recurring thematic ideas of a particular writer or group of writers. How do the New Testament writers speak of faith? What was St. Jerome's view of the religious value of virginity? Here is where Biblical theology and patristic theology develop. It is not possible to fix here any absolute labels, or to indicate inviolable canons of procedure; but, generally speaking, the organization which is done at this level is content to employ the vocabulary encountered in the documents themselves, or to make only such use of an outside terminology as makes the matter intelligible to a contemporary reader. It is not concerned to develop a universe of discourse within which the whole content of divine revelation can be seen in mutual interrelationships.

This work of partial synthesis and thematic study can be of immense, even of indispensable, help to exegesis. If a word occurs in a particular document fifty times, and in forty-five of these it is clear that the same fundamental meaning is operative, one is justified in supposing that, unless there are strong indications to the contrary, the other five instances will share this fundamental meaning.

Total Synthesis

But in theology, as in every intellectual discipline, the depth of understanding is not in proportion merely to the number of things known but to the insight into their underlying unity. The basic appetite of the human mind, the great problem whose answer is always being sought, is the desire for comprehensive, unified truth. The knowledge of many things does not satisfy, unless one grasps them in a totality—and this is to understand. Theology then seeks to see all the manifold riches of divine revelation in a synthesizing unity. This desire is not merely for the satisfaction of a kind of super-curiosity, but proceeds from the realization that anything less than this must involve, to some degree, distortion or misplaced emphasis. A partial view is not false for being incomplete; but it cannot provide the same inspiration or resolve man's deepest problems as does the total view.

In theology this presents two very difficult problems, so difficult indeed that this total synthesis must always remain an unattainable ideal to the realization of which we are constantly working. The first of these concerns the way in which the very thoughts contained in divine revelation are to be expressed. In order to combine many different ideas and modes of thought, it is first necessary to express them within the same system of discourse. It is like adding fractions with different denominators: $\frac{1}{2}$ plus $\frac{1}{3}$. To effect this combination it is necessary to convert both to a common denominator. (Thus: $\frac{1}{2}$ equals $\frac{3}{6}$, and $\frac{1}{3}$ equals $\frac{2}{6}$; hence $\frac{3}{6}$ plus $\frac{2}{6}$ equals $\frac{5}{6}$.) So also, if one is to combine the imagery of Genesis, the visions of Ezechiel, the teachings of the Synoptic Gospels, the reflective insights of St. John, and the sweeping view of St. Paul, it is not possible to leave these ideas simply in their original expression. The categories of thought of no one of these writers is adequate to say what all the rest of them are saying. Their ideas must be rethought and expressed in terms capable of being immediately interrelated. In working toward a solution of this problem, theology has developed or made use of terms which are not to be found in Sacred Scripture at all, or at least not in the same sense; for example, incarnation, satisfaction (as a mode of redemption), sacrament, merit, person, or freedom of choice.

The second problem is the actual work of interrelating, of synthesizing. After the ideas have been given a common denominator, the numerators must be added to form a unified totality. The essential impossibility finally of doing this in a completely satisfactory way lies in the fact that the ultimate unity of the truth of revelation is the divine truth itself, God, and he can never be adequately expressed in any of our formulas or comprehended in any of our systems. The highest achievement of theology as a science must be to glimpse the unity of the divine mystery which surpasses all understanding.

The Central Problem

From what has been said, it seems clear that the heart of the problem here is the search for the "common denominator," the categories of thought capable of expressing everything contained in divine revelation, without distortion or impoverishment. Theologians are not entirely agreed as to what these categories should be. But both the experience of seven hundred years and the special blessing of the Church indicate that they are to be found in the categories employed by St. Thomas Aquinas, i.e., the categories of the philosophy of being. For it seems that we can best see how things are interrelated when we have been able to say *what* they really are. This is not to make the thought of St. Thomas the final arbiter in all theological discussion, nor to say that he has explicated fully all the necessary categories of thought. But it does say that St. Thomas provides the speculative theologian with a fruitful and vigorous source of light and inspiration in working toward total synthesis—a task he himself advanced more than any other single person in the history of Christian thought.

The usefulness of employing the categories of being for expressing theological truth further is confirmed by the fact that, ultimately, the principle of analysis and the principle of synthesis must be the same. By a principle of analysis here is meant some one aspect common to all the matters to be ordered, but found in them in different ways. For example, in arranging books in a library, I can sort them out on the basis of size, or language, or author, or content, because each of these is an aspect found in every book, but in a different way. Having divided the books in one way, I can thereafter arrange them in an orderly way. But I cannot decide to put the large books on one shelf, the French books on another, those written by authors whose last name begins with "J" on another, and history books on another. The principle I use to sort them out in the first place must also be the principle I use to arrange them with respect to one another.

Theological analysis and synthesis on this level of total unity must proceed in a similar fashion. The realities which God has made known to us through His personal intervention at definite times and places must be grasped as far as possible in terms of what is most profound and universal in man's knowing experience: *being*. This aspect is found in everything that in any way is. The most trivial happenings and the most significant events, the most lifeless propositions and the most dynamic truths, all have this in common: in some way they *are*. To grasp them explicitly under the aspect of their *being* and then, on a basis of the categories of being, to relate them to one another, provides the procedure which theology has found most fruitful in working toward total synthesis.

A Fifth Kind of Activity

There is a further kind of activity that theology must engage in, in addition to those just described. It must endeavor to speak to the men of today in a language they can understand. Theology is not just a luxury or a pleasant way of passing the time. The work of criticism, exegesis, analysis, and synthesis which scholars achieve is not simply for their own profit and satisfaction; it is to enrich the Church as a whole. Hence, there must also be those who make it their business to proclaim these riches in a language and tone that will be meaningful to those who are not themselves directly engaged in the theological enterprise. They must address themselves to the whole multitude of believers who have accepted the word of God and thirst to drink more deeply of its living waters. This is the work of the so-called "kerygmatic theology."

Theological Method: A Summary

We may summarize what has been said about theological method in the following five observations:

(1) Theological method begins by asking questions which spring from the deepest concern of man about himself and his relationship to what is ultimately real. These questions take on more definite shape and detailed articulation as the evidence accumulates and partial answers are found.

(2) Asking questions is followed by investigating the evidence proper to theology. It is the evidence which has been accepted by faith: God's revealed word as transmitted within the Church in Sacred Scripture and tradition.

(3) Investigation of the evidence leads to an organization of such evidence. This means the formulation of an argument that bears upon the questions that are being asked.

(4) From this argument or organized evidence there issues a conclusion: the expression of the answer or truth that has been sought.

(5) Finally, theology emerges as a unified body of knowledge, an acquired wisdom of the believing mind, when all its

answers are seen in a coherent and mutually illuminating unity.

It may be appropriate to observe that the progress of theology toward its goal is not a rectilinear ascent of these five steps one after another; it is rather a spiral that goes falteringly upward, asking, investigating, organizing, answering, synthesizing, only to begin again.

II. Recent Developments in Theological Method

What we have said about theological method thus far has, in one way or another, always been true of the way theologians proceed. But, like every scholarly human undertaking, it is open to certain variations. The history of theology since Vatican Council I has shown some profound and important shifts in theological method.

Nineteenth-century theology contained much that was good, much which underlies present developments in theology. But, generally speaking, there were some notable defects that weakened theological method. We may sum up these under three heads: (1) lack of real contact with the sources of theological evidence, (2) verbalism, and (3) an exaggerated concern for polemics.

Neglect of Sources

Pope Pius XII in his encyclical letter *Humani Generis* wrote: "It is true also that theologians must always return to the sources of divine revelation; for it is their task to show how the teachings of the living magisterium are found either explicitly or implicitly in Sacred Scripture and divine 'tradition.' In addition, these sources of divinely revealed truth are so filled with innumerable treasures that they can never really be exhausted. Hence, the sacred sciences always take on new freshness from the study of these sources; on the other hand, speculation divorced from a deeper investigation of the sacred deposit becomes sterile, as we know from experience." (Denzinger, 3886) The concluding words of this quotation indicate that the pope was not merely describing a possibility, but a situation that had actually existed. Much of nineteenth-century theology was content with "proof texts," brief quotations culled from Scripture, the Fathers, and the Councils, cited out of context and deemed to support a thesis the theologian was bent on proving.

Perhaps the most notable defect here (aside from the fact that the "proof text" on closer examination often did not really prove) was that almost all sense of sacred history was lost. For instance, in a thesis on the government of all things by divine providence, often there was communicated no sense of an unfolding plan of God, a plan whose realization began with creation, grew to fullness in the Incarnation and work of Christ, and now tends to its climax at his Second Coming. Instead, theology labored under a mechanical concern for individual salvation, or else it developed curious but irrelevant problems because they challenged the speculative ingenuity of a particular writer or fitted into some *a priori* division of matter that he had worked out.

This meant that the emphases of theology were often far removed from the original emphasis of revelation. Father M. D. Chenu, O.P., observes that, at the beginning of the twentieth century, a well-known encyclopedia appeared which contained no article on Christ's Ascension, while devoting twelve columns to Our Lady's Assumption.[1] Easter was dealt with only to mention the controversy about the date. He also refers to a dogmatic treatise of the same period that has nothing to say about the Resurrection, and deals with the *parousia* only to refute the eschatological views of Loisy. He concludes the paragraph with a lament that theology could so lose sight of the fundamental facts of the Christian mystery.

[1] M. D. Chenu, O.P., *Is Theology A Science?* (New York: Hawthorne Books, 1959), p. 44.

Verbalism

In theology, as in every intellectual endeavor, a concern for clarity and precision is the mark of an energetic and disciplined mind. But it is possible to repeat definitions and formulas without any real depth of understanding. When this happens in theology, a kind of closed system is developed that is held together simply by the coherence of non-contradictory definitions. The endeavor to understand God's self-revelation loses all sense of mystery and is replaced by a kind of dialectical mastery. Instead of experiencing oneself everywhere surrounded by stretches of truth that point to the infinite, one gets the feeling that everything has been neatly disposed of in appropriate pigeonholes. Because a problem has been named, an answer labeled, a definition given, a reply formulated, the impression is given that everything has been taken care of. A perfectly valid formula such as *ex opere operato* ("from the very performance of the rite"), used by the Council of Trent to describe the way in which the sacraments cause grace, is explained in a way that does not really avoid the notion of magic. Nineteenth-century theology was suffering from this sort of thing in many areas.

Polemics

Finally, nineteenth-century theology was dominated almost wholly by a concern for controversy. The principal effort of the theologian was to refute some error, real or apparent, and to prove a thesis against some adversary. The effort to explore and understand the truth of revelation for the positive enrichment it would give the life of faith was overshadowed by the violence of reaction to various mistakes. The face of theology was shaped, not by the inner requirements of the wisdom of faith, but by the refutation of errors ranging from gnosticism and Pelagianism to Protestantism and rationalism. Generally speaking, little effort was made to discover what element of truth these positions may have contained, and still less to consider them in their original sources. Stereotyped caricatures drawn from hostile sources set out the positions to be refuted, and one's theological guns proceeded to demolish them. Again and again a manual of theology would introduce a thesis by stating: "This thesis is placed against the error of those who maintain . . ."

Unquestionably, the refutation of heresy is important, and in the history of theology it has often served the purpose of clarifying further and penetrating the riches of divine revelation. But a discipline almost wholly occupied with this essentially negative work is not well calculated to inspire the life of the Church along fruitful and positive lines.

Since Vatican Council I

The Vatican Council itself, as if to show the perennial vigor of Catholic thought, set forth an excellent explanation of theological understanding and how it was to be acquired. In the first place, the relations of the divinely revealed truths among themselves should be explored so that they may mutually illuminate one another. This method, if used exclusively, could mean a kind of static view of revealed truth. Hence, the Council enunciated a second principle of understanding: The mysteries of faith should be considered in relation to man's last end. Here is a basic formulation of the dynamism that should characterize Christian theology, an insistence that theology be relevant to the meaning of life. But faith is the perfection of knowledge as grace is the perfection of nature, so the Council laid down a third principle for the guidance of theology, lest the contemplation of revealed truth become lost in a world of eternal abstractions. Divinely revealed truths are to be understood by analogy with natural truths. The whole world of truth, natural and supernatural, is one coherent unity; there is no reason, therefore, why what is more easily understood by us should not cast light on what is less easily understood, even though this latter be in itself immeasurably more intelligible. However, despite this excellent conciliar formulation, it is difficult to see any immediate influence of it upon the method of theology.

The revitalization of theology and theological method was due to many causes, but three seem to me to have been the most decisive: (1) renewed scientific study of Scripture and the documents of tradition, (2) the revival of the study of St. Thomas, and (3) a more reflective awareness of the personal dimensions of human life at all levels.

Return to the Sources

The development of historical studies in the nineteenth century, especially in Germany, was destined to have profound influence upon Christian theology, for these methods of historical research were turned upon the origins and development of Christianity. The written record of these early events began to be submitted to rigorous investigation. Catholic scholars quite commonly felt themselves on the defensive, though some few saw the immense importance of co-operating with these efforts so as to deal from firsthand knowledge with the problems they posed and, even more important, to profit from the insights they provided. The nineteenth century saw great work being done, chiefly by non-Catholic scholars, on Biblical criticism and the history of dogma, even though many mistakes were made. Unfortunately, at this same time the religious heresy known as Modernism began to make inroads within the Church, pretending to find support in the conclusions of these studies. Modernism sought to undermine the whole supernatural foundation of Christianity and reduce revelation to the projection of a subjective religious need. Modernism was condemned; and the scientific study of Scripture according to the newly developed critical methods fell under suspicion. Work continued, nevertheless, and the shadow of suspicion gradually lightened until the monumental encyclical letter of Pius XII, *Divino Afflante Spiritu,* in 1943 marked the real renaissance of these studies within the Catholic Church, though a certain amount of hostility and suspicion continues even today.

A similar interest in the study of the monuments of Christian tradition was going forward. Editions and translations of the Fathers of the Church were published. Collections of the Acts and Decrees of Church Councils were brought out. Christian archaeology and the study of the liturgy threw new light on the life of the early Christian community.

This has meant the beginning of a profound revitalization of the method of theology and the ordinary way of presenting it. Questions are proposed without a primary polemical intent, and the sources of revelation are explored not just to collect proof texts, but to find in proper context all the evidence relevant to these questions. Not uncommonly, a treatise in theology is begun with a careful survey of the development of revelation and doctrine in a particular area down to the classical formulation of the revealed truth by the authentic, living teaching authority of the Church. Only when this has been done is any attempt made to search out, through speculation, the deeper implications and mutual relations of revealed truths. Thus, speculation is not divorced from the primary data of revealed truth grasped in its original meaning.

The Thomistic Revival

In 1879, the year following his election as pope, Leo XIII issued an encyclical letter, *Aeterni Patris,* on the study of St. Thomas Aquinas. It recalled Catholic thinkers to the great store of wisdom to be found in Aquinas' writings. The study of St. Thomas had never been entirely neglected within the Church, but it was confined in large part to the Dominican Order, whose great ornament he is, and to certain other religious communities. In the nineteenth century, the teaching of

St. Thomas provided no common basis for the education of priests. Pope Leo had become convinced, by personal study, of the immense profit for both philosophy and theology to be gained by a renewed study of his writings. Hence, the letter on St. Thomas was among the very first acts of his pontificate. The influence of the Thomistic revival was felt first and most strongly in the field of philosophy. This was to be expected, since one of Thomas' greatest contributions was the clear elaboration of a metaphysics based on the categories of being.

But St. Thomas was not primarily a philosopher; he was a theologian. His preoccupation with Sacred Scripture and tradition was an abiding feature of his relatively short life. His analysis of the deposit of faith in terms of *being* enabled him to sketch the lines of a magnificent synthesis of all theology, wherein he was able to make all the parts fit. It begins with the study of God in the unity of His nature and the trinity of His personality. And, from the inner power of trinitarian life, there proceeded by God's free creative act the multitude of finite beings, all joined to one another in the unity of a single universe on account of their relationship to God as end. And as all things proceed from God, so they return to Him, each according to its nature. Even man's sin, which turned him from God, finds its superabundant remedy in the work of Christ, the incarnate Son of God and our way to the Father. His work is made available to us through the Church and in the sacraments.

It is this sweeping vision of St. Thomas, combining metaphysical penetration with historical perspective, which rescued theology from verbalism and opened the way for a deeper understanding of the whole of God's revelation. The mistake, occasionally made, of taking a particular statement of St. Thomas about something as the last word on the subject, detracts in no way from the enormous value to be gained from a patient, thorough study of the development of the Thomistic synthesis. It is not a closed system of thought held together by abstract definitions, but a system open to indefinite growth, whose internal unity is only a reflection of the living oneness of objective truth.

Psychology of the Person

The third main influence which has served to affect modern trends in theological method is not something proper to theology itself, but rather is a more reflective awareness of subjectivity in all areas of human activity. "Subjectivity" is used here without any pejorative connotation, simply to designate the inwardness of the human person, his interior self-possession, the center of liberty within him (influenced though it be by many forces within and without) enabling him to say "I" in response to a "thou." Feuerbach, in *The Essence of Christianity*, published in the first half of the nineteenth century as a polemic against belief in God, made frequent use of the expression "I-thou" relation. In our day the Jewish philosopher Martin Buber has done much to popularize this insight. Further enlightenment on this way of viewing man came with the development of the modern study of psychology, which has set in a new light the essential importance of interpersonal relations for development of the personality. This is not all as revolutionary as it is sometimes made to appear, but the explicit insistence on these points is something characteristic of our own day and constitutes a most valuable contribution.

When it is remembered that the basic questions of theology are the ultimate questions, those which reach to the deepest significance of human life and man's relationship to the ultimately real, it becomes clear that theological method must take into account this fresh approach to subjectivity and intersubjectivity. It tends to make all theological truth more relevant to human needs, and it has injected new vigor into the understanding of the most varied parts of theology. Creation is seen not just as making something out of nothing, but as

God's personal initiative calling other persons into existence and inviting them to everlasting friendship with Himself—an initiative which awaits a response from the created person. Grace is thought of not merely as a physical participation in divine life, but as the foundation for entering into personal relationships with God in the activity of faith, hope, and love. The sacraments are not just efficacious signs of grace, but personal encounters between Christ and the human person. This enrichment of theology is only just beginning to be felt, and the years ahead should see most rewarding developments along this line.

Conclusion

All that we have said can perhaps be summarized by saying that modern trends in theological method are marked by a deeper awareness of what theology really is: the understanding of faith, and by an appreciation of the fact that this faith essentially is man's response to a message of salvation communicated by God at definite times and places, reaching its fullness in Christ, and transmitted by the Church. These trends are vitalizing theological speculation by genuine understanding. And they are causing fruitless polemics to be abandoned in favor of an effort to make the truth of God a significant force in the whole of human life.

Chapter III

REDISCOVERY OF THE BIBLE

by

John E. Huesman

Since the close of the Second World War, there has been a remarkable surge of interest in religion, particularly here in the United States. This interest is not to be measured exclusively by the increased number of churchgoers; it is to be noted as well in the new zest for religious discussion and controversy on the college level. Since the end of the war, numerous non-Catholic universities have put in courses in theology—courses that are attended to capacity. In addition to the private institutions, at least twenty-six state universities in our country have now introduced departments of theology. A further example of this new interest in religion and theology is to be seen in the eagerness with which American publishers are seeking manuscripts of religious books, for the simple reason that these religious books are selling. The reasons for this new interest in religion are not difficult to find, and although many factors have contributed to this new interest, three come quickly to mind. The first would be, paradoxically enough—the failure of science. Near the close of the nineteenth century, and in the early part of our own twentieth century, the amazing progress in scientific research brought with it a sense of supreme self-confidence. Science, we were told, held the key to all of man's problems. Religion came to be looked upon just as a crutch for the weak. Then came the holocaust of World War II, the development of nuclear weapons, and a series of traitorous incidents in which some of our scientists betrayed military secrets to the enemy. Gone today is that sense of self-confidence that science holds all the answers. In its stead there has grown a dread fear of this giant that man has created for himself. Men have come to realize that science, if left to itself, may well spell doom for all mankind. In this situation inquiring minds have turned to religion for some answers and assistance.

A second factor that has contributed to this growing interest in religion was the discovery, in 1947, of the Dead Sea Scrolls. These documents captured the fancy of men the world over and led to a renewed interest in the study of the origins of Christianity.

A third factor, and one far more important than the first two, has been our twentieth-century Biblical renaissance, which was already in full bloom at the close of the Second World War, and which had a wealth of information at its disposal to provide to those who were turning to religion for some answers to their problems. Why are we having this twentieth-century Biblical revival, or renaissance, as it is often termed? Assuredly it constitutes the most flourishing Biblical movement in the history of the Church. To answer this question, we must know something about the development of Scripture itself and its use within the Church.

Background to Biblical Understanding

To start, I would like to try to answer these questions and give an example of the methodology now being employed by Catholic Biblical scholars. The Bible presents us with a unique phenomenon, for in it we have some seventy-two books, all the work of one principal author, the Holy Spirit, who has made use of numerous human instruments in the composition of his message. Moses, the first of the human instruments to be employed by the Holy Spirit, wrote in the thirteenth century before Christ. The Apostle John, perhaps the last of the human instruments used by the Holy Spirit, wrote in the first century of our Christian era. Hence, we can see that the Bible gives us some fourteen hundred years of the development of God's plan of salvation, coming from Moses up to John.

This plan of salvation was not something just tossed off in the abstract. It was geared for a specific people, God's chosen people, the Hebrews. These Hebrews were Semites, had the psychology of Semites, felt and acted as Semites. If, then, this plan were to be understood by the Hebrews, it had to be couched in the language, in the psychology, in the literary forms, that were in vogue among Hebrews. These literary forms—or, as we might call them, literary fashions, literary genres—just like fashions in clothing, are constantly changing. If we need proof of that, take a copy of this morning's newspaper, then go down to the public library and pick up a newspaper from some area of a century ago, and see how much the literary form of newspaper writing has changed in just one hundred years. Or, by way of another analogy, take a political speech, of which we have heard plenty in recent times, and contrast the type of political writing that is being done today with, say, a speech of Daniel Webster, and see just how much the literary form of political writing has changed in just one hundred years.

As we have seen, the Bible gives us some fourteen hundred years of the development of God's plan of salvation. If then, we, from our vantage point of the twentieth century, want to understand that plan in its written Biblical form, we have to know something about the historical background, the psychology of the people, and the various literary forms that went into the composition of the Bible throughout this long period. And here is where our problem begins; because long before the coming of Christ, there were forces at work rendering ever more obscure our knowledge of the ancient Semitic Near East. As early as the seventh and sixth centuries B.C., the non-Semitic Medes and Persians swept out of the mountains from the East, bringing with them a non-Semitic culture which they attempted to implant in the Near East. Of far greater importance, of course, were the inroads made by the Greeks, who, after the time of Alexander the Great, made studied efforts to Hellenize the whole of the Near East.

The Jews, contrary to what Wellhausen was propounding in the nineteenth century, were not living in a cultural vacuum but were very open to the influences going on around them. And, whereas they maintained a very fervent affection for the letter of the Old Testament, even the Jews gradually lost contact with the literary forms that had gone into its composition. Finally, in His own good time, Our Lord and Saviour, Jesus Christ, appeared on this earth and brought with Him the Gospel message of the glad tidings, which was also to be handed to man via a Semitic idiom. While on earth, of course, He also founded His Church and gave that Church an infallible teaching authority. With the death and Resurrection of Our Lord, and the ultimate rejection of Christianity by the Chosen People, the Apostles turned, with this message of redemption, this Gospel message, to the Gentile world—to a world that was predominantly Greek in its culture.

It was to be God's Divine Providence that our dogma be built up within the framework of Greek philosophical thought. In the early centuries of Christianity, what do we note with regard to the use of the Bible? We can point to two general tendencies. The first was to study the Bible as though it were a Greek text, and not one of Semitic origin. The second tendency was to regard the Bible, and particularly the Old Testament, as though it were a *locus Messianicus*, a source of quotations pointing to the Messiah.

As I stated, these were general tendencies. There were exceptions, and one of those exceptions was St. Jerome, the Church patron of Scripture study. Jerome was convinced that if one really wanted to understand the Bible he must, as it were, immerse himself in a Semitic background. With this in mind, Jerome took himself to the Near East, hired rabbis to tutor him in Hebrew and Aramaic, and tried to absorb as much of this Semitic background as he could. We are all familiar with his great work, the Vulgate Version of the Bible.

But Jerome himself was limited by the shortcomings of his own mentors who, themselves, as I have mentioned, had lost contact with the literary forms that had gone into the composition of the earlier books of the Bible. Not long after the time of Jerome, we can note the rise of Mohammedanism in the Near East, to be followed by the long centuries of Turkish hegemony. And, throughout these long centuries, the Near East became simply a closed book to Western scholars.

In our quick survey, let's move over to the Christian West. What do we find there? We find a deep reverence for the Bible as God's own Book, which He has given to His Church. Once again, however, we can point to certain tendencies with regard to the use of the Bible. The first is going to be one already noted in the early centuries of the Church—a tendency to regard it as though it were a Greek text and not one of Semitic background. The second tendency, and one which flourished after the period of Scholasticism, was to regard the Bible as though it were a *locus theologicus*, a source book of quotations to back up the theses propounded by systematic theology. This would be the be-all and end-all of the Bible.

Biblical Problems in the Eighteenth and Nineteenth Centuries

Moving up now through the centuries, we find even darker days for the Bible, during the so-called Era of Enlightenment in France; from that period stem two great heresies, deism and rationalism. Deism maintains that, if there is a God, He is in His Heaven, we are down here, and there can be no possible contact between the two; this systematically rules out any possibility of revelation that God might make to His people. Rationalism attempts to divinize the mind of man, and simultaneously and utterly rejects the supernatural. In the nineteenth-century heyday of rationalism we can point to its two greatest advocates, both Germans, Julius Wellhausen and David Friedrich Strauss.

Wellhausen attempted a literary analysis of the sacred text, whereas Strauss, in his *Life of Jesus*, written in 1835, introduced the celebrated distinction between the historical Jesus and the Christ of faith. Take an example: in reading the New Testament we learned that Jesus walked down from Jerusalem to Jericho; Strauss would reason that anyone could walk down from Jerusalem to Jericho. Therefore, he would attribute that activity to the historical Jesus, the Jesus who actually lived. But if, in that same New Testament, we read something that smacks of the supernatural, of the miraculous, that must be attributed (he tells us) to the Christ of faith, who was merely a figment of man's imagination. Wellhausenism is dead today, thanks largely to the work of modern scientific archaeology. In certain very liberal circles, however, the influence of Strauss unfortunately is very much felt.

The era of Wellhausen and Strauss also saw the growth of higher criticism in Biblical circles, a movement that was to produce ambivalent reactions in the Christian world. To a small band of dedicated scholars and their loyal adherents this new research brought deeper interest in the Bible and results that were to stand the test of time. By the majority of eighteenth- and nineteenth-century Christians, however, the work of the critics was looked upon as a perilous hazard to the faith of ordinary folk. The resultant fear unfortunately strengthened the fundamentalist hold on the masses.

Thus far, we have mentioned a goodly number of negative influences which have affected the study of the Bible. Still, we have pointed out that we are in the midst today of our most flourishing Biblical movement. How are we able to explain it? Here, we have to make mention of something that at first glance seems wholly irrelevant so far as the Bible is concerned. In 1821 a very brilliant Frenchman by the name of Champollion succeeded in deciphering Egyptian hieroglyphics. Not many years later Grotefend (a German) and Rawlinson (an Englishman) solved the riddle of cuneiform writing. These two great discoveries, in combination with the new Anglo-French "sphere of influence" in the Near East, were once more to open up that area to Western thought. The nineteenth century would witness feverish archaeological activity throughout the region. Literally tens of thousands of cuneiform tablets were unearthed, tablets that enabled us to rediscover the languages, the cultures, and the literatures of the people of the Semitic ancient Near East. And, as the scholars began to study the documents, they noticed similarities in the type of writing found there and the type of writing found in our Bible.

In the van of scholars pursuing Semitic studies and their relevance for the Bible was the Dominican Père Lagrange, who set up the Ecole Biblique in Jerusalem. From its beginning in the nineteenth century down to the present day, this Dominican project has produced many of the outstanding Catholic scholars in the Biblical movement.

Developments during the Twentieth Century

The first significant results of this comparative work appeared at the turn of this century. Unfortunately for the Church, at that particular time Rome was embroiled in the crisis of Modernism—that heresy which says that doctrines are constantly evolving in such a way that the Catholic Church of the twentieth century would not be the same as the Catholic Church that Christ founded. And, unfortunately, some authorities in Rome thought that those who were interested in the comparative work between the newfound Semitic literatures and our Biblical literatures, were in some way influenced by Modernism. Catholic scholars in the Biblical field, including our most prominent figure, the eminent Dominican Père Lagrange, were effectively silenced at that particular time. At that time Rome also set up the Pontifical Biblical Commission, which was to serve as the watchdog of orthodoxy in things Biblical. At the same time it organized the Pontifical Biblical Institute in Rome, which was to be the sole institution in the Catholic Church where one could get a higher degree in Scripture. Rome, as it were, wanted all her future teachers of Scripture to get their training under her own watchful gaze. This period of silence lasted approximately forty years, until in 1943 we have the encyclical of Pius XII, *Divino Afflante Spiritu,* which was to be the Magna Carta of our modern Biblical movement. In that encyclical the pope urged Catholic scholars to shake off the shackles of silence and to "dig in" once more in their Biblical research; and this time it was to be in the light of the new knowledge to be found from the ancillary sciences of history, linguistics, and archaeology.

During the previous forty years, sound Protestant scholars had been doing very effective work. They, of course, were not bound by any restrictions from Rome, and we have benefited a great deal from the research they have made. But since 1943 there has been remarkable progress in Biblical research in the Catholic Church. In general it has taken a twofold direction. The first we might call the development of the traditional exegesis in the light of the new knowledge gained from the auxiliary sciences mentioned above. The best example of work in that field would be, by all means, the *Bible de Jérusalem,* the French Bible edited by the Dominicans in Jerusalem which, in my opinion, is the finest Bible in the world today. Other examples of Catholic work in this field are the Bonner Bible and the Echter Bible in Germany and, here in America, the Confraternity Old Testament. Of Protestant scholarship in this same vein, we can point to the Revised Standard Version; it is excellent and follows the same approach, using the knowledge gained from the ancillary sciences.

Biblical Theology

The second direction that Catholic Biblical work has taken since 1943 is in the field of Biblical theology. This can be defined as the study of God's doctrine as found in Sacred Scripture, analyzed and systematized according to Biblical categories. Let us take a brief example: the concept of sin. How does the speculative or systematic theologian define the concept "sin"? He makes use first of the magnificent synthesis of St. Thomas, who sees creation as an emanation of the goodness of God Himself. Men, as creatures, to gain their end must go back to God. Sin, then, is something that takes man off of the path back to God and is, therefore, aptly defined by the speculative theologian as a deordination. How does the Biblical theologian go about defining sin? He maintains that, adequately to define it, one must start with Genesis, work through the Bible, and find the various ideas that God Himself has revealed as highlighting the concept of sin. In the Bible we find sin described as disobedience, as rebellion, as treachery, as slavery, as death; and in the Prophets is found the poignant idea of sin as fornication or adultery, because it ruptures the spouse relationship between the soul and Almighty God. This is a very brief example, but I think it should shed some light on how much Biblical theology can contribute to the understanding of sin, over and above what the speculative theologian has to offer us. Many are the added nuances that the Bible shows in this particular concept. And this is just one example. One can take any concept and work it through the Bible, and find out what God Himself has revealed through the Bible, giving a fuller understanding of these Biblical themes.

Literary Forms

Perhaps the most significant contribution that the study of these ancillary sciences has added to Biblical progress is found in the new approach to the sacred text by the analysis of the literary form involved. Many people and, unfortunately, not a few clerics immediately grow disturbed when they hear the Catholic Biblical scholar talk about the "literary form" of a sacred document. They think he is either tainted with rationalism or treating the document as though it were something merely human; or else they think he is infected with Modernism and suggesting that the doctrines are changing.

The analysis of the literary form of a sacred document in no way affects the inspired sacred character of the document. We all know that the Holy Spirit has made use of human instruments in the composition of His message and, as is His wont, He uses human instruments according to their nature. That nature, however, is not an intellect and a will in the abstract, but an intellect and a will conditioned by the historical circumstances, by the psychology of the people, by the literary forms in vogue among this particular people at this particular time and place. This is extremely important, this matter of the new approach concerning the analysis of literary forms; and since it is still so suspect by some Catholics it is worth while to quote from *Divino Afflante Spiritu* itself to show that this is not simply one writer's opinion, but is what Pius XII has propounded:

> But frequently the literal sense is not so obvious in the words and writings of ancient oriental authors as it is with the writers of today. What they intended to signify by their words is not determined only by the laws of grammar and philology or merely by the context. It is absolutely necessary for the interpreter to go back in spirit to those remote centuries of the East, and make proper use of the aids afforded by history, archaeology, ethnology, and other sciences in order to discover what literary forms the writers of that early age intended to use and did in fact employ; for to express what they had in mind, the ancients of the East did not always use the same forms and expressions that we use today. They used those that were current among the people of their own time and place. What these were, the exegete cannot determine a priori, but only from the careful study of ancient oriental literature. This study has been pursued during the past few decades with greater care and industry than formerly, and has made us better acquainted with the literary forms used in those ancient times,

whether in poetical descriptions or in the formulation of rules and laws of conduct, or in the narration of historical facts and events. It has now clearly demonstrated the unique pre-eminence among all the ancient nations of the East, which the people of Israel enjoyed in historical writing, both in regard to the antiquity of the events recorded and to the accuracy with which they are related. A circumstance which is, of course, explained by the *charism* of divine inspiration, and by the special religious purpose of Biblical history.

At the same time no one who has a just conception of Biblical inspiration will be surprised to find that the sacred writers, like the other ancients, employ certain arts of exposition and narrative, certain idioms especially characteristic of the Semitic languages (known as approximations) and certain hyperbolical and even paradoxical expressions designed for the sake of emphasis. The sacred books need not exclude any of the forms of expression which were commonly used in human speech by the ancient peoples, especially of the East, to convey their meaning so long as they are in no way incompatible with God's sanctity and God's truth.

In this very important passage, the pope first of all tells us that different literary forms are actually to be found in our texts. Again, he proposes a criterion with regard to the use of these literary forms, for he tells us that any literary form may be found in the Bible so long as it does not contradict the holiness or the truth of Almighty God.

What, for example, would be a literary form contradicting the holiness of Almighty God? Pornography. Obviously there will be no pornography in the sacred text. What would be an example of a literary form contradicting the truth of Almighty God? A genuine myth, something which attempts to divinize a material element. With those two ruled out, any other literary form may be found in our sacred text. There we discover at least three different types of history. First we find history as it is understood by a modern professional—a Toynbee or a Sontag. (In fact, these historians are coming to recognize that our oldest form of true historical writing is found in the Bible, in the Second Book of Samuel, chapters 9–20, which give the history of David.) History of a far different type is to be found in the early chapters of Genesis. We find still a third type in the Books of Kings. A modern professional historian dealing with the kings of Judah or Israel would consider himself obligated first to search out material concerning their military, social, business, and diplomatic activities, and their personal affairs. Only then would he consider himself ready to give a verdict on any particular king. Not so the sacred writer, who wants to know only if this particular king furthered the true cult of Yahweh. We can better understand him once we find out what kind of history he is writing. We find beautiful poetry in the Bible, the lyrical poetry of the Psalter, where the psalmist wants simply to sing out his love of Almighty God. We have the dirge or the *Qinah* poetry of the Lamentations noting the destruction of Jerusalem and its precious Temple. We find saga in the Bible, stories, for example, about Samson and the Patriarchs. We find fable when the plants and trees in the Book of Judges talk to one another about raising up a king over themselves. And we find didactic fiction in the Bible. These are just a few of the literary forms to be found in our sacred text.

The Book of Jona

To illustrate the methodology currently employed in Bible studies we will take the extremely short Book of Jona, which in the Hebrew Bible takes just three pages. Everyone is familiar, of course, with the story of the prophet Jona. But we are interested in the literary forms of this book. The traditional view is that we are dealing here with history, and those who favor this position say that there was a real prophet by the name of Jona, who lived in the eighth century B.C. We find him mentioned, for example, in the Books of Kings, and the people who back this view tell us that among believing Catholics there should be no problem about all the miracles to be found in the Book of Jona. And they make a great to-do about the testimony of our Lord as found in St. Matthew's gospel. Since this is so important to them we should read the significant verses. They will be found in Matthew 12:39–42: "But he answered and said to them, 'An evil and adulterous generation demands a sign, and no sign shall be given it but the sign of Jonas the prophet. For even as Jonas was in the belly of the fish three days and three nights, so will the Son of Man be three days and three nights in the heart of the earth. The men of Nineve will rise up in the judgment with this generation and will condemn it; for they repented at the preaching of Jonas, and behold, a greater than Jonas is here. The queen of the South will rise up in the judgment with this generation and will condemn it; for she came from the ends of the earth to hear the wisdom of Solomon, and behold, a greater than Solomon is here.'" The traditionalists tell us that Christ here is putting Jona's experience in the belly of the great fish and the conversion of the Ninivetes on the same plane as his own stay in the tomb, and the coming of the Queen of Sheba. The latter two are historical events; the earlier two should also be considered historical.

What do the modern exegetes have to say about this traditional view? They challenge it on various grounds. First of all, for historical reasons: In the eighth century B.C. Ninive was the greatest city in the world. For our author it seems to have become just a memory, for he tells us that Ninive was. Again we can point to a substantial inaccuracy with regard to the size of the city. We know today from scientific archaeology that the circumference of Ninive in the time of the Assyrian monarch Sennacherib, was eight miles. We know too from ancient sources that, after the destruction of Ninive in 612, popular fancy blew up the size of the former city to incredible proportions. In line with this later exaggeration, our author says that Ninive was a city of three days' journey. Again, if we were dealing with history here, we would expect to find some mention of the details contained in this work in the strictly historical books of the Bible. However, we find not a word.

Again, the modern exegete challenges the old view for literary reasons. Today we know much more about the development of the Hebrew language than did scholars even fifty years ago, and we know quite definitely that the language of the Book of Jona is not the Hebrew of the eighth century B.C. but that of some three or four hundred years later—quite a difference. Again the modern exegete challenges the old view on the basis of what he calls the artificial character of the supernatural as we find it in this book. Of course, no Catholic can challenge the possibility of the supernatural, but in this particular work we find the supernatural multiplied at will, as it were. We have the miraculous storm, the miraculous choice of Jona as the one responsible for it, and his miraculous stay in the belly of the great fish.

Finally, the modern challenges the traditional view for what he calls the accumulation of improbabilities. What does this mean? In the Old Testament, no prophet was ever given the job of preaching to the pagans. Hence we find it very strange that this lone prophet Jona be assigned the role of preaching penance to, of all people, the hated Assyrians, who were at the height of their power in the eighth century B.C. Far more improbable is it that they were converted. If we are dealing with history, the conversion overnight of half a million souls would be a far greater miracle than that of Pentecost, when a couple of thousand were converted by the preaching of all the Apostles. Again, if we were dealing with history, we can be sure that Hebrew historians would have trumpeted this victory of Yahweh over the false deities of the Assyrians in every subsequent page of the Hebrew Bible. But we find no mention of it whatever. For these reasons, and for no fear of the supernatural, the modern exegete states that the literary form of this little book is *didactic fiction.*

What is to be said now of the testimony of Christ? We maintain that these narratives retain their force, whether the events alluded to be of a historical or of a parable nature. We have all heard many Sunday sermons, and we are familiar with the practice whereby preachers refer to the publican or the prodigal son as though they were real people. The Church does this in the liturgy; for example, in the Mass for the Dead, we are told to pray that, with Lazarus, the onetime pauper (not the Lazarus Christ raised from the dead) we may have eternal rest. Consequently, for Christ and the Apostles the whole of the Old Testament, both in historical and in parable content, prefigured in some way the coming Kingdom of God. Hence, we see no difficulty in the fact that Our Lord could make use of a parable element, this stay of Jona in the belly of the whale, to prefigure his own stay on earth, which was a historical thing. Nor do we see any difficulty that He would juxtapose the conversion of the Ninivetes, a parable element, with the coming of the Queen of Sheba, a historical event.

Thus far we have dealt with the negative evaluations of the Book of Jona. What have we to offer in the positive way now in our understanding, in our analysis, of this book? Pope Pius XII in *Divino Afflante Spiritu* says that we are supposed to make use of our linguistic background and knowledge in evaluating such a book as this. As previously noted, authorities categorically maintain that the Hebrew of this particular book is that of the fifth or fourth centuries B.C. What was the historical situation of God's people at this particular time? They had come back from exile in the city of Babylon. What did they find now in their beloved Palestine? They found that a goodly number of pagans had come in and settled down there. In a short time the Hebrews started intermarrying with these pagans, to the great detriment of normative Yahwism. In this particular crisis God raised up Nehemia to purge his people of this problem. We can see the fervor with which he went around breaking up these marriages in the Book of Nehemia. As a result of this cleansing movement a certain feeling understandably grew up among the Jews which we now refer to as particularism: the idea that Yahweh was their particular possession, and that He had no interest with anyone else. This, of course, was theologically unsound, and in this historical situation God revealed to the author of the Book of Jona the following truth: "I am the God of all men; no matter what your nation may be, if you repent of your sins, I will be merciful." That is the theological teaching of the Book of Jona.

How then was the author to get this across to the men of his times, who were steeped in the idea of particularism? Under the light of inspiration he chose the literary form of didactic fiction and built up this delightful, if pungent, story of a prophet who was given the job of preaching penance to the despised Assyrians. The prophet by no means relished this role. In fact he took off in the opposite direction to escape fulfilling it. He boarded a ship. God, of course, was not to be frustrated, so we see the drama of this story build up. We have the miraculous storm and the miraculous choice of Jona as the one responsible for it. The sailors threw him overboard, and he was taken in by the fish. After his three-day retreat in its belly, he decided he would go along with what Almighty God wanted. The fish conveniently spewed him out in the northern section of the Mediterranean. From there he proceeded to Ninive and preached penance to the Assyrians. And the worst possible thing happened. They were converted. As the little book ends, we find the prophet sitting under his gourd plant sulking at the mercy of Almighty God, to, of all people, these Assyrians.

How better could the author have gotten across the theological meat of this book than by this story? If we stop and study this theological analysis of the Book of Jona the sacred text will become more meaningful. And it is just such a deeper and fuller understanding of the theological content of the Bible—as salvation history—that our new approach seeks. By no means, then, are the intentions of the modern Catholic Biblical scholar negative. He does not seek to despoil his fellow Catholics of their heritage, as some mistakenly assert. In

God's unfathomable providence, it has been decreed that our day should enjoy the fruits of remarkable discoveries in paleontology, ethnology, and archaeology. Those efforts have provided us new insights into the Semitic mentality, and into the literary genres that the Semites employed to express themselves. In his analysis, then, of these genres, the Catholic Biblical scholar seeks not to supplant, but to supplement, our Biblical heritage, so that man in our age may come to know and appreciate the divine plan of salvation and thus participate more readily in the divine life it provides.

Chapter IV

COVENANT IN THE ANCIENT WORLD

by

Albert J. Zabala

The Bible presents the word of God in the words of man. Without a comprehension of what man is trying to say, it is impossible to understand the divine word. Sacred history was not written in a vacuum, nor did it drop from heaven. Today, our greatly increased knowledge of the ancient Near Eastern languages, literary forms, and customs enables the Biblical exegete of the twentieth century to have a richer appreciation of the gracious way in which God has accommodated His message to man's diverse cultures over the centuries. The covenant, a pact which binds together two parties, is at the heart of Israel and Christianity. It is one example of God adjusting Himself to man's way of expressing his personal and societal relationships. Pius XII, in his encyclical *Divino Afflante Spiritu* (which has been called the Magna Carta of Catholic Biblical studies), stressed the need of finding out the various literary forms of the Bible:

> What is the literal sense of a passage is not always as obvious in the speeches and writings of the ancient authors of the East, as it is in the works of our time. What they wish to express is not to be determined by the rules of grammar and philology alone, nor solely by the context; the interpreter must, as it were, go back wholly in spirit to those remote centuries of the East and with history, archaeology, ethnology, and other sciences, accurately determine what modes of writing, so to speak, the authors of that ancient period would be likely to use, and in fact did use.

Wellhausen, the nineteenth-century German Biblical scholar, struck at the very heart of the Israelite religion by denying the Mosaic origin of the covenant, and judged it to be no earlier than the sixth-century prophet Jeremia. On the other hand Mendenhall, a recognized American scholar, has shown that certain Hittite covenants of the fourteenth and thirteenth centuries B.C. are remarkably similar to the covenant of Moses. Only within the last half century has there been any sizable knowledge of these Hittites, whose kingdom occupied the site of present-day Turkey and flourished between 1900 and 1200 B.C.

These ancient Hittite covenants shed great light on the covenant of Sinai. Their basic structure will be seen to be imbedded in the Mosaic covenant, and thus will substantiate the Mosaic origin of this covenant. These ancient covenants of fealty were imposed to bind a king to his vassal, a vassal to his king. Their form is easily recognizable: the preamble, followed by a historical prologue, then stipulations, and the blessings and curses. In the preamble the Hittite king presented himself to his vassal through a messenger—a messenger whose role was to emphasize the power and majesty of the all-powerful king. The historical prologue recalled all that the Hittite monarch had done in the past for his vassal—usually a description of actual historical events. These deeds furnished motivation for the vassal's response, couched in the law. This bound the vassal to the sovereign in undivided loyalty and service. Further laws spelled out the mutual responsibilities of king and vassal in time of war—the treatment and disposition of fugitives, or captives. The gods of both the covenant-bound parties were then invoked as witnesses to this sacred treaty. Frequently, the heavens, the sea, and the clouds were called upon as witnesses. In order that later generations might make a personal recommitment, provisions were made for the periodic reading of the covenant. Finally, this sacred covenant was concluded by invoking blessings for fidelity and curses for infidelity. After the thirteenth century, with the disappearance of the Hittites, this form of the Hittite covenant no longer existed, except as it found expression in the Sinai covenant.

I. The Mosaic Covenant

It is one thing to assert that the covenant of Sinai bears a resemblance to the Hittite covenant of the fourteenth and thirteenth centuries B.C., and it is another thing to demonstrate this assertion. Only by an exegesis of the Biblical texts relative to the covenant can this claim be substantiated.

There are several accounts of the Sinai covenant. In Exodus (ch. 19) Moses is presented as God's messenger. ". . . Moses went up the mountain to God. Then the Lord called to him and said, 'Thus shall you say to the house of Jacob . . .' " (v. 3). The following verse presents the historical prologue. " 'You have seen for yourselves how I treated the Egyptians and how I bore you up on eagle wings and brought you here to myself' " (v. 4). By this liberation from the slavery of the Egyptians, Yahweh has revealed to Israel that He is their Saviour. The exodus is the first act of salvation history. Yahweh's rights over Israel are grounded on His intervention on their behalf. The people are to respond by fidelity to the law of the covenant. " 'Therefore, if you hearken to my voice and keep my covenant' " (v. 5). Here law is seen as a response to history. The sacred character of the law is evident by reason of the fact that it is a response to sacred history. Law and history are thus united in both the Hittite and the Mosaic covenants.

An analysis of the Hittite king-vassal covenant indicates that the superior power is regarded as a king; so, too, an analysis of the Mosaic covenant makes clear that Israel also regards Yahweh as king. By saving Israel from Egypt, Yahweh has formed Israel as His kingdom, the people of God, a holy people, set apart as the Lord's very own. Israel is not merely the creature of the Lord, nor His servant, but His covenant-partner. "'You shall be my special possession, dearer to me than all other people, though all the earth is mine. You shall be to me a kingdom of priests, a holy nation'" (Exod. 19:5-6). Israel's free acceptance and fidelity to the covenant will bring about this great blessing. The people freely enter into the covenant. "'All that the Lord has said, we will do'" (Exod. 19:8). The covenant has now created Israel and its faith and its law.

II. Exodus 20

The Decalogue, which is the law of Sinai, is the text of the Mosaic covenant. In this account we find the same union of history and law. "'I, the Lord, am your God, who brought you out of the land of Egypt, that place of slavery'" (v. 2). This is the historical prologue. And following this is the law: "'You shall not have other gods besides me'" (v. 3). It is worthy of note that the Ten Commandments give no details concerning the nature of divine worship. The law, which responds to God's election, makes two basic demands: one vertical, toward the worship of the one God—Israel is to have no other god as her king. This prohibition, too, is thoroughly consistent with the Hittite covenant form which demanded that the vassal have but one overlord. The other demand of the covenant is horizontal, relating Israelite to Israelite in justice and fraternal love. This social aspect of the covenant will be an essential characteristic of both the old and the new covenants. The fact is that, in the new covenant, Christ will say that the entire law is summed up in one—love thy neighbor.

Further analysis of the Decalogue shows that many of the Commandments have as their purpose the warding off of those dangers which may destroy the newly created community; namely, murder, adultery, and stealing. During the centuries Israel will manifest a growing awareness of the importance of this community aspect of law. As Yahweh has shown His love of the community, so, too, is each Israelite to love the community. "'The needy will never be lacking in the land; that is why I command you to open your hand to your poor and needy kinsman in your country'" (Deut. 15:11). If Israel obeys, it is guaranteed divine blessings; if it refuses, it will suffer the punishment of the Lord. "'If you heed his voice and carry out all I tell you, I will be an enemy to your enemies and a foe to your foes'" (Exod. 23:22).

III. The Sacred Meal

It was common in the ancient world for special symbolic rites to follow the conclusion of a covenant. When Abraham made a covenant with the Lord, he cut certain animals in half (Gen. 15:7–10). This was his way of saying: "May I be cleft in two, as these animals have been, should I be unfaithful to my covenant." After his covenant with the Lord, Moses sacrificed peace offerings of oxen. He then took the blood of these animals and sprinkled it on the altar and on the people.

> When Moses came to the people and related all the words and ordinances of the Lord, they all answered with one voice, "We will do everything that the Lord has told us." Moses then wrote down all the words of the Lord and, rising early the next day, he erected at the foot of the mountain an altar and twelve pillars for the twelve tribes of Israel. Then, having sent certain young men of the Israelites to offer holocausts and sacrifice young bulls as peace offerings to the Lord, Moses took half of the blood and put it in large bowls; the other half he splashed on the altar. Taking the Book of the Covenant, he read it aloud to the people, who answered, "All that the Lord has said, we will heed and do." Then he took the blood and sprinkled it on the people, saying, "This is the blood of the covenant which the Lord has made with you in accordance with all these words of his" (Exod. 24:3–8).

This blood was thought of as life (Lev. 17:11). It was sprinkled on the altar which represented Yahweh, and upon the people in order to symbolize the unity of life between Yahweh and Israel. The personal communion of life was established by the communion of wills. "'All that the Lord has said, we will heed and do'" (Exod. 24:7). The blood of the covenant will continue to play, in later generations, a prominent role in the sacrifices of Israel. Here there is no room for magic; Israel meets its Lord in the observance of His will.

The covenant is then concluded by a sacred meal. "After gazing on God, they could still eat and drink" (Exod. 24:11). It was a meal of fellowship and peace. There was no greater crime than for one to eat at the same table and then to attack his host.

> Even my friend who had my trust
> and partook of my bread, has raised his heel against me.
> (Ps. 40:10)

John the Evangelist will recall these words in his account of the Last Supper (13:18). The meal has united Israel to its Lord and has created a fellowship among the Israelites themselves.

IV. Gratuity of the Covenant

When later generations grew proud of the covenant and of Yahweh's choice, they were to be reminded that there was nothing in Israel that demanded Yahweh's intervention—nothing that demanded the covenant. Yahweh had existed before Israel. No necessary link existed between the two save the free election of the Lord, an election that was a divine grace.

> It was not because you are the largest of all nations that the Lord set his heart on you and chose you, for you are really the

smallest of all nations. It was because the Lord loved you and because of his fidelity to the oath he had sworn to your fathers, that he brought you out with his strong hand from the place of slavery, and ransomed you from the hand of Pharao, king of Egypt (Deut. 7:7–8).

The only reason for the covenant and for Israel's existence is divine love. The granting of the land, too, will be seen as an expression of divine love.

After the Lord, your God, has thrust them out of your way, do not say to yourselves, "It is because of my merits that the Lord has brought me in to possess this land"; for it is really because of the wickedness of these nations that the Lord is driving them out before you. No, it is not because of your merits or the integrity of your heart that you are going in to take possession of their land; but the Lord, your God, is driving these nations out before you on account of their wickedness and in order to keep the promise which he made on oath to your fathers, Abraham, Isaac and Jacob. (Deut. 9:4–5).

The very gratuity of God's choice makes the religion of Israel radically distinct from the nature religion of its neighbors, who had deified the moon, or the stars, or the vital forces of nature. But Israel was not allowed to forget the gratuity of God's love.

He found them in a wilderness,
a wasteland of howling desert.
He shielded them and cared for them,
guarding them as the apple of his eye.

As an eagle incites its nestlings forth
by hovering over its brood,
So he spread his wings to receive them
and bore them up on his pinions.

The Lord alone was their leader,
no strange god was with him.
(Deut. 32:10–12)

V. Renewal of the Covenant

Just as the Hittite covenants had made provisions for the renewal of the covenant, so, too, was the Israel of succeeding generations to renew its covenant with the Lord. Josue, the successor of Moses, led the people of God into the Promised Land and gathered together the various tribes at Sichem, near the grave of the patriarch Joseph. On this occasion, Josue reminded his people of those great deeds of salvation history. He began with the promise made to Abraham, which was a command to history. He then recalled God's intervention in Egypt on behalf of His people, the covenant of Sinai and, finally, the giving of the land. Here, once again, in this covenant renewal we find the basic Hittite covenant form of the fourteenth and thirteenth centuries B.C. Josue was the messenger of Yahweh, the great king. We have the historical prologue which manifests both Yahweh's love and choice of Israel. This was followed by a demand for a response, which was the law of Israel. "'Now, therefore, fear the Lord and serve him completely and sincerely'" (Jos. 24:14). The people were drawn into the covenant by their free acceptance. "'We will serve the Lord, our God, and obey his voice'" (Jos. 24:24). The covenant of Sinai had now been renewed.

For generations to come the covenant renewal will bring Sinai and its law to the people and will make them part of God's kingdom. They will meet their Lord not in the forces of nature, as their Canaanite neighbors will attempt to do, but they will meet the Lord in the faithful observance of His law.

And the king went up to the temple of the Lord, and all the men of Juda, and all the inhabitants of Jerusalem with him, the priests and the prophets, and all the people both little and great, and in the hearing of them all he read all the words of the book of the covenant which was found in the housc of the Lord. And the king stood upon the step, and made a covenant with the Lord, to walk after the Lord, and to keep his commandments, and his testimonies and his ceremonies, with all their heart, and with all their soul, and to perform the words of this covenant, which were written in that book; and the people agreed to the covenant (4 Kgs. 23:2–3).

At Sichem, and in all the covenant renewals, Sinai lives on, ever inviting Israel to respond to Yahweh's covenant love.

The Hittite treaties were inscribed on tablets and placed in a sanctuary and so, too, was the Israelite covenant. "So Josue made a covenant with the people that day and made statutes and ordinances for them at Sichem, which he recorded in the Book of the Law of God; Then he took a large stone and set it up there under the oak that was in the sanctuary of the Lord" (Jos. 24:26). The placing of the text of the covenant in the presence of the Lord shows the sacred character of this treaty with Yahweh. Every seven years the law of Sinai was to be read in public, as Moses commanded:

"On the feast of Booths, at the prescribed time in the year of relaxation which comes at the end of every seven-year period, when all Israel goes to appear before the Lord, your God, in the place which he chooses, you shall read this law aloud in the presence of all Israel" (Deut. 31:10–11).

VI. Theology of History

History plays a unique part in Israel. Yahweh is known first in history and, only later, as the Lord of nature. History is the epiphany of the Lord. In history Yahweh will make known to Israel both His saving will and His presence. For Israel, history is revelation. In the covenant, and the exodus with which it is identified, God spoke not so much by what He said, but by what He did for His people. In prayer and public worship, Israel will ever recall, with loving memory, God's love made known in those great deeds of salvation history. The principal religious feasts reactualize those deeds of the Lord, as seen in the covenant renewal at Sichem. The feast of Passover, which is connected with the exodus from Egypt, will bring succeeding generations to Sinai to renew the covenant.

"Observe the month of Abib by keeping the Passover of the Lord, your God, since it was in the month of Abib that he brought you by night out of Egypt. You shall offer the Passover sacrifice from your flock or your herd to the Lord, your God, . . . You shall not eat leavened bread with it. . . . that you may remember as long as you live the day of your departure from the land of Egypt; for in frightened haste you left the land of Egypt" (Deut. 16:1–3).

Just as Christians know that Christ did not die and rise solely for the inhabitants of Jerusalem, so the Israelites knew that Yahweh did not liberate a small band of semi-nomads and enter into a covenant relationship with them only, but with all succeeding generations who would willingly accept the law of Sinai. The feasts of other peoples—the Canaanites, the Egyptians, the Babylonians—were bound up with timeless myths, with the cycle, with the concept that all things would be repeated forever, and that the really important events took place before time began—in mythical time—and that men must repeat these archetypal gestures. Israel's feasts recall the unique, nonrepeatable events which are the revelation of Yahweh's saving love and purpose. Only Israel takes time and history seriously and bases its very existence and hope on them. For Israel, time will be educative; it will be the means of God's gradual self-revelation. Time in Israel will look forward. It will be linear and filled with hope.

Sacred history is a demand that calls for man's response, which is sacred law. In Israel, therefore, law never exists in isolation; it is always related to what God does for His people. As salvation history grows richer, as God does more for His people, then law, which is the response to salvation history, will change and will share the light which increased revelation brings. Because of this intrinsic principle of growth, Biblical law is dynamic. God expects a response in proportion to the revelation He makes in this gradual unfolding. More can be expected of Moses than of Abraham because God revealed more to Moses. Isaia should respond more than Moses because God's self-manifestation in history revealed more of the divine goodness to Isaia than to Moses at Sinai. Likewise, the law of the new covenant will demand a greater response because the historical deeds of Christian salvation history, the death and Resurrection of Jesus Christ, far surpass any of God's self-manifestations made in the Old Testament. This constant relationship of sacred law to salvation history is at the heart of any meaningful Judeo-Christian theology of history. It is in the gradual awareness of the meaning of the covenant that law and history are tied together by the Lord of history, who first chooses us and then calls for our loving response, which is law.

VII. Growth of the Covenant

The story of Israel is the story of the vital evolution of the covenant. In the exodus and the covenant of Sinai, God revealed Himself as King, as Saviour, and as Redeemer.

> I will sing to the Lord, for he is gloriously triumphant; . . .
> and he has been my savior.
> In your mercy you led the people you redeemed; . . .
> The Lord shall reign forever and ever.
>
> (Exod. 15:1–2, 13, 18)

Succeeding generations would not reject this understanding of the covenant relationship, for once anything enters the stream of revelation it remains; it is never lost, it may only be enriched. And it will be the task of the prophets by their lives, their reflection, and the word of the Lord which will come upon them, to enrich the theological meaning of the covenant.

The eighth-century prophet, Osee, who wooed back his faithless spouse, will speak of Yahweh's relation to Israel as that of a bridegroom to his bride. The desert period will be seen as the period of Israel's youthful and faithful love.

So I will allure her;
  I will lead her into the desert
  and speak to her heart. . . .
She shall respond there as in the days of her youth,
  when she came up from the land of Egypt.

On that day, says the Lord,
She shall call me "My husband,"
  and . . .

I will espouse you to me forever.
(Osee 2:16–21)

Osee was indeed bold to use such imagery when Israel was being seduced by the fertility cults of its neighbors, the Canaanites, who worshiped the male deity, Baal, and the female deity, Astarte (cf. Ezech. 16:8).

Later, Isaia, reflecting on this nuptial imagery that Osee had introduced, will speak of infidelity to the covenant as harlotry (Isa. 1:21). Isaia himself will speak of the covenant relationship as that of a provident vineyardist to his vineyard.

Let me now sing of my friend [Yahweh],
  my friend's song concerning his vineyard. . . .
The vineyard of the Lord of hosts is the house of Israel . . .
(Isa. 5:1, 7)

During the exile, when the people were deprived of their land and their temple, Ezechiel will remind the people that the Lord of the covenant is the Good Shepherd and Israel is His flock.

I myself will pasture my sheep; I myself will give them rest, says the Lord God. The lost I will seek out, the strayed I will bring back, the injured I will bind up, the sick I will heal, . . . shepherding them rightly (Ezech. 34:15–16).

"Thus they shall know that I, the Lord, am their God, and they are my people, the house of Israel, says the Lord God" (Ezech. 34:30). Each of these images tells Israel something more of the tender love and care of God and of their own failure to respond to that love. These images will all find their fulfillment in Christ's relationship to His kingdom, as Bridegroom and Good Shepherd.

VIII. Failure of the Covenant

The prophets sing of the steadfast love of the Lord, of His fidelity to the covenant, and they indict Israel for its repeated violations of the covenant. Of greatest importance is the fact that Israel is not only condemned for want of sincere worship, but principally for want of social justice without which no worship is pleasing to God. No prophet denounces Israel more for its failure to live up to the horizontal dimension of the covenant than the prophet Amos. He is rightly called the prophet of social justice.

I hate, I spurn your feasts,
  I take no pleasure in your solemnities;
Your cereal offerings I will not accept,
  nor consider your stall-fed peace offerings.
Away with your noisy songs!
  I will not listen to the melodies of your harps.
But if you would offer me holocausts,
  then let justice surge like water,
  and goodness like an unfailing stream.

(Amos 5:21–24)

This denunciation of sacrifice on the part of Amos, and of many other prophets, was not to be considered as a condemnation of sacrifice, nor was the prophet to be opposed to the priest, for the prophet Isaia received his vocation in the Temple. The prophets were, however, enemies of mere formalism, enemies of any attempt to use worship to manipulate God.

They attempted to bring Israel back to a more interior love in their sacrificial offerings. The best yardstick of one's sincerity in worship was the fulfillment of one's obligation toward his neighbor. Men can deceive themselves about the sincerity of their devotion to God in public worship, but the sincerity of man's acts toward his fellow man is not difficult to measure and judge.

IX. Knowledge of God

In the prophets, failure to practice social justice is the equivalent of a lack of knowledge of God. Israel would only know the Lord, in proportion, as the social demands of the covenant were fulfilled. If land meant salvation, then exile, the loss of Yahweh's land, meant loss of salvation. Exile, and ultimately the need of a new covenant, would be the result of this want of knowledge of God. Isaia cries out,

> An ox knows its owner,
> and an ass, its master's manger;
> But Israel does not know,
> my people has not understood.
> (Isa. 1:3)

Here there is no question of a speculative knowledge of God (the ancient Semites did not sit outside of their tents and gaze at the stars in wondering speculation), but of a knowledge that results from fidelity to God's will. It was a lived-out knowledge.

> There is no fidelity, no mercy,
> no knowledge of God in the land.
> False swearing, lying, murder, stealing and adultery!
> (Osee 4:1–2)

The want of knowledge of God is the result of those deeds which destroy the fraternal life of the community.

Let not the wise man glory in his wisdom,
  nor the strong man glory in his strength,
  nor the rich man glory in his riches;
But rather, let him who glories, glory in this,
  that in his prudence he knows me,
Knows that I, the Lord, bring about kindness,
  justice and uprightness on the earth;
For with such am I pleased, says the Lord.
(Jer. 9:22–23)

Because he dispensed justice to the weak and the poor,
  it went well with him.
Is this not true knowledge of me?
  says the Lord.
(Jer. 22:16)

No one is exempt from this sin of social injustice.

Small and great alike, all are greedy for gain;
  prophet and priest, all practice fraud.
(Jer. 6:13)

It is this that will bring about the exile.

Therefore my people go into exile,
  because they do not understand;
Their nobles die of hunger . . .
(Isa. 5:13)

Because of the social injustices the Mosaic covenant is doomed. The prophets in describing the new covenant do so in terms of the knowledge of God and the social justice which will exist in the new covenant.

The days are coming, says the Lord, when I will make a new covenant with the house of Israel and the house of Juda. It will not be like the covenant I made with their fathers the day I took them by the hand to lead them forth from the land of Egypt; for they broke my covenant, and I had to show myself their master, says the Lord. But this is the covenant which I will make with the house of Israel after those days, says the Lord. I will place my law within them, and write it upon their hearts; I will be their God, and they shall be my people. No longer will they have need to teach their friends and kinsmen how to know the Lord. All, from least to greatest, shall know me, says the Lord, for I will forgive their evildoing and remember their sin no more (Jer. 31:31–34).

Jeremia was the first prophet to announce the news of a new covenant. This prophecy was a step forward to that interiorization of religion which will culminate in the risen Lord's gift of the indwelling Spirit.

When the prophets foretell of the future Messias, they speak of the kingdom of justice which He is to establish.

From David's throne, and over his kingdom,
which he confirms and sustains
By judgment and justice,
both now and forever.

(Isa. 9:6)

The Messias himself will have this knowledge (Isa. 11:2) and so, too, will all the members of His kingdom, ". . . for the earth shall be filled with knowledge of the Lord . . ." (Isa. 11:9). Where there is not justice, there can be no true religion. This is the message of the prophets. It will, likewise, be the message of the new covenant. Christ sums up all of the commandments in this love of our neighbor. This is the means for us to know Him. Jesus will manifest Himself to the man who keeps His law. "He who has my commandments and keeps them, he it is who loves me. But he who loves me will be loved by my Father, and I will love him and manifest myself to him" (John 14:21).

X. From Shadow to Reality

The divine plan for man's salvation was not fully revealed to Moses or the prophets. They were given but glimpses of that plan which was to unfold gradually during the course of salvation history. To appreciate the interrelationship that exists between the Old and the New Testament, we must appreciate that God is the author of both Act I and Act II. Certain events, things, and persons are made by God, in His plan, to be rough sketches or types of events, things, and persons in the future. They are shadows of future realities. Our understanding of those types is made clear to us by the liturgy and the New Testament. "For the law [has] but a shadow of the good things to come, and not the exact image of the objects . . ." (Heb. 10:1). Adam, Moses, and David are types or prophecies of a new Adam, a new Moses, a new David. The kingdom, the Temple, the Passover feasts, the blood of the covenant, the priesthood of Israel, the covenant itself, were in the providence of God merely shadows or prophecies of a new kingdom, a new Temple, a new Passover, the blood of the new covenant, a new priesthood, a new covenant (Jer. 31:31). The same mystery of divine love is revealed, but it is revealed gradually in time. Once again, time and history are given a meaning by both Israel and Christianity.

The events of the past are, therefore, not without meaning for the Christian. In the womb of Israel, God was already fashioning His Church. Israel's history is our history. Typology is the name given to this mutual relationship between God's past and future manifestations. The prophesied reality always surpasses the expectation of the earlier image.

> Remember not the events of the past,
> the things of long ago consider not;
> See, I am doing something new!
> Now it springs forth, do you not perceive it?
> (Isa. 43:18–19)

The new exodus and the new covenant are predicted in terms of the old covenant; they are not related, as is the blueprint to the building. God's gifts exceed the expectations given us by the promises.

XI. The Synoptic Gospels and the New Covenant

The Jewish Passover, commemorating and revivifying the covenant of Sinai, gave way to a new Passover and a new covenant, sealed in the blood of Christ. The Gospel of Mark, the oldest of our Gospels, recounts the words spoken by Jesus at the Last Supper when He instituted this new covenant, which is likewise a new sacrifice. "And taking a cup and giving thanks, he gave it to them, and they all drank of it; and he said to them, 'This is my blood of the new covenant, which is being shed for many'" (22:23–24). Matthew adds the words "unto the forgiveness of sins." (26:28). The account of Luke has "'This cup is the new covenant in my blood, which shall be shed for you'" (22:20).

Just as the covenant of Sinai was ratified in blood, so, too, the new covenant was to be sealed in the blood of the Lamb. Jesus certainly had in mind the Mosaic covenant and the prophecies of Isaia (c. 53) concerning the suffering servant of the Lord. This sacrifice of the new covenant supplants the old sacrifice of animals. The prophecy of Jeremia (31:31) concerning the new covenant is fulfilled.

XII. Paul and the Covenant

Even when the covenant is not explicitly mentioned, it dominates all New Testament theology. The theology of Paul is a theology of the covenant. Paul is proud of his ancestry. ". . . who are Israelites, who have the adoption as sons, and the glory of the covenants and the legislation and the worship and the promises . . ." (Rom. 9:4). Proud as Paul is of his Israelite heritage, its covenant was one of slavery, while the new covenant of Christ is one of freedom (Gal. 4:24). The new covenant is of the life-giving Spirit. ". . . our sufficiency is from God. He also it is who has made us fit ministers of the new covenant, not of the letter but of the Spirit; for the letter kills, but the Spirit gives life" (2 Cor. 3:5–6). It is in the outpouring of the Holy Spirit that Paul finds God's love manifest (Rom. 5:5; 6:4–16). This Holy Spirit transforms men's hearts.

Our earliest account of the Last Supper is that of St. Paul in his First Epistle to the Corinthians. "'This cup is the new covenant in my blood; do this as often as you drink it, in remembrance of me'" (11:25). This account is identical with that of Paul's disciple, Luke (22:20), in referring to the cup as a sign of a covenant. Just as the covenant of Sinai created Israel, so, too, the new covenant creates a new Israel. At Sinai, a meal ratified the covenant and created a fellowship among those eating. The Eucharistic meal not only unites all Christians to Christ the King, but it unites each Christian, one to the other. "Because the bread is one, we though many, are one body, all of us who partake of the one bread" (1 Cor. 10:17). The Eucharist, which is Him who is Love, gives men the power to realize the demands of justice and charity that constitute the horizontal dimension of both covenants.

XIII. The New Law

John, in his account of the Last Supper, that "hour" which had dominated the life of Jesus, makes no mention of the institution of the Eucharist. He does, however, narrate Jesus' words concerning the new law (13:34). Law, as we have seen, is a response to God's gracious mercy made manifest in the covenant. Thus a new covenant demands a new response, a new law. This is as true as ". . . when the priesthood is changed, it is necessary that a change of law be made also" (Heb. 7:12). John, therefore, in recounting the new law is implicitly describing a new covenant, and the two are corollaries. A new law without a new covenant is unthinkable. No longer is it sufficient for men to respond to Yahweh's saving deeds by living the law of Sinai; a new response is demanded. Men are now to love as Christ has loved them in this new and everlasting covenant. The superiority of the new law is evidence of the superiority of the new covenant. Thus shall men know their God—in loving as Christ commands. The old law was like the Greek slave that led the child to his teacher; it led us to Christ. "Therefore the law has been our tutor unto Christ, that we might be justified by faith" (Gal. 3:24). John, just as the prophets of Israel, stressed the freedom of God's election. "'You have not chosen me, but I have chosen you . . .'" (15:16). God is ever the sovereign Lord; His choice is the supreme grace.

XIV. Letter to the Hebrews

The author of the letter to the Hebrews compares and contrasts the two covenants. His is a theology of the covenant and a theology of history.

> God, who at sundry times and in divers manners spoke in times past to the fathers by the prophets, last of all in these days has spoken to us by his Son, whom he appointed heir of all things, by whom also he made the world . . . (Heb. 1:1–2).

The covenant of Christ is superior to the covenants of Abraham, Moses, and Josue to the degree that Christ's priesthood is superior. Their covenants were binding for a brief period; His will endure. ". . . all the more has Jesus become surety of a superior covenant" (Heb. 7:22). Their priesthood demanded daily sacrifices; the priesthood of Christ is realized in the sacrifice ". . . in offering up himself" (Heb. 7:27).

The transcendence of Christ's covenant flows from the eternal redemption that is realized through His blood (Heb. 9:12). Judaism is thus compared to Christianity. Only Christianity is eternal and life-giving, for it alone has an eternal covenant, an eternal sacrifice, an eternal priesthood, and an eternal law of love.

XV. The Covenant as Revelation

The entire unfolding of salvation history is in relation to the covenants of Sinai and Calvary. By living the covenant, the priests, prophets, and evangelists sought to make it meaningful to their contemporaries. In the covenant they saw, little by little, how much the very name Yahweh was to mean in their lives: King, Shepherd, Bridegroom. And they saw too, little by little, how great was the dignity of man: covenant partner of the Lord. Gradually they saw what the response of man should be to such love, ". . . with all your heart, and with all your soul, and with all your strength" (Deut. 6:5). Thus, in this covenant relationship, there was the matter for an ever-growing theology of sin and a theology of spirituality. The faith, the confidence, the hope of Israel and of Christianity rest on the unshakable foundation of God's eternal Word pledged in His covenant.

God's first major revelation to mankind was in the covenant of Sinai. His supreme revelation was in the covenant of Calvary. At Sinai, Israel had become Yahweh's kingdom, but here the union was a juridical one. On Calvary the union between Christ and His Kingdom is infinitely more intimate; now the Christian becomes a member of the kingdom by his physical union with the King. Previously, King and kingdom were distinct, now they are one; Christ is both King and kingdom. The Apostolic Church believed that the words of the prophet Osee concerning Israel (Osee 11:1) were to be applied to Christ as the new Israel.

> But when they had departed, behold, an angel of the Lord appeared in a dream to Joseph, saying, "Arise, and take the child and his mother, and flee into Egypt, and remain there until I tell thee.

For Herod will seek the child to destroy him." So he arose, and took the child and his mother by night, and withdrew into Egypt, and remained there until the death of Herod; that what was spoken by the Lord through the prophet might be fulfilled, "Out of Egypt I called my son" (Matt. 2:13–15).

Chapter V

CONTEMPORARY LITURGICAL REVIVAL

by

Frank Norris

In recent years the number of participants in the annual North American Liturgical Week has soared to over five thousand. During the four days of study and prayer, bishops, priests, religious, and laity from all over the United States and Canada endeavor to deepen their knowledge and love of that great wellspring of the Christian life, the public worship of the Church. Among the participants there are always some few professional scholars, mostly priests, who have spent a lifetime in liturgical research and study. But the vast majority of those present are priests, religious, and lay people engaged in some sort of active work in the Church—priests in the parochial ministry, teaching sisters and brothers, and laity from almost every walk of life. Certainly one would have to be living in the backwoods of Catholicism not to realize that the current liturgical renewal is one of the most significant movements in the Catholic Church today.

When we recall the humble beginnings of the liturgical movement in this country, we can appreciate what is taking place in our day. The first liturgical week was held in Chicago in 1940, in the basement of a parish church. There were between two and three hundred people participating—and in more ways than one they were the Church of the underground! In 1940 a person had to stand up and be counted if he was brave enough to identify himself with the liturgical movement. For, in the minds of many, liturgists were those who were interested mainly in ecclesiastical millinery. Liturgists were people with an unbalanced interest in what was external and peripheral to the worship of the Church. This attitude toward the liturgical movement was all the more incredible when we realize that, in 1913, Pius X had, in the clearest terms possible, declared that eventually (for he saw the problems of putting this immediately into effect) there would have to be a thoroughgoing reform of liturgical books, a complete renewal of liturgical life in the Church. Still as late as 1940 many looked upon the liturgical movement as at best an attempt to make monks out of the laity.

The Liturgical Scene

Much has occurred since 1940. And the best thing that has happened is that we had Pius XII as our Holy Father for so many years. Pius XII was the first pope to take up what St. Pius X had begun. Benedict XV, the immediate successor of Pius X, was occupied almost exclusively with the problems of the First World War. Pius XI, because of the problems immediately at hand—the rise of Fascism and Nazism—simply could not occupy himself in any significant way with the liturgical revival. The remarkable thing is that Pius XII, in the midst of the Second World War, still found time to take up, in a striking fashion, the work begun by Pius X.

In 1943, we were given the theological basis for the present-day liturgical revival in the encyclical letter *Mystici Corporis Christi*. That document did not deal directly with the liturgical movement. It dealt with the nature of the Church; yet the liturgical movement is simply an expression of what the Church really is. In 1947 Pius XII gave his first extended teaching on the sacred liturgy in *Mediator Dei*. This encyclical had a partially negative purpose: to control and to correct certain notions concerning the nature of the liturgy. But, in the main, it was an eminently positive document. Its whole purpose was to spell out, in even greater detail than *Mystici Corporis Christi*, the doctrinal basis for liturgical renewal and to give a positive impetus, a positive encouragement, to that renewal.

In the following year, 1948, Pius XII gave a very solid proof of his intention to continue the work of Pius X by establishing the Pontifical Commission for the General Restoration of the Liturgy. He made it perfectly clear that it was not a question just of improving or correcting this or that particular item in the liturgy. It was a thoroughgoing reform that was to be effected. In 1955, we had the first major breakthrough in the Roman Liturgy since Patristic times, the restored rites of Holy Thursday, Good Friday, and Holy Saturday. Those who remember Holy Week before 1955 know that it was a sorry and sad sight by comparison with what takes place in many of our churches today. The services all took place in the morning. Often they were attended by just a handful of people. There was no participation by the congregation, no real understanding of what was going on. Certainly a pathetic climax to the greatest week in the liturgical life of the Church.

In 1956 there took place at Assisi and at Rome the first International Congress of Pastoral Liturgy. On that occasion Pius XII summed up in one sentence the mind of the contemporary Church on the present liturgical renewal. He said that the liturgical movement is seen as a sign of the providential dispositions of God for the present day, of the movement of the Holy Spirit in the Church to draw men more closely to the mysteries of the faith and the riches of grace which flow from the active participation of the faithful in liturgical life. The key phrase was, "It is a sign of the movement of the Holy Spirit in the Church today." It is not a fad, it is not a work for an elite within the Church. It is an indication of the will of the Spirit for all of God's people—the Church today. Two years later, in 1958, we received the instruction from Rome calling for active participation in the Mass throughout the entire Western Church.

Since 1940, much has been said about the liturgy by the

highest authority in the Church. And much has been done. Much no doubt needs to be done. It is not simply that we need a much greater implementation of some of the reforms already initiated in the Church. Far more basic is the need for deeper study concerning the real nature of liturgy and of liturgical participation, for there still exists even in the minds of those who are mightily concerned with liturgical renewal a certain amount of misunderstanding as to the nature of liturgy, and consequently, the profound nature of the liturgical movement. Sometimes persons who have a natural and spontaneous attraction to the liturgy will explain their interest by exclaiming: "It's the spirit of our times. We live in a democratic age. Of course everyone should take an active part in the Church's worship." Or sometimes we hear, "Liturgical participation is wonderful for children and for young people. It gives them something to do." Priests, too, have been known to remark: "Active liturgical participation is wonderful—very good for the laity. But it is hardly necessary for those who have a more profound understanding of the meaning—the inner reality of the Mass." I hope we shall come to see that a fully participated liturgical life is just as necessary in a Carmelite monastery, a seminary, or a university chapel as it is in the simplest of Catholic parishes. The question at hand, then, is what is the liturgy and, consequently, what is the liturgical movement.

What Is the Liturgy

Very simply and briefly, the liturgy is worship. The liturgy is the official public worship of the whole Christ, Head and members, of the entire Mystical Body. Concretely, this means that the liturgy is the Mass and the sacraments. It is true that the Divine Office and the sacramentals are part of the liturgy, too; but principally the liturgy is the Mass and the sacraments, and above all, *it is the Mass.* This is important to emphasize, because we must see that the liturgy is not something extra, something over and above the Mass and the sacraments. One cannot say, "I am all for the Mass, but I am rather indifferent to the liturgy." The Mass *is* the liturgy. The liturgy *is* the Mass.

The liturgical movement, then, is no more than an attempt on the part of Catholics, and of the Church, to make this concrete reality—this action which is the Mass—exactly what Jesus Christ intended it to be for his Body the Church. It is no more than that, and it is no less than that. The liturgy, therefore, and the liturgical movement, are not "art for art's sake." They are not archaeology for archaeology's sake. The liturgical movement is not concerned with monastic spirituality. It is not based upon a subjective liking for participation, for singing together, for Catholic fellowship or togetherness. The liturgical movement is simply taking the action of the Mass, in its full reality, seriously.

Another way of putting it is this: The liturgical movement is mightily concerned with the virtue of reverence. Christ gave us the Mass with a specific nature. We have only one thing to do, therefore: to know the nature of the Mass and to respond to it. Consequently it is "irreverent" for us to latch on to one or another aspect of the Mass and to put other aspects of it into the background of our consciousness. We simply have not the right to do that. If Christ gives us the Mass in a certain form, a certain "shape," if He gives it a certain dimension, then we must respect it as it is. We must have reverence for it in its totality. What we have done for many centuries now is to focus on a very real aspect of the Mass, namely the presence of Christ (considered, above all, in His divine nature), and to relegate into the background of our thinking such tremendously important aspects as the corporate and social dimensions of the Holy Eucharist. The liturgical movement, then, is concerned with the virtue of reverence for the sacramental order that Jesus Christ has established.

Theology of the Liturgy

To understand the liturgical movement we must have some very accurate theological notions. Briefly put, we may state it thus: The Mass and the sacraments (or, in a briefer fashion, simply the Mass) must be seen in light of the mystery of the Incarnation, because the principle that underlies the whole sacramental system, the principle that alone explains the full reality of the Eucharist, is the selfsame principle that underlies the mystery of the Incarnation of the Son of God.

The Incarnation is the central mystery of our Christian Catholic faith. There has always been, however, in the life of the Church from the very apostolic age on, a real hesitancy to take this mystery—admittedly a frightening mystery—seriously in all of its dimensions. The mystery, I say, is frightening when we really think of what it means: that God, the inaccessible God, takes to Himself a human nature, a human nature weak and frail of itself, and so possesses that human nature that the Son of God is *its* personality, so that we can say of this God, *He became man. He* lived. *He* suffered. *He* died upon a cross. When we ponder the Incarnation we see that it is a frightening mystery. It is understandable, certainly, that there will be some difficulty in comprehending it. St. Paul, in his First Letter to the Corinthians, speaks of the mystery of the redemptive Incarnation—God becoming man and its ultimate outcome, His dying upon a cross—as foolishness to the Greeks, and as a scandal, literally a stumbling block, to the Jews. We see, too, reflected in the Epistles of St. John, the beginning of the Docetist heresy. This was a heresy, in the first century of the Christian era, which could not face up to the scandal, the foolishness, of the Incarnation. The Docetists said, in effect, that the Logos, the second person of the Trinity, merely *appeared* to be incarnate. It was no more than a fantasy, however, created by the Logos in order to make Himself visible to us. But there is no genuine, true human nature in the Logos. Against this incipient heresy of Docetism we find St. John the Apostle, in his old age, vehemently protesting when he says, in his first letter,

". . . every spirit that confesses that Jesus Christ has come in the flesh, is of God. And every spirit that severs Jesus [regards the Christ and Jesus as two distinct persons], is not of God, but is of Antichrist . . ." (1 John 4:2–3).

In subsequent periods of early Christianity we find that same stumbling over the mystery of the Incarnation. This was particularly true in the late fourth and fifth centuries. The Nestorians, for example, did not deny either the humanity of Jesus Christ or His divinity. But they did not see the two united in the one person of the Word of God. For the Nestorians, Jesus Christ is two persons. He is totally and completely a human person, totally and completely a divine person. He is, of course, a divine person who associates Himself very intensely with the man Jesus. But this union is no more than the highest type of moral association between two persons. It is not the mystery of the Incarnation. The Nestorian cannot say that God became man, suffered, died, and rose for man. All he can say is that God most intimately associated himself with a human person who suffered, died, and rose for man.

In the years following the condemnation of Nestorianism, there arose the Monophysite heresy, which began with a great concentration on the fact that Jesus Christ is One and that Jesus Christ is God. But it puts so much emphasis on the divine nature of Jesus Christ that His humanity is forgotten. His humanity is spoken of as a drop of wine which is put into the ocean, and disappears within the ocean. So the humanity of Christ is joined to, and absorbed, as it were, into the infinite reality of His divine nature. So much for very real denials of this central mystery of our faith.

Even within the Catholic faith, within the area of belief which we would characterize in the main as correct and orthodox, there has always been a tendency in the Church (and that tendency exists today) to flee from facing up to the full implications of the doctrine of the Incarnation. It is not really a theoretical denial, but rather a failure to see spelled out in detail what the theoretical doctrine means. There has always been a tendency among Catholics to play the Monophysite, so to concentrate upon the divinity of Christ (apparently in an excess of piety) as to relegate into the background of our thinking the role of the humanity of Christ here and now. At least in the past, and perhaps too in the present, any number of young children, on being asked, "Whom do you receive in Holy Communion?" would answer, "God."

The mystery of the Incarnation tells us, therefore, that Jesus Christ as man is the great sacrament of God, the great sacred sign revealing God and things divine to us. The mystery tells us also that God became man and used this humanity, His full manhood, to redeem us. It is not enough to say that the actions of Christ as man—His living, His suffering, His dying on the cross—were the occasions upon which God redeemed us. We have to face up to the full mystery. And it is simply this: God the Son used His human nature so that the actions and the sufferings of that human nature were the true, instrumental cause of our salvation. It is not enough to say that Christ as man redeemed us simply by thoughts—by acts of His spirit, of His mind, of His soul. Christ was a concrete and specific man and He used His full human powers, of body as well as soul, to redeem us. He used the sweat and stench of His body, everything that He underwent as man and embraced in His full humanity, to bring us salvation.

The principle that is established, therefore, in virtue of the Incarnation, is this: the invisible divine life of God, the invisible mysteries of God, are shown forth to us in the person of Jesus Christ in His manhood, and those inner mysteries are brought to us and are communicated to us by means of the actions of this visible human man, Jesus Christ. This is the background, the realistic understanding of the Incarnation which alone can give us the proper setting for understanding the Mass, for understanding the sacramental system. When we speak of the Mass and of the sacraments as being signs, it is not a question of the bare minimum that might be sufficient in extreme cases to have a valid sacrament.

The Sacraments as Signs

The sacraments are no more than the continuation in time of the principles inherent in the mystery of the Incarnation. Just as the Incarnate Word during His historic life upon earth used His full human nature with all the powers of body and soul to show forth to us the invisible God, and to bring to us a share in the life of God, so now Jesus Christ uses water, wine, bread, oil, human gestures, speech and song, bodily movements, vestments, space, buildings—the elemental realities of life—to show forth divine mysteries, and to effect for us a participation in those divine mysteries.

We say that the sacraments, therefore, just as the human nature of Christ, are signs. They are things which tell us invisible realities.

Theologians for years have been writing volumes letting us know what we would make do with, for example, on a desert island if things were really tough and we only had a thimble of water. Again, what are the absolutely essential words we would have to use if someone were at the point of death and wished to be baptized? No doubt the professional theologian and the parish priest should know what to do in such circumstances. But that is the bare minimum. The trouble is, we have been making a norm out of a bare minimum.

When we say the sacraments are signs, we do not mean they are lifeless, shrunken, shriveled up little indications which the initiate, after much reading and with tremendous faith, can see as a sign of things invisible. We mean that Christ gave us a sacramental system wherein we are to use full, rich, material, and human elements. This is the way of the sacraments because it is the way of the Incarnation. Christ was not a skeleton without body and blood. He was a concrete and specific personality. He was not just "man" in the abstract. He had a certain height and certain dimensions; He had a certain weight, a certain color to His skin, a certain manner of speech (He spoke like a Galilean peasant.). He had the manners of His people. The whole of His humanity spoke to us of the God He was.

Western sacramental theology—the sacramental theology of the Latin Church—has been the victim of pragmatism, of minimalism, for many years now. Let us give two examples: Baptism and the Eucharist.

St. Paul tells us that Baptism is the mystery wherein we die and are buried with Christ, and wherein we rise to newness of life with Christ. The basic element that Christ gave us to show forth this inner dying, burial, and new arising, is water. As this mystery came to us from Christ and as it was lived out in the early Church, it was shown forth by full immersion in water. A man was literally buried—immersed—in water and rose from it. This use of water could certainly show forth, with the words, "I baptize you in the name of the Father, and of the Son, and of the Holy Spirit," inner, spiritual dying to the old Adam and rising to newness of life, to the mystery of the Resurrection, with the second Adam who is Christ.

It is true that in extreme cases one can use a minimal amount of water, a bit of water flowing on the principal organ of the human body, the head, to symbolize the immersion of the whole man. However, because this may be done *in extremis,* because in some circumstances it is feasible and desirable to use this procedure, we have for many centuries made what is acceptable for some occasions the absolute norm. And we have completely forgotten the use of the full, rich sign of the sacrament of Baptism by immersion.

The second example is the Holy Eucharist. Christ gave us the Eucharist under the form of a meal. From the beginning, it was always a sacred meal. It had a sacred character to it. It was never considered simply an ordinary meal, so that it is perfectly understandable that there will be stylistic elements in this sacred repast. But what have we done in the Western Church? We have departed as far from the meal aspect as we possibly can. We have reduced the shape, the size, the texture, everything of the bread, till it is paper-thin and tasteless. For centuries, too, we have withdrawn the use of the chalice from the laity. Doubtless, in certain cases, it is necessary to give the Eucharist by means of bread only. And we know that this is valid because the gloriously risen Christ cannot be separated, and He is truly present in His totality under the form of bread. But certainly this is not the full, rich use of the sign that Jesus Christ gave to the Holy Eucharist. Certainly one liturgical reform that is mightily desired by many Catholics today is that there will be *some* restoration (at least on some major occasions) of the chalice to the laity.

I cite these examples simply to show how far we have gone in minimizing the sign value of the sacraments. In a way we are playing the Monophysite again. We are pretending that we are so interested in the inner mystery of the Mass, its Divine content, that we do not want to be distracted by the externals. Our Lord, however, gave us the sacraments in a form which corresponds to the whole principle of the Incarnation. We have no more right to underplay the importance of the external rite of the sacraments than we have to minimize or neglect the sacred humanity of Christ.

This, then, is the theological justification of the liturgical movement. In other words, the liturgical movement is no more than an attempt on the part of the Church to restore the full, rich, sign value of the Mass and of the sacraments; to make them be totally what Christ intended them to be. This is not indulging in pure externalism. Obviously, the external of a sign must lead us to the inner mystery. But let us not be deceived. We can neither apprehend nor enter fully into this inner mystery unless we accept the full external sign.

The person who tells us that he prefers to concentrate upon "the inner mystery" of the Mass, the presence of God, of Jesus Christ and His redeeming sacrifice, and has little or nothing to do with the "distracting" elements of the external—one who loves so dearly his silent, morning Mass with not a sound to disturb him, does not in fact enter fully into the inner mystery. For the inner reality of the Mass is not simply the presence of Christ. It is the presence of Jesus Christ *as Head of His Body which is the Church.* It is Jesus Christ, invisibly leading the entire community in worship, making us more perfectly members of his One Body. The whole purpose of the meal-structure of the Eucharist is to show forth, and to make it easy for men to enter into, the full mystery of the Eucharist, a mystery which essentially is corporate because it concerns the *Totus Christus,* the Whole Christ, Head and Members.

The Beginnings of the Liturgy

We can approach the liturgical movement and see its justification from still another viewpoint; namely, the historical. Such an approach acts as a powerful corroboration of the somewhat abstract theological notions we have seen. I am more and more convinced that we cannot put aside as secondary, or as unimportant, the development of Christian worship during the first five or six centuries of the Church's life. What took place then tells us how the Church instinctively and consistently viewed the reality of the Mass, indeed the reality of all the sacraments.

We begin with the Last Supper. The Last Supper was, in all probability, a Passover, a paschal meal. The very least that can be said was that it was a sacred Jewish meal, celebrated in close proximity to the Passover, and filled with Passover themes and Passover theology. The Passover, we know, served to rally the Jews together, to make them conscious of being God's people. It was, at the same time, a sacrificial meal which recalled their past deliverance at the time of the exodus. It was, furthermore, a pledge of even greater redemption to come. Our Lord engrafted the Holy Eucharist onto the very structure of the traditional paschal meal. We must not think that Christ and his apostles celebrated the Passover, then cleared the table for a "quick little Mass." Rather Christ took two moments in the paschal meal, moments and rites which were part of the traditional service, and He simply transformed them into the Christian paschal mystery. At the beginning of the meal, the father of the family would take unleavened bread and say, "Behold, the bread of affliction which our fathers ate in the land of Egypt!" Our Lord took that very action and transformed it by saying, "This is my body, which is being given for you." Toward the end of the meal, when the third cup of wine, "the cup of blessing," was ritually passed around the table after an act of thanksgiving had been pronounced over it, Our Lord observed the traditional usage; He ended his act of thanksgiving, however, with the additional words, "This cup is the new covenant in my blood." Thus, our Saviour engrafted our Christian Eucharist onto the very structure of the Passover meal, thereby indicating that this new rite, this "Passover transformed," was to participate in the "theology" of the ancient Passover. It was to be the perfection, the fulfillment, of the Jewish Passover. It, too, will have an eminently corporate nature. It, too, will make a new Israel more conscious of its oneness in Christ. It, too, is to recall to this community its past redemption. It, too, will be a pledge of a future glorious act of redemption, the second coming of Christ. It, too, finally, is an act of communal sacrificial worship.

For many centuries, the Church maintained in a very fine form the basic meal structure of the Holy Eucharist. Even though there was, relatively soon, a liturgical development, a certain stylization and an addition of other elements, basically the meal structure of the Eucharist was wonderfully preserved. When we examine the early anaphoras or canons of the Mass, what do we find? The Mass, stripped to its essentials, is this: bread and wine are placed upon a table. Then a prayer of thanksgiving ("grace") is offered to God. Finally, the food over which thanks has been given is consumed. The basic structure of the Canon of the Mass, therefore, despite later additions, is that of an act of thanksgiving addressed to God the Father. It is one unified prayer, thanking God for His saving actions of the past to the people of Israel but, above all, for Jesus Christ who lived, suffered, died, and triumphed over death for us and, on the eve of His glorious Passion, gave us this memorial meal which would enable men of all ages to enter into saving contact with the power of His death and Resurrection. The essential "shape" of the Mass, then, is grace over food which is then consumed.

The early Church never forgot that the Eucharistic meal is a communal celebration. Even in the fourth and fifth centuries, when a rich and rather rapid liturgical development took place, the basic "shape" of the Eucharist was clearly preserved. True, the liturgy became more solemn, more elaborate; but there was always a proper distribution of roles. No one man pre-empted the activity of the community. Prominent, of course, was the presiding celebrant, bishop or priest. He was now assisted in solemn and elaborate fashion by a deacon, a subdeacon, and minor ministers. The choir had its special role to perform. So, too, did the congregation. If one were to ask a Christian in the fourth or the fifth century who it was that celebrated the Holy Eucharist, the only possible answer would be, "*We* celebrate the Eucharist." In his experience, the Eucharist was not just one prayer, one action, but the total reality of the communal service of worship. He knew that the deacon, and the deacon alone, performed certain actions—he alone proclaimed the Gospel to which the celebrant himself listened with reverence. The subdeacon, and the subdeacon alone, read the Epistle. The celebrant alone recited the essential prayer of thanksgiving, although aloud and in the people's name (always in the first person plural). The choir sang its proper parts. The congregation made the common responses and acclamations. In those early centuries, the full reality of the Mass came from all the roles which were performed by the various members and units of the entire worshiping assembly.

In summary, throughout the whole Patristic period of the Church, the external celebration of the Mass followed out honestly and authentically the law of the Incarnation, the great sacramental principle that the external elements are to be full, rich signs of the internal realities conveyed by the Holy Eucharist.

One reason that the celebration of the Eucharist in East and West was so splendid during this period was that the liturgy followed the language of the people. This was the law of the early Church. There was no such thing, in East or West, as a sacred or hieratic language. Obviously, the language of the Holy Eucharist was never the language of the street. It always was a dignified, literary language, one which had a beauty and cadence worthy of the sacred liturgy. And, in that sense, perhaps the very ignorant would not understand every single word or phrase of the Eucharistic celebration. But, basically, the language was the language of the people. It never occurred to anyone in the Church to create a "mystique" of a sacred language, to suggest that a sacred language was a sign of unity or that it added to the mystery of the Eucharist. The early Church realized that Our Lord gave us mystery *aplenty* when He gave us the reality of Himself and of His sacrifice. It was not the Church's task to add to the mystery of the Holy Eucharist. The essential mystery of the Eucharist, the Church perceived, is the presence of Christ and His redeeming sacrifice. It is not the language. We see clear evidence of this mentality even in the West (the East has always kept fairly close to the ancient principle). In Rome, for the first century and a half or so of the Church's life, the language used for the celebration of the Eucharist was Greek. Not for any mystical devotion to the original language of the New Testament, but simply because the majority of Christians living in

Rome were Greek-speaking. When it came about, somewhere in the third century, that this was no longer the case and the majority of Christians spoke Latin, then the Church in Rome quite simply switched to Latin. One is tempted to wonder, perhaps, if even in those days there were a few diehards who said, "No, we'll never have Latin in the liturgy. What was good enough for our parents and grandparents is good enough for these young people today!"

The History of Liturgical Life

We come now to the breakdown of liturgical life. This begins, roughly, with the conversion of the barbarian tribes. Certainly the rapid acceptance of Christianity by whole new peoples created real problems for the Church. Let me mention just two of them. The first was an entirely new attitude, toward religion and "the divinity," which was not characteristic of Christians in the Graeco-Roman world. It was a love of the mysterious in the sacramental rituals and ceremonies of the Church. This attitude of the new converts to Christianity was a carry-over from their attitude to pagan divinities. Hence, there was no great disturbance on the part of the newly converted tribes if they did not perfectly understand the rites of the Church. So long as they were sacred, majestic, and sonorous, all was well. Understanding of itself was not of the first importance.

Secondly, there was the language problem. From the fifth century on, in the West there began the gradual, almost imperceptible emergence of the Romance languages. Everywhere a more and more corrupt Latin was being spoken. Yet there was no consistent form of the increasingly debased Latin dialects; none of them were, over a long period, anything like a written language. The standard Latin of the Church remained the only acceptable literary form of communication. Here the Church faced a real dilemma. There was no decent, stable vernacular tongue suitable for the sacred liturgy. Latin was the only language that could be kept; and yet the people understood it less and less. This is one reason why the Canon of the Mass, which was composed to be sung aloud—and was so sung for centuries—very gradually came to be recited silently. This happened because the people no longer could follow the sense of the words. The priest simply lowered his voice and sang the sacred words to himself. Still later he began to *recite* the text to himself. Before long, the silent canon, to which we are accustomed, was a *fait accompli.*

There are other factors to note in this period. The first is the beginning of the widespread abstention from Holy Communion. This came as a result of a rather late reaction in the West to the fourth-century heresy of Arianism, which had denied the divinity of Christ. Wherever there was excessive concentration upon the Godhead of Christ, the faithful gradually received the Holy Eucharist less and less frequently. People feared to receive God the Almighty, the terrible, the inaccessible. They lost their realization of Christ's humanity as the bridge between the infinite God and sinful man. By the early Middle Ages, for example, the faithful received Holy Communion *at best* once a year. Even devout laymen such as St. Louis IX, King of France, who were wont to hear sometimes two and three Masses a day, received Communion at most three or four times a year.

In the thirteenth century, the chalice gradually was withdrawn from the faithful. Because the people no longer had an active role at Mass, and because they no longer received Communion frequently, the Mass came to be viewed more as a theophany, as the dramatic appearance of God upon our altars, than as a communal sacrifice. With this notion of the Mass as "God becoming present," there developed the cult of seeing the Host, or, as the expression had it during the Middle Ages, of "seeing God." The elevation of the Host in the Mass, which came into prominence in the late thirteenth century, was, in a way, simply a substitute for receiving the Eucharist. People did not receive Communion, and yet they had great faith in the presence of "God" at the Celebration of Mass. Thus, the elevation began as a concession to their desire to "see God," to see the Host.

At the time of the Reformation, the Protestant reformers had important insights into the nature of Christian worship—a real awareness, for example, that the Mass was a communal action of the people, and not just an action which proceeds from the power of the ordained priest. As regards the language of worship, the reformers saw rightly that the use of a living tongue was of vital importance to the people. It was a mighty part of the full sign of the Holy Eucharist. Unfortunately, some of them went too far. They said, in effect, that unless the Eucharist and the other sacraments are celebrated in a living language they are useless. The Church could not accept that. She had to say that even though the use of the language of the people at worship is useful, still it is not absolutely required for a valid and fruitful celebration of the liturgy. Unfortunately, however, in the centuries following the Council of Trent, any discussion by Catholics of the advantages of the vernacular was looked upon, in practice, as a concession to the ideas of the Protestant reformers. We know, for example, that in the seventeenth century in France there was an initial movement (in many ways quite good but perhaps tinged with Gallicanism) to promote the use of the Missal (with vernacular translations) by the people. Strange as it may seem to us, this practice was forbidden by the Holy See under pain of excommunication. As late as the pontificate of Leo XIII in the last century, the ruling still remained on the books. One could find prayer books even in the early years of this century which did not dare give the people a word-for-word translation of the Canon of the Mass, but which substituted for it a paraphrase, more or less close to the words of the priest but still not a translation of the words themselves.

With Pius X, we hear the first clear, authoritative call to a renewal of liturgical worship. In quick succession he restored frequent Communion to the faithful, enunciated the great principles of liturgical renewal, began the restoration of Gregorian chant and decent modern music to the Church and, in the last years of his pontificate, declared that, eventually, there would have to be a total and thoroughgoing reform of the liturgy of the Western Church. What is taking place in the Church today is no more than the effort, some fifty years later, to carry out the program sketched by that sainted and farseeing pontiff.

As for the present-day liturgical renewal, the following points are worthy of note. First, there is a growing awareness of the necessity of making liturgical adjustments according to the needs of specific areas of the Church. For all too long, we have thought of the Western Church as an absolutely uniform section of the Church Universal. We are just beginning to realize that there is no reason why we must have maximum uniformity everywhere within the Western rite. The Church now is much more willing to contemplate the possibility of a variety of forms of liturgical worship suited to the needs of various areas within the Western Church, forms in which the full sign of the sacrament may best be spelled out, for the good of the faithful.

We have come to see, too, the importance of a structural reform of the liturgy. An example will best illustrate my point. The present Mass needs a clearer, a neater, a more incisive articulation of its parts. As it is now, it resembles an Italian primitive: the parts of the picture are all there but proper perspective is lacking. The Mass appears to many simply as a long series of prayers by a priest at an altar. Yet, the Mass has clearly defined parts which should stand out vividly. There is first of all an Entrance Rite. It consists of the Entrance Hymn (the Introit), the Kyrie, and the Gloria. It concludes with the Collect. This is a distinct unit of the Mass. It has nothing to do with an action at the altar. It is not sacrificial. It belongs in the sanctuary, but not at the altar. Secondly, the Mass has an instruction service, a Scripture service which likewise does not belong at the altar. An altar is for sacrifice. The reading of the Epistle and Gospel, the response of the people, the breaking of the bread of the Word in the homily—these actions should take place facing the people. The whole first part of the Mass (the so-called fore-Mass) badly needs a structural reform.

The same holds true of the Offertory which, in its present form, is excessively verbose and insufficiently active. It is basically a presentation of the gifts of bread and wine by the people. Its most important prayer is the Secret—which should be said aloud. Its name in times past was *oratio super oblata* —the prayer over the gifts.

The one part of the Mass which clearly belongs at the altar is the act of thanksgiving (the Canon) which is, at one and the same time, a prayer of gratitude to God and an act of consecration which transforms our gifts into the body and blood of Christ. The Canon clearly belongs at the altar. If the priest did not go to the altar until the Canon—the truly sacrificial part of the Mass—then this great prayer of Thanksgiving and Consecration would stand out with much more prominence than it does today and its significance would thereby be enhanced.

With the awareness of the advisability of greater liturgical variation within the Western Church and of the need for a considerable structural reform of the liturgy, particularly of the Mass, there will come, almost naturally and spontaneously, appreciation of the desirability of a much more extensive use of the vernacular at Mass. A structurally "correct" Mass, truly adapted to the real needs of the various peoples of the Church, scarcely can be celebrated, from beginning to end, in a language none of them understands.

Postscript

Since this chapter was first written—or rather, given as a spoken lecture—the Second Vatican Council has convened and has enacted changes of far-reaching consequence for the worship of the Church. On December 4, 1963, Pope Paul VI solemnly promulgated the *Constitution on the Sacred Liturgy*, which had been drawn up and overwhelmingly approved by the Fathers of the Council. Almost all of the most cherished aims of those engaged in the work of liturgical renewal have now been vindicated in principle. The underlying theology of the Constitution, it must also be stressed, is one of extraordinary depth and beauty. A full and rich understanding of the mystery of the Incarnation as the basis of the whole sacramental life of the Church; the necessity, consequently, of clear and honest "signs" in sacramental celebrations; the explicit and reiterated declaration that there is to be a thoroughgoing reform of all liturgical rites; and the repeated insistence that "all the faithful should be led to that full, conscious, and active participation in liturgical celebrations which is demanded by the very nature of the liturgy" (para. 14)—these are a sampling of the great themes of this magnificent document.

Most of the details of the Council's liturgical reforms are generally well known: the wide initial introduction of the people's tongue into the celebration of Mass and of the sacraments; the promise of an increased lectionary of Scripture pericopes; a spelling out of the important principle of a distribution of roles in liturgical services; a cautious reintroduction of the rite of concelebration by many priests of the Mass; the partial restoration of the chalice to the laity. These are some of the concrete ways in which the Council has decided to bring about a renewal of the Church's public worship.

We would be naïve in the extreme, however, to think for a moment that all has been won in the long and difficult struggle for liturgical reform, a movement which has been going on in the Church for over half a century. What we have been given is a blueprint for reform and renewal. An immense task of formation and education of clergy and people alike remains. Unless there is intelligent understanding of the inner meaning of the liturgy, the active participation of all the people will never become, in practice, "the primary and indispensable source from which the faithful are to derive the true Christian spirit" (para. 14).

We may therefore rightly rejoice at the promulgation of the *Constitution;* but let us see it as it is, a glorious and challenging potential for the revitalization of God's holy people which all of us, in however modest a way, are summoned to actualize in our lives and in the lives of our brothers.

Chapter VI

THE LAYMAN IN THE CHURCH

by

Joseph M. Powers

Introduction

Theological discussions on the layman's situation in the Church are characterized today by a certain amount of tension. The existence of this tension is understandable. To the extent that these discussions center around the layman's "being in the Church," the religious meaning of the layman is well stated. But to the extent that the approach to the consideration of the layman in the Church departs from the point of view of his situation as distinct from that of the cleric, there is a real danger that we will prejudge the reality of the Church and consequently prejudge the layman's situation in the Church. The reality of "being in the Church" basically is neither a clerical nor a lay reality; it precedes, both historically and theologically, any lay-cleric opposition.

However, there is a basis for the theological tension in the current discussion of the layman's position in the Church. It is to be found in the fact that there are two aspects in the reality of the Church itself. Unfortunately, the historical evolution of the theology of the Church has traditionally overemphasized the opposition between these two aspects. The opposition is actually a *datum* of Christian tradition, but its meaning is rooted in a deeper unity which gives to these two aspects of the Church the character of correlatives rather than antitheses.

St. Paul presents these two aspects of the Church in his twofold presentation of the Church as the mystical "Body of

Christ." On the one hand he presents the Church in its identity with the heavenly Christ (1 Cor. 12:12–13, 20; Rom. 12:4–5). From this point of view, the Church as a whole constitutes the visible presence of Christ in our world, and its members, regardless of their situation in the Church, carry on the mission of Christ to the world in a "horizontal identity" with Him. From this point of view, Christ *is* the totality of His members. On the other hand, St. Paul also presents the earthly Church as distinct from the heavenly Christ, opposite to Christ, distinct and opposite as the members are from the head of the body (Col. 1:18; Eph. 1:22). In this view there is a "vertical distinction" between Christ and His members, Christ is the *source* of grace, the life of the Body; the emphasis is on the structural distinction of parts rather than on the organic existential identity between body and members.

Against the background of this Pauline presentation of the Church we can distinguish two poles of being and action within the reality which is the Church. The first, which we may call the "life-pole," emphasizes the communal character of the Church. It presents the Church as Christ immanent in this world, incarnate in His mind and hands and heart in our world. It emphasizes the life of all believers inasmuch as they share a Christian vocation in grace and truth. It emphasizes the reality of grace which is produced by the Church as a sign of salvation. The other pole, which we can call the "structural pole," emphasizes the hierarchical character of the Church—Christ's transcendence over the world, his "being established in power" (Rom. 1:4), his having all things subjected to Him by God (1 Cor. 15:25–28). It highlights the Church as a means of salvation, an organ of grace in which life in Christ descends to the members through a structured hierarchical institution.

In the light of these two poles of being and action, then, the members of the Church can be considered from the point of view of the life-pole (and here all members of the Church are equal in their Christian vocation) or from that of the structural pole (and here each member finds himself in a distinct ecclesiastical situation). It is from the latter viewpoint that the lay-cleric dichotomy derives its meaning. But it is essential that we keep in mind that these two poles are dimensions of one reality and must be seen against the background of the one Christ who is at once present in a basically equal manner in all His members, and also acts as source of grace and life in the Church in and through its hierarchical structure. Even in the structured hierarchy of the Church, the movement of grace and life must not be considered as a purely downward movement from the higher to the lower situation; rather it must be considered as the result of a true partnership, in which the total experience of the Church is the result of the diversified experiences of variously situated members within the Church's hierarchy.

The unity which underlies this bipolarity in the Church is to be seen in the "pre-given" character of the Church. St. Luke suggests this pre-giveness of the Church in his treatment of the phenomenon of Pentecost (Acts 2:1–41). The three thousand persons baptized on that day are described as being "added to" the Church (Acts 2:41). The Church as it is mentioned here would seem to indicate the body of the Apostles and disciples inasmuch as they have been constituted into a community by the action of the Spirit. But even here, the action of the Spirit is to add the Apostles to something which is pre-given, namely, Christ. As St. Paul remarks: ". . . we are all baptized *into* one body . . . of one Spirit" (1 Cor. 12:13) (italics mine). Thus the Baptism of the Apostles "in Spirit and fire" served to incorporate them into the pre-given Body of Christ. In this sense, neither the Apostles nor the faithful who are added to them in the events of Pentecost actually constitute the Church. Rather, they are united by the Father, in the sending of the Spirit, to the pre-given center, Christ. In this manner the members of the Church are made into a community to the extent that they are united with Christ through the action of the Spirit. Thus, it is the heavenly Christ who is the pre-given principle of unity and reality in the Church. The Church is one because Christ is one.

I. History of the Growth of Lay-Cleric Opposition

Here we will trace briefly the history of the theology of the Church from the point of view of the status of the layman and the cleric. We want to follow the growth of two opposite theological attitudes within the framework of our question. These attitudes appear most clearly in their most extreme manifestations, and it is in the light of these extremes that we intend to synthesize a truer position for the layman in the Church.

The Old Testament

We should note at the outset that the Scriptural sources, besides noting the basic unity of the Church, also present us with the existence of two situations within and the two dimensions of the Church—its communal and its structural character.

The words "lay" and "cleric" derive from the Greek terms *laos* (people) and *klēros* (portion, lot), which, in turn, are translations of the corresponding Hebrew words *ʿam* and *goral.* It is interesting to note that these terms have the same religious significance in the Old Testament. The *laos,* by a gradual shrinkage in meaning from the idea of *any people* or community, came to mean *the* people: that people which was called by God and established as *His* people (Ex. 6:7; Lev. 26:12; Deut. 26:17; Jer. 7:23; Ezech. 11:20). This is a people which is chosen from among the *gôyîm* (the other nations of the earth), separated from them, and made heirs to His promise. The portion assigned by lot to the priestly tribe was this very people of God. This tribe was dedicated to the religious service of the people, and for this reason did not receive a share in the division of the land. There is, then, an existential identity in the content of these two terms. But there is also a clear distinction between the persons designated by these terms. It is a distinction of situation within this people as well as one which only has meaning in the framework of the religious reality of God's people, and is based on religious service rendered within that community.

New Testament

New Testament usage of *laos* corresponds to some extent with the Old Testament use of the term. It reflects both the traditional Jewish mentality (e.g., Luke 2:32 corresponds to the ideas in chapters 42 and 36 of Isaia) and the more universal messianic expectations of the prophetic tradition. The prophets have a wider concept of the people of the Promise. The remnant of the people which is to form the post-exilic people of God is one which will be drawn from all the nations (Is. 45:20), from the pagans as well as the Jews. St. Paul is particularly clear on this point, emphasizing the election of the Gentiles as God's people (Rom. 9:24 ff cites Osee to this effect), designating the Christian as the Temple of God (2 Cor. 6:16 cites the promise of Leviticus and Exodus to this effect). The council of the Apostles at Jerusalem, alluding to the question of the conversion of Cornelius, saw quite clearly the raising of God's people as something which now took place among the non-Jewish peoples (Acts 15:14). In this way the New Testament carries on the religious significance of the Old Testament usage of *laos*. The people of God are those who hear His voice and keep His covenant. This is a people founded on faith (Gal. 3:26) and whose fidelity to the Christian "way" is a fulfillment of the New Covenant with the New Israel (Gal. 6:13–16; Rom. 9:6 ff).

But there is also a distinction of status within this people.

St. Paul calls attention to the diversities of ministries within the Christian community (1 Cor. 12:4–31). But even here the diversity of ministries is meaningful within the unity of the Christian people and is devoted to its service. Thus, the total mystery of the Church embraces both life and structure, and the total experience of the Church is the result of an organic cooperation of all the members, each operating in the Church within the limits of its own situation.

First Christian Centuries

Early Christian use of the concept of the *laos* corresponds, as is to be expected, to Biblical usage. This is particularly apparent in the treatment of the Church as a cultic community. Early descriptions of the liturgy present us with the liturgical dialogue of "people" and "president" or "elder" or "bishop." But the daily life of Christianity did not seem to know the distinction of clergy and laity to the extent to which we know it today. There is a consistent emphasis, of course, on the predominant station of the bishop as teacher and shepherd of the young community, but even here there is a much closer involvement of the cleric with ordinary Christian existence. St. Paul set an example in this matter, working at his trade of weaver while he evangelized the communities of Asia Minor. Thus, though there is a distinction made between cleric and laity within the Christian community, one cannot escape the constant emphasis on their unity rather than on their distinction. There are several possible explanations for this emphasis. Besides the intimate involvement of the lower level in the ordinary world of trade and family life, the mind of the East tends to stress existential unities and totalities rather than the analytical distinctions which are so meaningful to the Western mind. Also, the relatively small numbers of the Christian communities would naturally lead to a desire to feel a sense of communion with one another and with other Christian groups. Thus, both in practice and in theory, these centuries saw an insistence on the organic unity of the Christian community, within which the states of laity and clergy were seen as correlative rather than as opposite elements.

Monastic Movement

By the early third century there arose in the Church a force which was to contribute greatly to the sense of distinction between the cleric and the layman: monasticism. Monasticism is, in its whole way of life, a testimony to God's transcendence of this world and human history, and it incorporates into its practice a strong emphasis on the eschatological character of the Christian calling. In addition, monasticism introduced another distinction into the structure of the Church itself. Besides the basic condition of Christianity in the laity, and the life of dedication to the service of the altar and the Christian community in the clerical state, there was now present a third situation in which the Christian could experience his vocation: that of complete withdrawal from the stream of secular life, complete dedication to God and the things of God, and preparation for the life of the world to come in contemplation and penance.

Almost from the beginning, monasticism exerted a strong influence on clerical life. By the end of the fourth century there existed communities of clerics with monastic ideals. The communities of St. Jerome, St. Ambrose, St. Augustine, and St. Eusebius of Vercelli all practiced a more or less monastic way of life. They assumed the tonsure and its subsequent obligations in the monastic traditions. Further, with the growth of monasticism in the West, there occurred a coincidence of the monastic and liturgical traditions. The development of liturgies after the eighth century was due in great part to the growing monastic communities. The life of the monk came to be centered more and more about the altar, and the monk, whose condition in the structure of the Church was that of a layman, came to consider himself a cleric. The twelfth century saw bitter struggles in this matter between the monastic communities and the diocesan clergy.

The barbarian invasions of western Europe drove Christian learning into the shelter of the cloisters, and the monasteries developed a virtual monopoly on education. The classics of Christian and pagan learning became the property of the monasteries. The education of the upper classes became the duty of the monks. The prevalent ideas on the meaning of the Church and the status of the Christian in the world were therefore expressed within a monastic frame of reference. Clerical training, to the extent that it existed at all, was largely a monastic training, and there came about a gradual assimilation of the clerical to the monastic ideal. Further, the reservoirs of documentation which are the traditional sources of theology were located in the monasteries, and consequently the theology of the Church which comes to us from the Dark Ages is a monastic theology.

The period following the Dark Ages saw the emergence of another tradition: the canonical. In its primitive form, this tradition was largely collative, gathering together the sources of Christian thought with a view toward some regulation of ecclesiastical life and practice. Such tradition, with its juridical bent, stressed the societal character of the Church, and in particular its hierarchical power. Taken in this light, the distinction of cleric and layman in the Church is defined in terms of their respective competence with regard to the Church's hierarchical power. Thus, the cleric is seen as the subject of ecclesiastical power, and the layman is seen as the object of that power.

The traditional sources for a theology of the Church, therefore—the monastic and the canonical traditions—came to define the position of the lay Christian in the Church (1) in opposition to the monastic state and (2) in opposition to the clerical state. In the first case, the lay condition is a state which is granted by God to those who are incapable or unwilling to embrace the full consequences of Christian vocation. In the second case, the lay condition is defined as that state in which the Christian is ruled, taught, and sanctified by the holder of hierarchical power. Thus, far more than a distinction, there is a cleavage introduced into the Christian vocation itself. This is strikingly expressed in a statement which Gratian, in his *Decretum*, attributes to St. Jerome:

> There are two kinds of Christians. There is one kind which is set aside for divine service, dedicated to contemplation and prayer and finds it proper to withdraw from the noise of the world, as in the case of the cleric; and those who are completely devoted to God, namely the religious. . . .
>
> There is another kind of Christian, as in the case of the laity. . . . These are allowed to possess temporal goods. . . . To these are granted the *concessions* of marriage, tilling the soil, judging between man and man . . . and thus they can be saved, provided, however, that they avoid evil by doing good. *Decretum*, Causa 12, quest. 1, c. 7. (Author's translation and italics.)

The transition from the concept of the lay state as the basic condition in which the Christian calling is experienced to that of a *concession*, granted to those who are incapable of living a life of complete devotion to God, is quite startling when we see it expressed so neatly.

However, we cannot ignore another aspect of Christian tradition—that found in the lives of those who lead a genuine Christian existence. We cannot hope to document this in the same way as the monastic and canonical traditions, but its existence is an integral part of that indefectible character of the Church and its members as they live in Christ under the guidance of His Spirit. There is a documentation of sorts for this awareness of the basic dignity of Christian living in the manifestations of Christian art. Of particular interest in this respect are those carved and painted images of the Last Judgment which have always formed such a prominent part in Christian architecture. Here we find no distinction when it comes to the rewards and punishments of the Parousia. True, there are representations of different situations in Christian life, but the company of the damned and that of the elect are both peopled with Christians of every station, from king to menial, from pope to deacon. It is in these representations that we find so striking a statement of the consciousness of the ultimate *responsibility* for the work of Christ in this world. And this responsibility is shared alike by cleric and layman, of low station or high.

It is against the background of this ultimate Christian responsibility that we can understand the deviation of clericalism. This excess of the clerical mind loses sight of the inwardness of daily and secular life and looks on life in this world as of merely symbolic value. Its meaning can only be seen in reference to the life of the world to come, and its values are subordinate to their purely religious meaning. The elements of secular life can only have meaning in reference to salvation in the hereafter. It is this attitude which leads the clericalist (and not necessarily the cleric) to introduce or to prolong clerical guardianship over matters which lie within the competence and responsibility of the laity. We can see how anticlericalism, insofar as it is a protest against this confiscation of competence and responsibility, is basically a Christian attitude in reaction to the clericalist mind. As an attitude which insists on the inner value of the things of this world, a value enhanced by the transforming action of Christ's Incarnation, this is sound and useful in the life of the Church. As a movement against clerical*ism,* it is an affirmation of the basic dignity of the Christian vocation.

II. The Growth of Communal-Structural Opposition in the Theology of the Church

Historically, the evolution of the *Tractatus de Ecclesia* (Treatise on the Church) as a distinct theological discipline has its origins in the conflict between movements which stressed the Church's communal aspect to the detriment of the structural and vice versa. This does not imply that there was no theological reflection on the Church's nature and meaning prior to these conflicts. On the contrary, we find penetrating theological treatments of the Church in the earliest Christian writers, beginning with the New Testament. We are concerned here with the evolution of the Treatise on the Church as a distinct part of theological science. This theological formulation came about as a reaction to movements which overstressed the Church's communitarian aspect. Thus our treatment of this development naturally falls into a consideration of the communitarian exaggerations and the theological reaction to these exaggerations.

Exaggerations of the Communitarian Aspect

The first movement characterized by a formulation of this exaggeration is the Spiritualist movement, dating from the twelfth century, which found a characteristic formulation in Joachim of Flora, an Italian friar. Joachim distinguished three ages in the religious history of mankind: The first age is that of the Father, the Old Testament, in which God reveals his wrath against sinful man; the second age is that of the Son, which is the age of the Redemption and the establishment and growth of the Church; the final age, which Joachim insisted had already begun, was the age of the Spirit, in which the faithful were to be ruled by the direct pneumatic influence of the Spirit. Of particular importance is his insistence that this direction takes place independently of any structure in the Church. The Spirit rules the Church by ruling the individual. The true Church is that collection of the saints who live in union with the Spirit, and authority within this collectivity corresponds to the personal holiness of the individual. In its strong reaction to early Scholasticism, this movement rejected any structured concept of the Church and insisted that the Church's character is constituted by individual persons gathered together in and by the Spirit.

This movement took many forms in medieval Europe: in the Beguard and Beguine movements of France and the Balkans, in the many Flagellant movements, in the rise of the Fraticelli in Italy. But they all share the same spirit: a conviction that the Church is constituted by its members. In its opposition to any structural reality, it completely ignored the pre-given character of the Church.

Another formulation of communitarian exaggeration is to be found in early democratic movements. Some of these movements, because of a peculiar mixture of Aristotelean politics and Nominalist theology, brought about the first stirrings of popular government in western Europe. Their spirit is even apparent in the rules of some religious orders which found their origin in the high Middle Ages. Though this movement was stifled by the growth of state absolutism, its influence on the theology of the Church was genuine, both because of what it had to say about the Church and what theologians had to say in reply.

One of the most prominent figures of this movement was Marsiglio of Padua. His statements on the constitution of the Church reflect the background of the struggles of Boniface VIII and John XXII against Philip the Fair and Louis II. These conflicts centered on questions of competence concerning the temporal possessions of the Church. Boniface VIII's famous bull on the unity and power of the Church, *Unam Sanctam,* defended the rights of the popes over temporal rulers. It is against this historical background that Marsiglio developed his thought on the Church. From Nominalist theology, Marsiglio adopted the principle that the Church as a community adds nothing to the members which compose it. The members are the constituting factor of the community and, as such, have complete equality within the community. Cleric and laity thus have equal competence in the Church. The question at issue was the right of emperors to seize the possessions of monasteries, and the principle of Marsiglio's solution was the equal competence of layman and cleric in the Church. We find the most startling extreme of Nominalist theology in Marsiglio in his contention that the Church can subsist even in a single soul, and that that individual soul can be the soul of a baptized infant. This remarkable individualism is the paradoxical extreme of the communitarian exaggeration which begins with an emphasis on the equal competence of all individuals in the community, and ends with the elimination of the community itself.

Conciliarism united Gallican and democratic tendencies in the peculiar situation of the Western Schism. Faced with the aspirations of three claimants to the papal throne, the conciliarists looked with longing eyes toward Gerson's contentions that the council of bishops has the right to depose a pope. Here we have an opposition between pope and "Church" in which the members of the hierarchy itself claim equal competence with the pope. It is a remarkable attempt to reject the structured character of the hierarchy itself and inject a communitarian spirit into the area where one would least expect to find it.

Gallicanism found its most vehement expression in the apogee of French royal power under Louis XIV, in the seventeenth and eighteenth centuries, and continued in many different forms into the nineteenth century; but its origins lay in the writings of the Parisian theologians of the twelfth century, whose opinions were the basis of the conciliarist movement. Out of its resentment for the authority of Rome, Gallicanism asserted the inferiority of the pope to royal power (in regalist Gallicanism), to the Council (in conciliarism) and to French customs and faith (as it appears in the Clergy Declaration of 1682). The same movement appears in the statism of Febronianism in Prussia and Josephinism in Austria.

Of all the communitarian exaggerations, however, none has had such a vast influence on the theological treatise on the

Church as the Reformation. This enormous religious rebellion against Rome formed the negative pole against which the classical theology of the Church reacted. In the framework of our question, we can call the Reformation a clash between ecclesiastical machinery and individual faith. In the theology of the Reformation, the Church's interiority was stressed to such an extent that any visible manifestation of the Church was judged to be either of simply human institution (as in Lutheran theology) or humanly sinful (as in Calvinist theology). The true Church is considered to be the interior and invisible union of believers in their common commitment to Christ in faith. The visible Church is simply consequent on the free association of believers into visible groups in a given locality. These free associations are not divine institutions, nor are they sanctifying realities. God alone sanctifies, and the visible Church is of man's making. Preachers and ministers receive their vocation from the community and are completely equal, even subject to, the community in the exercise of their ministerial calling.

The positive statement of the Church's interiority is not utterly false in itself. What is false in this movement is the extreme emphasis in the interiority of the Church to the exclusion of any visible hierarchical structure. We have seen the extreme manifestations of communitarian emphasis in the Church's theology. It is in this light that we can understand the anti-Protestant polemic which comprises such a great part of classical ecclesiology.

Theological Reactions to Communitarian Exaggerations

The first explicit treatises on the Church date from the anti-Gallican treatises of the early fourteenth century. Though they were written in the context of the conflict between Boniface VIII and Philip the Fair, they are still genuine theological treatises, drawing their conclusions from the sources of Christian tradition. What we wish to point out in these treatises, however, is their orientation and emphasis. The first treatises, in and about 1300, all stress the *power* of the Church in contrast to the power of rulers and states. James of Viterbo writes *De Regimine Christiano* (On Christian Ruling Power); John of Paris, *De Potestate Regia et Papali* (On Royal and Papal Power); Giles of Rome, *De Ecclesiae Potestate* (On the Power of the Church). In the context of regalist Gallicanism, the Church is seen as the subject of divine power and authority. The treatment of the Church, therefore, is purely from the structural point of view. As an institutional Church, it is clerical.

Of course, this treatment of the Church is not false. The Church *is* institutional, it *is* clerical when we consider it as the subject of hierarchical power. Canonical tradition defines the cleric in precisely this context. The question with this presentation is rather one of adequacy, particularly its adequacy for an understanding of those who do not have this legal competence in the Church. Given this approach, it is to be expected that the layman, insofar as he is not the subject of ecclesiastical power, will be treated as the object of that power and his role vis à vis the cleric will be a passive one: that of being taught, being ruled, being sanctified by the hierarchy. Taken from this point of view, the dignity and richness of the Christian vocation loses its dynamism and its legitimate theological stature.

The continuing occurrence of Gallicanism and parallel movements throughout the fourteenth and fifteenth centuries tended to harden this theological approach to the understanding of the Church and to establish it as the classical theological treatment of the Church. In the sixteenth and seventeenth centuries, the flowering of statism and nationalism resulted in a heavy concentration of works on the philosophy and theology of law, a body of writing which had its effect on the theology of the Church. This brought about an even stronger emphasis on the Church's societal character, stressing its rights and competence as a divinely established monarchy for the ruling of all believers, kings and subjects alike. Some authors concentrated so thoroughly on this aspect that they considered the Church a particular type of human society, a supernatural species of the natural genus of society —a characteristic which still persists in some theological manuals.

Counter-reformation ecclesiology insists on this same societal character in its reaction to the Reformation theologians' insistence on the Church's interiority. The writings of Pighi, Melchior Cano, Suarez, Bellarmine, d'Este, and others "proclaim," in the words of one of their theological heirs, "the basic fact that the one and only true Church of Jesus Christ, according to the dispensation of the New Testament, is truly visible, a society composed of parts or members who can be recognized as such in this world."[1] From this time, the defensive insistence on the structural pole of the Church becomes an integral part of ecclesiology. It becomes the basic point of reference for the whole discussion of the Church. Even the four qualities of the Church, its unity, sanctity, catholicity, and apostolicity are treated in this light—unity being given in the absoluteness of papal authority, sanctity explained in terms of the legal machinery for canonization, catholicity explained in terms of geographical distribution, and apostolicity treated as a claim to historical authenticity. These four aspects become "notes," diagnostic characteristics which are aimed at forcing consent to the Church's claims. The reality of these four characteristics of the Church because of its relation to Christ is passed over in favor of a defensive vindication of its right to the obedience and assent of all mankind. Its theology, in brief, gives way to an apologetic, a polemic.

Such, then, is the not always fortunate development of the Church's classical theology. Its reactionary character is not something which is wrong. The expression of the Christian mystery must always be framed in terms which are meaning-

[1] J. C. Fenton, "Cardinal Ottaviani and the Council," *The American Ecclesiastical Review*, Jan. 1963.

ful to an era. In this way, different aspects of the mystery of the Church have found expression according to different historical circumstances. For this reason, the development of a "hierarchology" rather than an "ecclesiology" is understandable. But this reactionary character of ecclesiology has resulted in a onesidedness, an inadequacy. If we had to choose between the two alternatives offered us in the history of the theology of the Church, we would have to choose between a hierarchy divorced from a people or a people divorced from a hierarchy, between a structure without life and a life without structure. Which of these alternatives is worse would be problematical, although, because of the pre-given character of the Church, we would be forced to admit that the first alternatives are less undesirable. Cardinal Salieges was not far from the truth when he exclaimed, "Poor theologians! They have forgotten two things: the laity and the Holy Spirit!"

The past fifty years have witnessed a new emphasis on a more total theology of the Church. The Thomist revival has emphasized anew the inwardness of the created and the material and tied the mystery of the Church closer to the mystery of Christ; the strengthening of dogmatic tradition has resulted in a fruitful return to the sources of theological tradition and emphasized the total message of Sacred Scripture rather than its value as a source of polemic; the liturgical renewal, with its emphasis on the communitarian character of Christian worship and its insistence of a greater involvement of the whole Church in its worship, has re-emphasized the priestly mission of the whole Church; the social renewal in Catholic thought has called new attention to the necessity of the co-operation and participation of the laity in the Church's mission to the world. All these developments have given a new balance to the theology of the Church and, consequently, to the understanding of the status and function of the lay Christian.

We have seen, in this brief exposition of the vicissitudes of ecclesiology, the extreme developments of two opposite positions. In the light of these extremes, the tensions in the classical treatment of the Church should be understandable. With this background we may now approach a more positive exposition of the station and function of the layman in the Church. Our development will be threefold, corresponding to the threefold messianic function of the Church as it continues the mission of Christ to this world. This mission is one of The Anointed One, with historical overtones of priestly, prophetic, and royal status and function. It is from this aspect that we will approach the layman—in the light of his priestly, prophetic, and royal character.

III. The Layman and the Mission of the Church

The Priestly Mission of the Layman

Priesthood, as a religious reality, is intimately bound up with sacrifice. And when we look at the inner reality of sacrifice, we can reach some understanding of the deepest dimension of meaning in priesthood.

The soul of religious significance in sacrifice is in the inner awareness of God's transcendent, creative action. God's creating reaches into the innermost core of the human person, confronting the person in all of his truly free actions. The inner recognition of this transcendent creativity and the free acceptance of and subjection to it is the inner state which man in turn exteriorized in cultic sacrifice. The Old and New Testament treatments of sacrifice seem to bring this out in their insistence on "inner sacrifice" as the necessary complement of ritual sacrifice. The Letter to the Hebrews puts the words of Psalm 39 on the lips of Christ precisely as a priest: "Sacrifice and oblation thou wouldst not. . . . 'Behold, I come—(in the head of the book it is written of me)—to do thy will, O God'" (Hebr. 10:5–7). It is total subjection to the all-pervading creative action of the transcendent God which gives inner meaning to the visible cultic act of sacrifice.

The history of salvation presents the sacrifice of Christ as one of its central themes. Malachy's vision of the new Israel was phrased in precisely these terms. The New Israel is to be a people gathered from the ends of the earth which will offer a clean and acceptable sacrifice to God (Mal. 1:6–11), and in the context of the tradition embodied in Psalm 39, we can see that the cleanness of this sacrifice lies to a great extent in its total devotion to God's majesty. This clean oblation is accomplished in Christ. We tend to think that His death on the Cross was *the* sacrificial moment in His life. This is true to the extent that His death is the ultimate expression of everything which His life was—all sacrifice in the sense we have just described. We cannot ignore the sacrificial character of the whole of Christ's life in His total subjection to the will of the Father. He does what the Father commands; his words are the words of the Father; His very food is His Father's will (Jn. 12:44–50). It is the unequivocal revelation of this total subjection in worshiping obedience which is heard in the cry: "It is consummated!" Nor is this the end of Christ's sacrificial work. His sacrificial life and death have an eternal validity (Hebr. 9:24–28; 10:11–13). Seated at the right hand of the Father, Christ continues to act sacrificially, interceding for men, it is true, but more fundamentally sacrificial in his subjection of all creation to the Father Who gives Christ mastery over everything (1 Cor. 15:25). It is from this heavenly Christ that the people of God derive their sacrificial and priestly mission. Baptism incorporates the Christian into Christ's sacrificial life and death and raises the Christian up into the eternal and glorious priesthood of Christ (Rom. 6:7–11). This is the basis for the existence of priesthood in the Church. There is priesthood in the Church because the people of God *are* priestly, the visible earthly manifestation of the heavenly priest, Christ, continuing His priestly work in the world here and now.

The earliest level of Christian literature seems to be conscious of this in the fact that it used the classical term for the priest (*hieros*) only to designate Christ or His priestly Body on earth. When it comes to speak of the official priesthood within the structure of the Church, it uses the terms "elder" (*presbuteroi*), "overseer," or "bishop" (*episkopē*). It is the total Church which *is* priestly, because only Christ *is* priest—the unique priest from Whom all other priesthood derives. The total Church, then, continues Christ's priestly and sacrificial work on earth. Within the Church, individual members, through their incorporation into the priestly Christ, take on a dynamic relationship to Christ the priest. This is one aspect of what we call the "character" conferred in the sacraments of Baptism, Confirmation, and Holy Orders.

Thus, from the point of view of the "life-pole" of the Church, every Christian has a priesthood in and through incorporation into the priestly Christ. For this reason, we can see the unacceptability of the expression "the universal priesthood of the laity." The universal priesthood is an aspect of the *life* of the Church, and is neither lay nor clerical. It is a basic condition of Christianity as such and cannot be claimed as the exclusive condition of any part of the structured Church.

However, priesthood, as an aspect of the life of the Church, can and should be considered from the structural pole of being and action in the Church, if we are to arrive at any balanced appreciation of the priesthood of the laity. The concrete, historical, salvific dispensation of God shows us that men are to be saved in and through the community, and specifically in and through the community which God has gathered together in Christ. Within the structured character of this community we find the distinction between hierarchical and lay priesthood. The hierarchical priesthood makes visible in and to the Church the reality of Christ's opposition to His members as their mediator before the Father. Under this aspect, Christ and the hierarchical priesthood are opposed to the rest of His members. But this opposition is based on a distinct ministry in the Church: a dedication to the religious and, in this case, the specifically priestly service of the Christian community: "It is the duty of the priest to bless . . . and to offer sacrifice" (*Pontificale Romanum*). It is the priest who, *in the name of the heavenly Christ*, effects the sacrificial presence of Christ in the Church. And it is only in function of this presence that the Christian community can offer its sacrifice in and with Christ. Thus it should be clear that the opposition between lay and hierarchical priesthood is the opposition of correlative, complementary elements in the structured Church, and not that of antithetical opposition.

Salvation and worship are both *ecclesial* realities. They take place within and according to the conditions of life in the Christian *community*. Within the community, each member has his station, a situation in which there is a distinct experience of the Christian vocation. This situational distinction is necessary for the life and total experience of the priestly "Body of the Lord" (1 Cor. 12:18–21). The desire of any part of the community to claim for itself the prerogatives of another part is, reductively, a desire to be a Church unto one's self: it is destructive of the life of the Body.

Today, the Church calls for a much closer involvement of the total community in its worship. If the layman is to come to a deeper appreciation of the meaning and validity of his own priestly character, it is to be within the experience of the life of the Church as a cultic community. It is that experience in community which gives meaning and dimension to his priesthood. And no amount of explanation can substitute for the work of God which is accomplished in us in that experience.

The Prophetic Mission of the Layman

Here, as before, we must distinguish between structure and life, because the prophetic mission in which the layman shares is the prophetic mission of the Church, which, in turn, continues the prophetic mission of Christ.

This prophetic mission of Christ forms the life-pole around which the prophetic calling of the Christian gravitates. It consists of the revealing witness which Christ gives to the redemptive love of His Father. In this sense, Christ fulfills and perfects the prophetic function as it is presented in the Old Testament. There, the prophets serve as conscience and guide for Israel, pointing out the divine dimension and reality of its existence as a people, excoriating its deviations from God's plans. When the prophets look to the fulfillment of Israel's life in the coming of Christ, they allude to the transcendent prophetic reality which will characterize the new Israel. Then the people of God will be enlightened and active because of an *inner* principle of illumination and action, rather than because of the exterior proddings of the prophets (Jer. 31:33, 34; Is. 54:13; Joel 2:28, 29). It is in its very being that the new Israel will give uncontrovertible witness to God's redemptive work in Christ.

The theme of Christ as the revelation of the Father is, of course, a constant of the New Testament (John 12:44, Matt. 10:40). Christ is so completely filled with the Will of His Father that the very sight of Christ is the sight of the Father (John 14:9). In everything which Christ is, says, and does, He is the revelation of the Father to the world. This shows us the deepest meaning of Christ's words: "I am the light of the world" (John 8:12). It is this light and illuminating force which Christ pours out on His Church (John 1:7–9) in the anointing of the Spirit. In virtue of this inner illumination in Christ, the Christian can let his light shine before men so that they will see his good works and give glory to the Father in heaven (Matt. 5:16). The body of the Lord is thus *the* sign which gives testimony to this world and leads men to the knowledge and love of God. It testifies to the Resurrection and glorification of Christ. It testifies to the whole body of truth which is subsequent to this central Christian fact (Acts

2:22–36). And by everything which it is, it testifies to the truth and validity of a way of life the existential basis of which is to be found in the glorious Christ. Thus the Christian is a "sign raised up among the nations" not only in the logical sense of a phenomenon which leads to the knowledge of something else; far more important, he is a sign in that he makes visible to the world the inner divine light of love and grace which is the "spring of living water" which nourishes his own existence.

Every Christian, lay and cleric alike, shares this same prophetic illumination in Christ. But each person experiences the work of this inner light in a situationally different manner, depending, from the structural point of view, on whether he is situated within the *teaching* or the *taught* Church. We must remember that the glorified Christ, as head of His Mystical Body, shares this light with the Body also through the structured hierarchy which represents His character as "Lord." The timeless witness which the Church gives to the Resurrection and its consequences is ultimately Christ's own witness to the glory which the Father has given Him. From this point of view, the Church is "taught" by the splendor of the glorified Christ, and receives from above the light which it sheds on the world.

The reality of these two dimensions within the Christian prophetic vocation indicates the necessity of continued and earnest dialogue between the laity and clergy in the Church. The experience of this calling on the part of the layman and cleric respectively is, of necessity, one-sided. Each has his own inalienable contribution to make to the total experience of this prophetic mission in the Church. Each side of this dialogue has meaningful experience to contribute to the other's experience of the central Christian mystery as it illuminates every dimension of human endeavor. And let us recall that this dialogue, far from implying merely speaking to one another, implies *listening* to one another with the previous conviction that the other has something valid and meaningful to say. This conviction is based on the realization that each Christian has been given his situation in the Church *by God*—that situation in the Church is a proper vocation, be it clerical or lay (1 Cor. 12:18; Rom. 12:3–4). From this frank and sincere exchange of experience within the Church's community must arise that total experience of the Church which will motivate the Christian to "let his light shine before men so that they will see his good works and give glory to the Father who is in Heaven" (Matt. 5:16).

The Royal Mission of the Layman

Once again we find the meaning of the Christian's royal status and mission in that of Christ. Christ's kingly mission was one of restoration (Eph. 1:10). He was sent precisely in the context of man's rebellion and consequent loss of earthly dominion which was his from the beginning (Gen. 1:28). The restoration of this earthly kingship also involves the restoration of a kingship in heaven (Matt. 25:34). But it is through Christ and in Christ that the Christian can "come into his kingdom." Christ's obedience to His Father has merited for Him the exaltation as Lord of heaven and earth (Phil. 2:5–11). He rules as "Son of God by an act of power" (Rom. 1:4), to whom everything is subjected so that, in turn, He might subject everything to His Father (1 Cor. 15:25–28).

But Christ's Kingship also belongs to the Christian. He has prepared this kingdom for us (Matt. 25:34), and His victory over the world is the source of our strength and confidence (Matt. 16:33). St. Paul stresses our royal vocation in his emphasis on our being heirs to the same kingdom in and with Christ (Rom. 8:17) and in the fact that our glorious resurrection in Christ is a resurrection to kingship (2 Tim. 2:12). Our faith, our commitment to Christ is the basis of this status (1 John 5:4).

The "Body of the Lord," then, carries on the royal mission of Christ, just as it carries on His priestly and prophetic mission. And this is understandable, because these three vocations are but three aspects of one anointing which Christ and the Christian share in the Spirit of God. The life of the Christian is a royal, a priestly, and a prophetic life in the Church. Sharing in the death of Christ, the Christian shares as well in His Resurrection and glory (Rom. 6:3–6). Perhaps we can understand slightly what it means to "be in Christ."

The royal status of the Christian is experienced in the world by way of engagement and by way of transcendence and refusal. The Church is the presence of Christ in this world, and if His kingship is to span the earth, it is to do so through His members, who make his kingship a moving force in human history. And this obviously demands involvement of the Christian in the historical streams which move about him. But this involvement must be a *Christian* involvement, an involvement which does not surrender to the values and convictions of that "world" which is opposed to God and the work He has accomplished in Christ. The incarnation of the mystery of iniquity in human history thus demands an estrangement of the Christian from the world inasmuch as it is opposed to Christ. Hence the necessity of a transcendent refusal of the "worldly."

Again, this experience of the kingship of the Christian corresponds to God-given status within the structure of the Church. Christianity as a historically motivated force is directed by the kingly Christ through His members in accordance with their status in the governing function which the Church has over men. That power, even in the highest grades of the hierarchy, is still a "power of the keys": the vicarious ruling power of the masters of the Lord's household. The hierarchy exercises this power with a twofold responsibility—toward the heavenly Christ and toward His earthly members. This ruling binding power is *Christ's* power, not man's, and it must be exercised in the way that He determined. Further, it must take into account the genuine ecclesial responsibility of the members of Christ, who though they be bound from above, are still ultimately responsible for their self-determined activities within the Church. Thus it is that we see so many self-determining organizations operating within the Church, choosing apostolic works and carrying them out with the blessing of the hierarchy as genuinely *ecclesial* apostolates.

The responsibility of the hierarchy toward the members of Christ also serves as the basis for the legitimate function of public opinion within the Church. Only a foolish ruler would claim a universal competence with respect to his subjects. The Church does and must look to her members for competent professional guidance in areas of lay competence. Further, we must recall that public opinion has a positive as well as a negative function. It is exercised in agreement as well as in disagreement. The essentially corporate, ecclesial character of the life and activity of the Church also demands the positive influence of public opinion, both in the occurrence of positive suggestions from the ranks of the laity and in the "Amen" with which the laity lends universal support and agreement to hierarchical initiative. Of course, negative action in public opinion has influenced the Church—the history of such people as Catherine of Sienna, Bernardine of Sienna, Francis of Assisi, and Joan of Arc is well known. Only in the assumption of a corporate ecclesial responsibility for the work of the Church can the Christian, be he lay or cleric, experience the total effectiveness of Christianity as a moving force in history.

Conclusion

These remarks are an indication of the guidelines for some appreciation of the basic dignity of Christian vocation. This is the basic *datum* of Christian experience, the basic condition in which pope and layman alike must experience the meaning of life in Christ. But we must also remain constantly aware of the fact that God has given to each person in the Church a definite situation within the Church, and the very immensity of the mystery of Christianity demands that its total experience be a corporate reality resulting from the cooperation of every member of Christ. The measure of faith which God grants makes us all members of Christ and of one another (Rom. 12:3). The ministries which the Spirit grants to each within our corporate unity (1 Cor. 12:11) are all aimed at one goal: our common attainment of the perfect stature of the fullness of Christ (Eph. 4:13).

Chapter VII

SALVATION—A SACRAMENTAL ENCOUNTER

by

Paul Palmer

Basic to Judeo-Christian tradition is the belief that man is saved in and through the community. As Professor J. A. T. Robinson expressed it in his perceptive work, *The Body*, the ancient Hebrew "could not make his unique answer to God as an isolated individual."[1] If he has to live at all, he had to be one with the community, one with the people of God. To be separated from the community was death. To be restored to the community was life.

Similarly, the early Christian did not believe that he could be saved apart from the community. But for him the community was the new people of God, the Body of Christ, which is the Church. Entrance, or, better, incorporation into this Body of Christ which is the Church was had through baptism, "For in one Spirit we were all baptized into one body, . . ." as St. Paul tells us (1 Cor. 12:13). Separation from this body was death, incorporation into it was life. To be cut off from the community was to be severed from the principle of life. To be reconciled to this body through the sacrament of penance was life. For outside this body there is no salvation. Thus, early in the third century, Origen has the sinner ask three questions, but they are really one. "How can I who have fallen be saved? How can I have access to God? How can I return to the Church?" (*In. Ps. 36, Hom. 4*).

[1] J. A. T. Robinson, *The Body*. Chicago: Henry Regnery Co., 1952, p. 15.

Problem of Individualism

The idea of corporate salvation, of salvation in and through the Church, is a stumbling block to many Christians today. For many, salvation is a personal encounter with God in the innermost temple of the soul, where man can worship God in spirit and in truth. For many, the Church is an intruder, an interloper in this personal encounter with God. To some Christians, even Christ Himself is regarded as a distraction in the soul's meeting with its Creator.

These men will admit that man's encounter with God found its highest and noblest expression in the soul of the man Jesus, but Jesus has relevance today only as an example or pledge of what can happen to all of us. To paraphrase Paul Tillich, "We can all become Christs by sharing the experience of the man Jesus who became Christ."

Although this individualism in religion is foreign to Catholicism, something of its spirit has rubbed off on Catholics. Until recently, to quote Emile Masure, "The impression was frequently given that God is never faced with anything but an untold number of individuals, every one of them regulating on his own account the measure of his personal relationship with God."[2] True, Catholics come to church to worship God along with their fellow Catholics, just as Protestants do. But until the great liturgical revival of recent years, there was little solidarity in prayer, little communal worship. The praying community was often regarded as an obstacle or a distraction from one's personal piety and devotions.

Again, it is quite true that Catholic theologians have always stressed the essential mediatorship of Christ and the secondary mediatorship of the Church, but all too frequently Christ and His Church have been regarded as outside agents, as catalysts, arranging the meeting of the soul and God, but somehow external to the unifying process.

[2] Emile Masure, *Semaine Sociale de Nice,* Nice: 1934, p. 230.

Social and Ecclesial Aspects of the Sacraments

Today there is a growing awareness that salvation is not just *mediated* by Christ and the Church through the sacraments; rather, the life of grace is produced and maintained through *union* with Christ and the Church. Before encountering God, we must encounter Christ; before encountering Christ, we must encounter the Church. Union with God is had through union with Christ, and union with Christ is had through union with the Church, Christ continued and made visible in time. Henri de Lubac, in his extraordinary work *Catholicism,* has written:

"Grace does not set up a purely individual relationship between the soul and God or Christ; rather, each one receives grace in the measure in which he is joined socially to that unique organism in which there flows its life-giving stream. . . . All the sacraments are essentially sacraments in the Church; in her alone they produce their full effect, for in her alone, the society of the Spirit, is there, normally speaking, a sharing in the gift of the Spirit."[3]

This social or ecclesial churchly concept of salvation, in which the Christian is united to God and to Christ in the Church through his union with the community, is regarded by De Lubac as the "constant teaching of the Church," although De Lubac confesses that "in practice it is too little known."

The purpose of this chapter is to explore a long-neglected aspect of sacramental theology in order to make better known the social or ecclesial dimensions of the whole sacramental system. Instead of beginning with the sacraments themselves, the seven symbolic actions of Christ and His Church, the seven sacraments which are familiar, we prefer to begin with the concept of sacrament in a larger context, which is

[3] Henri de Lubac, *Catholicism*. New York: Longmans, Green & Co., 1950, p. 57.

coextensive with the economy of salvation realized first in Christ and then in His Church. We shall consider three basic points: (1) Christ is the sacrament of God; (2) the Church is the sacrament of Christ; (3) the seven sacraments are the symbolic actions of Christ and His Church in effecting our union with God. We shall conclude with man's response to this sacramental action.

Christ as the Sacrament of God

When we speak of Christ as the sacrament of God we mean Christ in His human nature, which he shares with us and in which He was visible to man. In this sense we can refer to the man Jesus without denying that He is God. Thus, we shall refer to His human will and actions, without denying that they are those of a divine person. We shall discuss Christ as the sacrament of God, as the visible manifestation and sign of the invisible God.

God's initial encounter with man was through the visible manhood of the God-man. That encounter might have been wholly spiritual; God, who is Spirit, might have revealed Himself directly to the human spirit; God, who is Holiness, might have directly sanctified man by the outpouring of His transforming love. Instead, the Word became flesh. He took a body and in and through that body established contact with man, redeemed him, and sanctified him. In doing this He graciously condescended to man's needs.

After all, man is neither pure spirit nor just a body. He is rather a spirit embodied. In the present life he is completely dependent on the body in his dealings with other men. Did you ever stop to think that all human interchange, all human encounter, is accomplished through the body? The body is the instrument of the spirit both passively and actively. Our encounter with other men, no matter how intellectual and spiritual the dialogue, is made possible only through the instrumentality of the body, through the functions of speech and hearing, of sight and touch. The human spirit cannot communicate directly with another spirit, but must use the instrument of corporeity, the body. What is true of your intellectual encounter is also true of the encounter with love. Two people in love can live the whole day through—a day pervaded by that warm, gentle, inner love. But unless that love is given expression in words and deeds it cannot grow. It will die if denied expression. And God, knowing the stuff of which we are made, condescended to our nature, and in His encounter with us became man. The Word became flesh.

To Philip's request at the Last Supper, "Lord, show us the Father and it is enough for us," Jesus replied: "Have I been so long a time with you and you have not known me? Philip, he who sees me sees also the Father" (John 14:8–9). Christ is the visible image of God. In this sense He is the sacrament of God. Knowledge of and access to God come through Christ. At Capharnaum Jesus cured a paralytic. But He did even more—He reconciled the sinner to God. He restored God's love to man. " 'But that you may know that the Son of Man has power on earth to forgive sins'—then he said to the paralytic—'Arise, take up thy pallet and go to thy house' " (Matt. 9:6). Matthew relates that the bystanders marveled that God should give "such power to men" (v. 8). As God, Christ could have directly cured the paralytic. But He did so as the Son of Man, as the visible instrument of the Godhead, the sacrament of God, acting in His visible humanity. During Christ's earthly career man's knowledge of and saving encounter with God involved an encounter with Christ. And ever since, our way to God has been through Christ.

The first to bypass Christ and seek a direct encounter with God were the Gnostic heretics of the early second century. To these fringe Christians the Incarnation was preposterous. That God should become man and take the flesh of a virgin was scandalous to them. They believed that the flesh was evil and incapable of the gift of the Holy Spirit; the body was the prison house of the spirit, and salvation could come only when the spirit was freed from the body and returned to the primal spirit whence it had come. Against the Gnostics the Church formulated her earliest creed, that of the Apostles: "I believe in . . . Jesus Christ, His only Son, Our Lord; Who was conceived by the Holy Ghost, born of the Virgin Mary, suffered under Pontius Pilate, was crucified, died, and was buried," and on the third day "arose again from the dead." The Church asserted the reality of the Incarnation, and the underlying principle of corporeity which states that Christ in His visible humanity is the sacrament of God.

The Church as the Sacrament of Christ

Strictly speaking, God could have sanctified man without becoming flesh, so too Christ could have applied the fruits of His redemptive death directly from heaven. There was no need for God to become man. So too there was no need for the God-man to continue Himself in a visible Church. And yet just as Christ in His visible humanity was the sacrament of God, so too the Church in all its visibility and human weakness is the sacrament of Christ. There is indeed no hypostatic union between Christ and the Church, as there is between the humanity and divinity of Christ. And yet, between Christ and His Church there is a mystical union, one so real that the Church can be called and is the Body of Christ. The Church is the Incarnation continued in time. It is the Incarnation made visible to us. Just as Christ was the visible and effective sign of the mercy of God in His earthly career, so too the Church is the visible sign or sacrament in human history of redemption accomplished and the effective sign of redemption communicated to men. And just as we cannot bypass Christ in our encounter with God, so too we cannot bypass the Church in our encounter with Christ.

Christ was the visible image of the invisible God. In much the same way for the Christian today the Church is the visible image of the invisible Christ. To Philip, Christ said:

". . . he who sees me sees also the Father" (John 14:9). To the Christian today, Christ says in effect: "He who sees the Church also sees me." For the Church is the Body of Christ, His visible manifestation in time. The mission of the Church is the continuation of His mission. Speaking to the Apostles as representatives of His Church, Christ says: "He who hears you, hears me; and he who rejects you, rejects me; and he who rejects me, rejects him who sent me" (Luke 10:16). On the night of the Resurrection, Christ's ministry of forgiving sins is continued in His Church: "As the Father has sent me, I also send you. . . . Receive the Holy Spirit; whose sins you shall forgive, they are forgiven them; and whose sins you shall retain, they are retained" (John 20:21–23). At Capharnaum, the Jews marveled that God should entrust to men the power of forgiving sins. And the world has marveled ever since. And yet, the power the Church claims today is a power which she received from Christ, a power which Christ received from God in His sacred humanity. It is the power of the Holy Spirit, the Spirit of Christ, the Spirit whom Christ promised to send when He was glorified.

In saying all this we are not extolling the Church for her own sake. The Church after all is a sign, and we do not stop at signs. We pass through them to find the object to which they point. The Church is the sign or sacrament of Christ, just as Christ is the sacrament or sign of God. Again, we must painfully admit that the Church, or, better, ourselves, her members, have not always pointed clearly to Christ. Christ wanted his bride the Church to be free of all spot or wrinkle; he wanted her beauty and radiance to shine through in every age, and to mirror forth the invisible Christ of Whom she is the image. And yet, despite the caricature that others have made of her, despite her own failure at times to live up to the ideal that Christ has set for her, she is still the only bride of Christ, the only image of Christ, the only sign pointing to Christ, as Christ is the only sign or sacrament pointing to the Father.

There is a tendency among some Catholics today to criticize the Church, to speak of her, as one has done recently, as a sinful Church. Admittedly there are sinners in the Church, but as Pius XII, in his encyclical on the Mystical Body of Christ, insists, her holiness will always shine forth "in the sacraments with which she begets and nurtures her children, in the faith which she preserves ever inviolate, in the holy laws which she imposes on all, and in the evangelical councils by which she admonishes and, finally, in the heavenly gifts and miraculous powers by which out of her inexhaustible fecundity she begets countless hosts of martyrs, virgins and confessors" (*Mystici Corporis*). Can any other Church make a similar claim?

Such is the Church, a mystery which has proved as great a stumbling block to many Christians as the mystery of the Incarnation. For the two are intimately related. The Incarnation is the enfleshment of God; the Church is the visible embodiment of the God-man. The Gnostics of the second century rejected the mystery of God made flesh. The Montanists of the third century rejected that of the God-man continued in a visible Church, a Church made up of bishops, as Tertullian the Montanist referred to the Catholic Church. True, these early heretics believed in a Church, but a spiritual one composed of men who would be taught directly and be led by the Spirit without any earthly intermediary.

Spirituality without the Church

Heresy has a strange way of repeating itself. In the twelfth century the abbot Joachim of Flora proclaimed the advent of a third covenant or age, supplanting the first covenant of Moses and the second covenant or New Testament of Jesus. It is the age of the Spirit, the age of the contemplative who will listen only to the inner voice of the Spirit. To quote Joachim, "Just as the veil of Moses was drawn aside by Christ, so that of Paul will be drawn aside by the Holy Spirit" (*Concordia Novi et Veteris Testamenti*). To all of this St. Bonaventure, the Seraphic Doctor and true contemplative, replied quite tersely: "After the New Testament, there will be no other" (*Commentarium in Sententias*).

Characteristic of all these Pentecostal movements, beginning with the Montanists of the second century and continuing in many Protestant sects today, is the endeavor to shake off the visible Church as a burdensome yoke or cumbersome intermediary in man's encounter with God. But, as De Lubac observes, they have all ended up embracing a void or worshiping false gods.

Truth demands that we acknowledge the fact that we are men and not pure spirits. The body is not evil as the Gnostics believed, nor must it and the material world be held as irrelevant or thought out of existence as the Christian Scientists demand. The Word became flesh and in that flesh He redeemed us, making a new body, the Church. But it is still His body, animated by the Holy Spirit, whom we first encounter not in some pentecostal room or in the temple of the individual soul; rather he is normally encountered in the Church, the domain of the Spirit.

St. Augustine sums it up quite beautifully: "What the human spirit or soul is to the members of our own body, the Holy Spirit is to the members of Christ, to the body of Christ, which is the Church" (*Sermon* 261, 14). And referring to those who knowingly separate themselves from the Church, he echoes the warning of Origen: "He who cuts himself off from Catholic communion" and goes out "of the house of salvation, makes himself responsible for his own death" (*Jesu Nave, Hom.* 3, 5). Augustine gives the reason: "For the Catholic Church alone is the body of Christ. . . . Outside this body the Holy Spirit vivifies no one. . . . and so those who are outside the Church do not receive the Holy Spirit" (*Letter* 185, 2, 50; PL 33, 815). This unqualified statement needs qualification.[4] But Augustine is expressing a general truth which is basic to Christianity.

[4] See Note at the end of the chapter.

Between Christ and His Church there is "a mystical identity." As Augustine puts it: "Head and members, one Christ," (*In Joannis Evangelium*, 21, 8) the whole Christ. In Pauline terms, "Christ and his bride the Church, one flesh" (cf. Eph. 5:23–30). For all practical purposes, then, for us Christ is His Church. If we are separated from Christ we are separated from His Spirit, the Holy Spirit.

The Church Is Catholic

In referring to the Catholic Church as the Body of Christ we use the word Catholic as understood by Origen, Augustine, and the Fathers of the East and West. The idea that there could be more than one Church of Christ was inconceivable to the Fathers of the early Church, just as it is incomprehensible to Catholics today.

Here is the heart of the matter. And Christians of all persuasions are beginning to realize it. The reality underlying the metaphor of the Church as the bride of Christ must necessarily stir all Christians to unite and to become in fact members of Christ's bride, members of one family. Writing in the third century, St. Cyprian, the great doctor of Christian unity, cites the text of St. Paul (Eph. 5:23–30) which refers to marriage as the symbol of Christ's union with His bride the Church and concludes: "How can he who is an apostate be one with Christ, who is not one with the spouse of Christ, and who is not in the Church of Christ?" (*Letter* 7).

The Sacraments as the Symbolic Actions of Christ and His Church

In the Church Christ sanctifies men and communicates to them the gift of the Spirit in seven sacraments, actions of the glorified Christ made visible in the external rites and liturgy of His visible body.

Baptism and Penance are good examples in explaining the

manner in which our first encounter with God is had through encountering Christ in His Church, and how our reconciliation with God, in the event of sin, is made possible by our reconciliation with Christ in His Church.

Baptism is frequently referred to as the sacrament of regeneration, of rebirth. And it is that. We are incorporated through Baptism into the body of Christ, receiving the Holy Spirit. This incorporation is the first effect of Baptism. Theologians refer to it as the sacramental character. We are stamped with the image (character) of Christ, becoming the object of the Father's love. If we place no obstacle in the way, divine life flows into our souls from Christ and we are transformed into heirs of God and coheirs with Christ. Thus the Church is central in the making of a Christian.

The sacrament of Penance is similar to Baptism. In fact, the Fathers of the Church refer to Penance as the second and more laborious Baptism. Through Baptism we are incorporated into the Church and made one body with Christ; through Penance we are reconciled with the Church, and thus reconciled in Christ to God. For the Church's ministry of forgiveness is actually the continuation of Christ's ministry of forgiveness. On Easter night Christ is speaking to the Apostles, but He looks beyond them to the successors of the Apostles as ministers of His Church. "As the Father has sent me, I also send you. . . . Receive the Holy Spirit; whose sins you shall forgive, they are forgiven them; and whose sins you shall retain, they are retained" (John 20:21–23). Whom the Church forgives, Christ forgives, since it is Christ acting in and through His Church who forgives. And whom Christ forgives the Father forgives. St. Augustine expressed it perfectly: "The peace of the Church forgives sins, and estrangement from the Church's peace retains sins." (*On Baptism*, 3, 18, 23). And his reason goes to the heart of the matter: "Since the forgiveness of sins cannot be granted except in the Holy Spirit, it is granted only in that Church which has the Holy Spirit." (*Sermon* 71, 20).

The Individual's Response

Thus far we have discussed the initiative of God, the working out of His redemptive love in and through Christ and His visible manifestation, the Church. However, we cannot speak of a personal encounter with God without considering the response of the individual to God's advances. The sacraments are symbolic actions of Christ and His Church. But the sacraments are not works of magic. Without denying that the sacraments have an efficacy far above that of sheer human striving, we must insist that they can neither save nor sanctify unless there is a personal response of faith, hope, and love on the part of the knowing recipient. In the case of infants, this triple response is made by the Church in the person of the child's sponsors, a response which the child will make on his own when capable.

In the case of an aware person, the response must be made by the individual. And yet the response is not wholly individual. The candidate for Baptism is caught up in the faith and worship of the Church. The faith he professes is not his own personal belief, individually come by. It is the faith of the Church, as it has been handed down for centuries and as it is enshrined in the Church's creed, the Apostles' Creed. We do not ask of Catholics their personal beliefs in matters of faith.

Again, the worship of the baptized Christian is not wholly individualistic. He is encouraged to practice private devotions and acts of piety and thus deepen his religious life. But even these private acts are caught up in the communal worship of the Church and receive a new significance and efficacy. In virtue of his Baptism, the Christian is stamped with the image of Christ, he is configured and made like to Christ, and he is consecrated to carry on the priestly role of Christ, which is to offer the Eucharistic sacrifice in concert with Him and the Church. In a sense the whole of the Christian's life of prayer, suffering, and devotion is subsumed and heightened in the daily sacrifice of Christians which is the sacrifice of the Mass, Calvary continued in time. The individual Christian is called upon to join Christ in the community of the faithful in offering a communal, social, and ever-expanding hymn of praise and thanksgiving to God. In doing so his personality is not suppressed nor absorbed by the community; rather he is called to the highest form of self-expression, a self which becomes ever more identified with Christ in His mystical community.

To sum up, our encounter with God is personal, but it is sacramental. It is personal but it is also social. Salvation is the personal encounter with God, but only as God is met in and through Christ and His Church. In a sense, this encounter with God is veiled and enveloped in signs, and yet it is real. One day the sacramental veil will be removed, and faith will yield to vision, hope to realization, love to possession, when we shall encounter God, face to face, in the Beatific Vision.

Outside the Church No Salvation. A Note

The basic problem raised by this paper is the lot of those who die outside the Roman Catholic Church. Origen, Cyprian, Augustine, and the Fathers of the Church are agreed that those who knowingly separate themselves from the Catholic Church and who never return cannot be saved. And it is in this context that the expression "outside the Church no salvation" is repeated time and again in the official documents of the teaching Church. The statement is usually directed to those who have been members of the Catholic Church and who have either actually withdrawn from the Church or who are contemplating such a withdrawal.

But what of those who have never been full members of the Church? What of those who have been born into a schismatical or heretical sect, and what of those who have not even been baptized as Christians? St. Augustine makes an important distinction relative to heretics which can be applied equally to schismatics. "They who defend their position, although it be false and perverse, without stubborn animosity, particularly when their own brazen presumption has not given it birth, but rather have inherited it from parents who have been deluded and have fallen into error, and who moreover with care and discretion search for the truth, prepared to amend should they discover it—these are in no sense [*nequaquam*] to be regarded as heretics" (*Letter* 43, PL, 33, 160). In the light of this statement, we can understand why Catholic theologians distinguish between formal heretics and material heretics, and why, more faithful to St. Augustine, even the word heretic is not used of those who are in good faith. In the words of Pope John XXIII, they are our "separated brethren."

But what of those who are not baptized, of those who are in no sense actual members of Christ's Mystical Body? Once again, St. Augustine's teaching is enlightening and has shaped contemporary Catholic teaching. Admitting that martyrdom "can supply for the lack of baptism," Augustine continues: "But faith and conversion of heart will do the same, if for want of time recourse cannot be had to the celebration of the mystery of baptism" (*On Baptism*, 4, 22, 29). True, Augustine is speaking of catechumens preparing for baptism, but the principle has been extended by Pius IX to all those who are invincibly ignorant of the true religion. Ignorance is considered invincible when lack of knowledge of the truth persists even though all the care has been taken that ordinarily prudent and conscientious persons would use in the circumstances. The quotation from St. Augustine (*Letter* 43) already cited describes possible circumstances which could render a person invincibly ignorant of the true religion or the need for baptism. After insisting on the general principle, "outside the Roman Apostolic Church no one can be saved," the pontiff continues: ". . . but we must hold it as equally certain that those who labor under ignorance, provided that it is invincible, are in the eyes of God not bound by any sin in this matter," a statement that surely implies that they can be saved, even though the pontiff leaves their lot to God (cf. Allocution, *Singulari quaedam*, Dec. 9, 1854, DB, 1647).

To conclude, actual and full membership in the Catholic Church, which is coterminous with the Mystical Body of Christ, is God's design for all men, but, considering the ignorance and prejudices even of men of good will, partial membership or membership in desire coupled with faith in God and true conversion of heart will be accounted by God as a substitute for His revealed Will for all men. In a wider sense we can say that no one is saved unless he belongs or is associated in some way with Christ's Church. Formal or full membership is had only by those who are united with Christ in one baptism, one faith, and one obedience. Partial or radical membership is had by all who are validly baptised, since baptism is the root or radix of all actual membership. Virtual membership is had by those who have the desire of baptism, even though this desire is not explicit but remains implicit in faith in God, and a true conversion of heart has the virtue or efficacy of preparing the soul for the indwelling of the Holy Spirit, who is normally given only to those who are members of Christ's Mystical Body which is the Catholic Church.

Chapter VIII

AUTHORITY IN THE CHURCH

by

James A. Mara

Pope John XXIII said that the purpose of the Vatican Council II is to work hard at whatever on the Catholic side needs to be healed and strengthened according to the teaching of our Lord Jesus Christ. When we have carried out this task, then we will point to the Church, in all her splendor and beauty, and say to our fellow Christians: "Look. This is the Church of Christ." That is the main purpose of the Council. That was what he had in mind when he first called the Council. Until we have done this healing work we cannot offer the Church to the Christians of the world in expectation of reunion. Pope John uses the word *aggiornamento* as designating the purpose of the Council. This simply means "bringing the Church up to date"—bringing it up to date by looking back at the Gospels.

There is no area where this attitude of *aggiornamento* is more needed than in the question of authority in the Church. The term "authority" collides with a whole system of memories and experiences and passions and feelings and exerts such pressure that I feel threatened to the core of my being. The very word seems to cause one of two reactions in everyone: either I feel it as something over against me, a threat to my existence as self, so that the word transforms my mood from discussion and relaxation to tension and combat; or else it triggers an explosion of fear. In the unconscious what is really feared may be authority itself. But on the conscious level we do not experience it that way. We experience a distaste for discussing it, a distaste amounting to abhorrence of entering into any dialogue with authority, or about authority. Perhaps we are afraid of losing the faith or injuring the faith of another. At any rate we do seem to fear that authority is so dreadfully alien that it is a threat to our existence as free agents. And so all our defenses are mobilized and that particular kind of anxiety ensues which always results in aggression. This is what we consciously fight against in considering authority. While we are considering the evidence we must struggle against this interior tension because otherwise we will not hear the evidence at all. Very few Catholics have heard what the New Testament has to say on authority.

These instinctive reactions to authority in the Church illustrate well the different possible levels upon which the subject may be discussed in Catholic theology or Catholic life. There are three possible attitudes to take about a discussion of authority, and Catholics tend to assume one of the first two. There is the attitude of polemics, secondly the attitude called apologetics, and lastly the attitude of dialogue. Polemics is a word for combat, a battle whose weapons are words instead of atomic bombs or rifles. The polemist is a man at war. He is trying to conquer someone whom he considers to be his enemy, and everything he says is directed toward this end, toward forcing his enemy to capitulate, and failing that, to reduce him to silence. In the last four hundred years polemics has been practiced a great deal between Catholics and Protestants, and often among Catholics themselves.

Apologetics is not combat. The word apologetics comes from a Greek word that has nothing to do with apology. The apologist is one who is attempting to convince a friend of something in order to convert him. Sometimes we have arguments of that sort in America on a political plane, though more usually we are engaged in polemics. The apologist wants to convert. Usually the person toward whom the apologetics is directed feels much more a victim than a friend, and from an attitude of anticipatory interest in what the apologist has to say or to write, he passes to boredom, and from there to resentment, and finally to bitterness. Then, of course, he replies, and both go right back to the field of polemics again.

A Dialogue on Authority in the Church

Dialogue is quite different. It is something that Catholics must learn to do. Non-Catholics also must learn it. But that does not excuse us, nor concern us here. Many Catholics like to get into polemical arguments about authority in the Church, but they rarely enter into true dialogue with non-Catholics, whether Christian or non-Christian.

A dialogue involves two partners, two collaborators, two equals. I have no right to enter into a dialogue with a person if I feel he is beneath me on any level that is touched upon in our dialogue. We are equals, and each one in the dialogue must recognize himself for what he is, the equal of the other, and the other for what the other is, my equal. The moment we find ourselves face to face with someone who attacks us or the community to which we belong, we are thrown on the defensive at once. We instinctively tighten up and get ready for battle. When someone tries to change my deepest convictions, I am going to feel threatened at the core of my being if I have real convictions. That is what is important about making a distinction between polemics, apologetics, and dialogue. When we decide upon the approach we are going to take we should do it deliberately, never fall into it because of our unconscious tendencies. If I am going to argue polemically with someone on the subject of authority in the Church, then I should know that I am doing it, and do it deliberately, not because unconscious tendencies have led me into it. After the Cuban missile crisis the relief felt in America was not a manifestation of fear; it was delight in becoming fully ourselves again. The same sort of thing took place at the end of the Second World War. Man is naturally a peaceful being, and no matter how strong the urge to war, war does in fact contract a person. And it destroys some of him too. Everyone is a casualty in war, even in a war of words.

Who has ever lost an argument? A dialogue about authority in the Church is neither an argument nor a war. If I enter a dialogue with another it is not because I want to convince him, conquer him, or force him to assent to anything. I do not want him to abandon one single conviction. That is true when one is speaking as a priest to fellow Catholics, or as a Catholic layman to non-Catholic Christians, or as a Christian to non-Christians. I have no right to assume an attitude that expects the other person to abandon any sincere conviction. Dialogue means that I want to seize upon the truth the other person possesses when he offers it to me, and to show him the truth that I believe I possess. Therefore, dialogue is outside the situations where polemics and apologetics can exist. Our Lord said in the Gospel that a man who intends to build a tower should sit down first, and then He says that the man should stay there, just sit there, until he has figured out how much the tower is going to cost. That is the position we want—to sit down, relaxed, and simply look at the evidence about authority in the Church with our minds completely open to the truth. Unless we can do that, with the truth of the faith that we mutually possess as Catholics, we can certainly not do it in discussing the truth of our faith with anyone else. There is a time for everything. There is a time to have war, I suppose, as well as a time for peace; a time to look and a time to act. Our Lord tells us in the Gospel that we should always look before we act. We should take a long, hard look. Otherwise our action may be a leap in the dark, the beginning of a long fall. In the spirit of the dialogue, then, what can be said about authority in the Church? The answer to such a question can come only by an attempt at *aggiornamento,* bringing the Church up to date by looking back at the Gospels.

Authority in the Church

The ordinary meaning of authority, of course, is the power to command obedience. That is what the dictionary tells us. Unless the President had real authority, America could not act in a crisis. Unless parents had authority over their children no child could receive a genuine education. A child cannot construct for himself that interior discipline that is the root of any mature personality. Unless the Church has authority there can be no unity of belief. This is true of authority in every human society: the state, the family, and the Church. We could pursue this theme along lines that must be familiar to everyone. The discussion has been so pursued for four hundred years now.

But it is also true that authority in the Church is revealed authority. It is not necessarily what we think the Church should have in order to be a society, but what God the Son decided to give it. It often happens that God's decision undermines our preconceived notions. This is because our notions are inevitably drawn from natural experience. When we think of society, it is of our father and his use of authority or of our own President or our legislatures that we are thinking.

If God created a supernatural society on earth He could certainly make it on the model of human societies, with the same sort of authority at its base. But He could do otherwise. He is not tied to the categories of our experience. We can only look at what He did. We cannot prejudge it. We cannot force His actions into our mold.

Authority in the Church is just as real as authority in human societies like the family or the state. But it is different. It is different because the society in which it is exercised is different from every human society. In the New Testament the Church is called *ecclesia*—that is, the people called together by God, chosen for His purpose; and *tou Soma tou Christou*—the Body of Christ because it is nourished by Christ

Himself Who gives to His members the Eucharist as their food and the Holy Spirit as the source of their life. But the New Testament word most used in Apostolic times and for centuries thereafter is *koinonia,* the common life that Christians share with the Trinity and one another. And the name for this common life is *agape.*

Agape and Authority

God the Son became man in order to communicate to mankind the life of the Trinity. This life, he tells us in St. John's Gospel, is *agape.* He does not say, as our English translations do, love. We do not know what Aramaic word Our Lord used, but we do know that when the Apostles and the authors of the New Testament translated Our Lord's word into Greek they used a neologism—an unaccustomed word, a word that deliberately forbade the reader to put it alongside his own experiences, incorporate it into his own heritage, his culture. The word *agape* scarcely appears in the *koine*—the Greek as spoken and written during and after the lifetime of the Apostles. The Apostles taught the early Christians that they must have *agape* for God and *agape* for one another. *Agape* meant something like love and at the same time something utterly different from their human experience of loving and being loved.

When Our Lord said this is the sign by which men will recognize you as my disciples—that you have *agape* for one another as I have *agape* for you—he was giving a sign, a mark, one mark alone by which His Church is recognized. This *agape* can only be learned by watching Christ. *Agape* in all the actions of His life, *agape* in His death, *agape* in His Resurrection and Ascension. He explains the interval between His Ascension and His Parousia—the interval between Easter Sunday and the end of the world—as the time when His disciples practice *agape.* The reason for the interval is this special and unique love that human beings are to have for one another.

All the other activities of the human race, the discoveries, progress, inventions, explorations, all the sciences elaborated and arts created, have reference to this *agape* or to nothing. The existential crisis so much discussed in our day comes to this: however much a man is caught up in human activities, however absorbed he is in those very movements which are man's natural glory, if he remains totally isolated from this *agape* of God he finds his existence absurd, his experiences all sharply focused on his own anguish.

Since the essential nature of Christ's Church is *agape* (St. Ignatius of Antioch calls the Church *agape*), everything in the Church exists as a means to create and communicate this *agape*. Everything, including authority.

The usual New Testament word for authority and power is *exousia*. Our Lord says, "All authority in heaven and on earth has been given to me" (Matt. 28:18). He does not say to the Apostles or Peter or anyone else, "And I give all this power to you." At the Last Supper He says, ". . . thou hast given him [Our Lord] power over all flesh, in order that to all thou hast given him he may give everlasting life" (John 17:2).

The Apostles were always arguing over who was to be the greatest among them; who was to have the most power. But Our Lord said, "The kings of the Gentiles lord it over them [*kuriuousin*], and they who exercise authority [*exousia*] over them are called Benefactors. But not so with you. On the contrary, let him who is greatest among you become as the youngest [*diakonos*], and him who is chief as the servant [*doulos*]. For which is the greater, he who reclines at table, or he who serves? Is it not he who reclines? But I am in your midst as he who serves" (Luke 22:25–27).

After instituting the Eucharist, Our Lord washes the feet of His Apostles and then says: "You call me Master and Lord, and you say well, for so I am. If, therefore, the Lord and Master have washed your feet, you also ought to wash the feet of one another. For I have given you an example, that as I have done to you, so you also should do. Amen, Amen, I say to you, no servant is greater than his master, nor is one who is sent greater than he who sent him. If you know these things, blessed shall you be if you do them. . . . he who receives anyone I send, receives me; and he who receives me, receives him who sent me" (John 13:13–20).

Our Lord's Apostles are servants of His disciples. Whoever welcomes these servants welcomes Our Lord. And the Apostles themselves throughout the New Testament call their office *diakonia* and call every Christian function *diakonia*, service—the duties performed by a true servant. One of these duties is authority. But authority in the Church does not raise one above the status of servant. It puts him into a life entirely devoted to service—into a life in which giving is always preferred to receiving (1 Cor. 15; 2 Cor. 7:2; 2 Thess. 2:7; 2 Cor. 9:7; Acts 20:35).

All the New Testament writings repeat Our Lord's teaching which identifies superiority of rank with the maximum degree of service. Not only do they call themselves *douloi* (slave laborers) of Christ and *diakonoi* (servants of the members of the Church), but they also teach that they do not wish to domineer over the faithful, to be their masters and lords.

The whole New Testament concept of authority as service is derived from the example of Our Lord's *agape*—an *agape* which led Him to a slave's death on the cross and to the Resurrection and Ascension.

Agape and the Power to Teach, Rule, and Sanctify

When Christ died on the cross He earned all the graces necessary for the salvation of every human being from Adam to the last man and woman. But when it comes to distributing these graces, He does not act alone. He has decided once and for all that these graces be distributed to the men of each generation through the free collaboration of the members of His Church. In order that each member might be sure of his part in this work of collaboration and love, He gave the Apostles and their successors (including Peter and his successors) the authority (power) to preserve his teaching intact so that our human attempts at deeper understanding would not result in deformation of what remains always revealed mystery. This is the power to teach. He gave them the power to direct the distribution of His grace through the sacraments so that in our enthusiasm for *agape* we would not be able (even though tempted) to deform *agape* into something low and weak. This is the power to sanctify. He gave them the power to formulate His law of love in words that each generation could clearly understand lest we make self-love the norm of true love. This is what is called the power of ruling.

Our Lord, then, gave to certain members of His Church sacred power, *hierarchē*. These members are not the Church. They are a part of the Church. It is ridiculous, therefore, and we ought not say, "The Church tells lay people," as though lay people were something other than the Church. These members possessing power possess it strictly and exclusively for the good of the Church and each member in it. But not for themselves. The hierarchy, therefore, exists for the Church as a means exists for the end. That is why the popes call themselves servants of the servants of God. That is what a pope, a bishop, a priest is. No more, but no less.

Authority exists in the Church because the Church is a life of service for all its members. What we call sanctifying grace is the created means by which the uncreated Spirit can dwell in us, and we with Him in the Father and the Son. God to us, God for us, God in contact with us, as St. Paul says. Each one of us must see that he is "My God" and see that he is not exclusively mine. I cannot know God or possess him in isolation. In fact an isolated person is a contradiction in terms. Even God who is absolutely one is not a solitary person and cannot be. Every gift to me is from God and for everyone else. Any gift that I keep for myself ceases to be God's gift.

Therefore, authority in the Church exists for all. Not only ought the hierarchy to live its life in the Spirit of serving the members of the Church. It *must* serve the members—willy-nilly because it is service and nothing else.

This service consists of infallible power to teach the truths Our Lord taught in another language to other people over nineteen hundred years ago; to control the means of grace, not in order to limit them but to direct them to their greatest fruitfulness; to interpret the law of Christ, not in order to destroy our liberty but to release it.

Authority within the Church, divinely instituted, is an authority of service. And it is meant along with grace to transform all the authority of human affairs. Every relationship that involves subordination—between man and woman, parents and children, rulers and citizens—is to be transformed into a relationship of *agape*. A husband can no longer merely love his wife; he is called upon to give his life for her as St. John and St. Paul explicitly say. A parent must love his child the way Christ loves him. No earthly relationship is left in its natural state. Each is to be transformed in the Lord. This demands a profound conversion on the part of Christians.

But what of this authority in the Church? What has been described does not seem to reflect experience. But it does reflect our experience. We are nourished with the Body of Christ and the truth of Christ. We are given the Holy Spirit. We are taught to be sons of Our Father who is also the Father of Our Lord Jesus Christ.

If it is difficult to exercise authority in the Church with great purity of heart, if those in authority (whom authority possesses) sometimes fail, they may fail because of our failures. It takes as much courage and humility to be truly served by those in authority as it does for the man in authority to be truly our servant.

Chapter IX

NEW APPROACHES TO MORAL THEOLOGY

by

Robert H. Dailey

Morality cannot be separated from religion without sacrifice of the imperative. The moral act is a good act in the religious sense of the term; the immoral act is a sin. However, for the Christian this proposition has a richer, profounder, more meaningful content than it has for one, if such there be, who cultivates natural religion. Here our purpose is to set forth a descriptive history of the development of moral theology, an appreciation and a criticism of our present moral theology, the needs which must be fulfilled in the reformulation of moral theology, and a description of the more worthy attempts to fulfill these needs at the present time.

At the very outset it would seem proper to give a definition of moral theology. The definition given by Father Henry Davis, S.J., at the beginning of his four-volume *Moral and Pastoral Theology,* would seem to be sufficient for our purposes here. He says, "Moral Theology is that branch of Theology which states and explains the laws of human conduct in reference to man's supernatural destiny, the vision and fruition of God. As a science, it investigates the morality of human acts, that is, the moral good and the moral evil in conduct in relation to man's ultimate end. It is a practical science because it has to regulate action."

Descriptive History of the Development of Moral Theology

The Apostolic Era. The Gospels reveal the long-heralded and long-awaited entrance into human lives of God, as a Father, by sending His divine Son. The Son is a man in form, appearance, and reality; but He does not cease to be God and He does not lose anything of the divine. This is Jesus Christ. In Him, by Him, and with Him we become sons of God and return as sons to our Father of whom we have been deprived by our sin.

Morality is not delivered in the Gospels in the form of a system of laws. Christ does, indeed, refine the Decalogue; but He goes much farther: be perfect as your heavenly Father is perfect; the Kingdom of God is within you; love one another as I have loved you. It is the loving response to the call of the Father to return to Him; a call, inspired by God's love, made in Christ, the response to which is possible by Him and will be made with Him or not at all. The Christian seeks to belong to Jesus . . . abide in Me . . . and by assuming His life to make with Him his way to the Father.

The epistolary writings of the Apostles, Peter and Paul, James, John, and Jude, will take up cases of conscience and give moral instruction, but the foundation will be the same as in the Gospels: the love of the Father, the mystery of Christ and His teaching, the Holy Spirit sent by Him, grace by which we become like Him and with Him return to the Father just as in Him and by Him we have returned to the Father in principle. It follows as a consequence of the Incarnation and the Redemption that moral living is the building of a new temple of God, a new creation, an undreamed of and undeserved perfection of the image of God which is man, worthy of an honored place in our Father's house. The imperative is the profound duty of loving response in human living to the call of a loving Father in Christ Jesus, His Son.

The Post-Apostolic Era. About the end of the first century was initiated the reflection of the communities of believers, the Church, on the moral message of Jesus as given us in the Gospels, the writings and the preaching of the Apostles. Two lines of development are followed: that of a clear listing of good works and of sins and that of a growing development of a system of moral science in terms of the Christian mystery, of theology, of the philosophies of the times and of law.

In the earlier period one finds a relatively simple moral catechism consisting in the catalogue of the moral instruction of the Old and New Testaments under the formalities of the Way of Life and the Way of Death. Christ is present spiritually and mystically in the faithful as He is in the Church because of their faith and charity. Therefore St. Ignatius of Antioch would write: "Let us perform all our actions with the thought that God is present in us; and then we shall be His temples, and He will be God dwelling within us" (*Epistle to the Ephesians*, 15, 3). Seen as clearly related to grace, to life in Christ, to life in the unity of His Mystical Body, the Church, the moral imperative of Christians is to believe in Christ and to follow Him faithfully in love without condition.

There is a casuistry, too, which served to solve moral problems created by the extension of Christianity into a hostile, pagan world and by the growth and development of the Church itself.

Martyrdom is one of the great questions. The martyr is a witness of Christ and Christ is present in His witness who realizes in his death the ideal of perfect oneness with his Lord. Correlative with the oft-repeated example of steadfast martyrdom is the problem of what to do about the many whose courage failed them when confronted by the supreme test . . . the apostates or *lapsi*. Virginity early came to the fore and earned its meaning of a bloodless martyrdom or giving of witness before the world, of faith in Christ, of hope that he will come to take possession of His Kingdom, of devoted love of Him. The virgin's life is characteristic of the eternal kingdom which Christ will offer to His Father, where "they shall neither marry nor be given in marriage but shall be like the angels of heaven" (Matt. 22, 30). At the same time there was agitated the problem of repeated remission of actual sins and the atonement of them by public penance. The bishop was Christ in the local church. His faith, when identical with the faith of other bishops and the Bishop of Rome, was the norm of faith for the people and obedience to him was the norm of life for the Christian. Unity of faith and charity among the bishops themselves, particularly with the Bishop of Rome, and among bishop and people, was most dramatically expressed by Eucharistic Communion, participation in and sharing of the same Holy Bread, the Body of Christ, by all. Toward the end of this era, desert spirituality arose to emphasize, as bloody martyrdom became less frequent, a new kind of witness to Christ through the struggle of the follower of Christ to free himself of the devil in his own flesh and to outwit his cunning invitation to succumb to the spirit of the world. By his asceticism he fled from moral ruin and entered into life.

Later Patristic Times. From the very beginning of the Church, cultivated men were attracted to Christianity and offered to its service their minds and energies. At this time began the systematization of Christian morality in terms of a purification of and an integration with the best of pagan philosophies. In the East, Clement of Alexandria, the moralist, and Origen of the Alexandrian school attempted to discover and to illuminate the relation between the positive values of pagan philosophy and the morals demanded by the Christian revelation. Wishing to offer the cultivated man of their time an authentic Christian morality in his own philosophical language they wrote about free will, virtue, and vice, Christ as the center of the Christian life, and thus tried to place pagan wisdom at the service of Christian theology. St. Cyril of Alexandria followed them to provide growth in Christian living with a solidly theological basis in sanctifying grace which connects Christian holiness with the substantial holiness of God (of which it is a participation effected in us by the action of the Holy Spirit, who was in the humanity of Christ only that He might be communicated to us).

In the West, arose a doctor who became one of the most influential in the Church, St. Augustine. His teaching was frankly and outstandingly moral. Holding to free will by the side of grace, he insistently recalls the necessity of voluntary moral activity. Such activity in the Christian flows from docility to the guidance of the Holy Spirit so that he may act through charity. Essential to Augustine's teaching is the fact that man has a necessity to seek happiness, and this happiness is rest in subsisting Goodness, Being, and Truth—God. But God commanded man to respect the order of nature and to seek his true happiness. So there is a law which supposes a natural order of things and a divine will which imposes it. Sin is a violation of the order willed by God, and virtue consists in the love of the law, of the good which is commanded and of the good which is simply counseled. Virtue is a force which enables a man to act in spite of his inherent weakness. Augustine teaches that all of the moral virtues come from the four cardinal virtues (prudence, justice, temperance, and fortitude), and that these cannot lead a man to his last end unless he has the theological virtues of faith, hope, and charity. Faith is the necessary basis of all supernatural and Christian life; hope is the condition of all faith working through charity and the source of true joy; charity truly unites man to God. In the wide sense charity is the love of good which is implied by every virtue and in the strict sense is the queen of all virtues, the sum of all Scriptural precepts, the virtue to which all the other virtues lead and through which they achieve their final purpose, union of man with God.

Christian moral perfection, therefore, resides in charity which accomplishes the law and sums up every virtue in itself. It is the source of pure love which makes God loved for Himself because of His perfections. From this Augustine goes on to develop his ascetical theology, the aim of which is the restoration of the image of God in the soul. Beginning with sanctifying grace, this renewal is consummated by perfect faith, hope, and charity. These three virtues are aided by actual grace, in the absence of which nothing can be done in the supernatural order, by the moral virtues, by the spiritual combat and good works, by prayer and piety which relates a man especially to Jesus Christ, Incarnate Wisdom.

If the influence of St. Augustine was far reaching so was that of St. Gregory the Great, the first monk to become a pope. This theologian and doctor of the Church was orientated toward the practical aspects of the Christian life and found in Holy Scripture examples and counsels on the moral and ascetical life of the faithful. His greatest works are the moral ones: the *Moralia*, the *Pastoral*, and the *Dialogues*. His Augustinianism is undeniable.

Early Middle Ages. For the next six centuries no great work on moral theology appeared. Emphasis was upon the practical points made in the writings and sermons of the Fathers, upon the decrees of Popes, bishops, and Councils issued against abuses in order to maintain the moral ideal. The Penitentials appear. These were compiled "so that priests should more fully understand how they ought to receive confessions and indicate penance to the penitents according to the canonical institution." (Council of Reims, 813, can. 12.) Lists of sins were provided and the penance corresponding to each sin was recorded, e.g., "If anyone exacts usury from anybody, he shall do penance for three years, one year on bread and water." (So-called *Roman Penitential*, #47.) Little is left to the judgment of the confessors. The expiatory and satisfactory nature of penance was emphasized. A legitimate complaint can be lodged at the end of this era to the effect that a static and almost mechanical attitude had taken possession of the moral guidance of the Church, which is reflected in the Penitential Books. There is no doubt that these books exercised an important influence in the evolution of moral teaching and practice.

The twelfth century ushered in the era of the canonists. Roman Law was rediscovered, and on the foundations of this law and ancient conciliar and Patristic texts was built Canon Law. The canonists concentrated upon the constitutional aspect of the Church, and the influence of their views remains strong today. Being members of a spiritual society, naturally they took up moral problems too. From positive law they went to law in general; from contracts they developed ideas on justice; from the study of crimes they went on to ideas of sin; in marriage they concentrated upon its contractual nature. Moral theology has not yet shaken off the influence of the canonists.

At this time there was the tendency to reserve to theology the study of God and the divine mysteries and to leave to philosophy the study of morals. No one of the great theologians—and theology was at the beginning of a golden age—constructed a clearly defined moral theology. This defect occurred again and exists today.

St. Thomas Aquinas. It remained for St. Thomas Aquinas to write a grandiose synthesis of the different tendencies of tradition and to initiate, after a fashion, the establishment of a real moral theology.

The moral theology of Aquinas is contained in the *Secunda Pars* of the *Summa Theologica.* Divided into two parts, the *Secunda Pars* presents a general moral theology in the *Prima Secundae* and a special moral theology in the *Secunda Secundae.*

The general moral theology begins with the consideration of the last end of man and proceeds to the exploration of the means of attaining it. These means are human acts. Therefore, Aquinas proceeds to analyze the human act and then goes on to discuss the principles or dynamic origins of the human act. The analysis involves an extended examination of the act of will and freedom of choice, good and bad acts, their merit and demerit before God, and terminates with an extensive study of the passions. The principles or dynamic origins of human acts are internal and external to the individual. Internal to him are the virtues and the gifts of the Holy Spirit and the actions proper to them, i.e., the beatitudes and fruits of the Holy Spirit. Internal to man too but moving him to his ruin are vices and sin. Origins of human acts which are external to man are the devil, who moves man to evil, and God, who moves him to his end. God does this by instructing him through law and by moving him by grace.

Special moral theology, according to the division of Aquinas, studies particular human acts. He proceeds by studying first the theological and moral virtues, the gift of the Holy Spirit which corresponds to each virtue, the vices which are opposed to each virtue, the affirmative and negative precepts of each virtue, and concludes his moral theology with the consideration of different states of life.

The influence of Aristotle in this moral theology is very strong. Aquinas resolves, better than his predecessors, the thorny problem of the relation between natural and supernatural morality, between reason and faith in the moral life, by exposing reason as the means of perceiving God and our way to Him which is revealed in nature and, when supernaturally elevated, illuminated, and moved by God, as a means of knowing the content of divine revelation. But his moral theology has its more profound roots in Patristic theology. Beatitude, which is the end of man, is blessed communion with God in face-to-face vision arrived at by love. The virtues receive their orientation and their meaning from love, from docility to the Will of God, from docility to grace, to the Word and the example of Christ.

Within the unity of the *Summa Theologica,* the *Secunda Pars* follows, by intellectual necessity, the *Prima Pars,* which is about God in his trinitarian life as Creator. It precedes the *Tertia Pars,* which is about Christ the Saviour, the sacraments which are Christ's symbolic actions effecting our salvation, and the culmination in eternal life which is a coming to Him through resurrection from the dead. Thomas therefore begins with God, Creator. His moral theology considers the motion of man to God, his final end, by his human acts: Christ as Man is our way to God. Following His example, reborn, sustained, repaired, and made to grow by His gifts which arc His sacramental actions, within the body of His elect which is the Church, we come finally to the culmination of mortal life after resurrection from the dead, to God from whom we first came.

The *Secunda Pars* is the longest of the three parts of the *Summa Theologica.* It is a mistake, however, to wrest it from its place in the unity of the whole and treat it simply as a moral theology apart from what precedes and follows it. Nevertheless, a separation did take place and it endures until our day. Great theologians, even among the Dominicans, have done this and moral theology has suffered.

Nominalism. The roots of separation are in the decadence of Scholasticism which occurred in the fourteenth and fifteenth centuries. Into this vacuum stepped Nominalism, which affected the development of moral theology in two ways: by its voluntarism, and by its evisceration of metaphysics.

In metaphysics, the universal was reduced to a sign, a pure creation of the mind, lacking all reality, the object of abstract knowledge, the knowledge of the ideal or unreal. The concrete, the singular, and the individual achieved a preponderating importance. It taught the unique value of the singular as opposed to the universal, of the individual as opposed to the species, of the concrete human person. Only the individual is real and is apprehended even intellectually by intuition. Thus a free act is the act of a singular being at a singular instant, the very essence of the soul, independent of intellectual representations of the good. Whereas Thomas saw the moral life as growth in virtue, the Nominalist, while recognizing in man the existence of dispositions to good or bad, to the virtues and the vices, nevertheless saw the moral life as a succession of decisive acts. His interest was less in the study and arrangement of the virtues and more in the consideration of each decision in its meaning and precise circumstances. The door is open to emphasis upon casuistry.

Nominalism was voluntaristic. The will has an absolute power of self-determination. Its decision is freed from reasonable motives. Whereas the Scholastic saw that the object of the will act is the good and the good is identified with being, the Nominalist taught that the good is the result of a free and arbitrary act. The good is whatever God freely and even arbitrarily wants to be good. The good is the law, and the law is whatever God wants it to be. Such voluntarism gave birth to legalism. Moral theology will, from now on, be less interested in virtue and more interested in law, in the commandments. Moral life became less of a response of man to God's Will in charity; it was less of a motion toward God. These ideas belong to ascetical and mystical theology but not to moral theology.

Nominalism was disastrous for speculative moral theology. To do it justice, however, it did contribute much to the knowledge of the moral act in its singularity and in its subjective aspects. Interest was centered on the new and the concrete problems that arose during these centuries from the rise of European nationalism and the economic changes in society.

The Sixteenth Century. This century saw a Thomistic renaissance. Authors like Cajetan and the Doctors of Salamanca, Vitoria, Cano, Soto, Medina, Mancio, and Bañes, all Dominicans, brought moral theology to a point of high development. The School of Salamanca, or the Salamanticenses, as they were called, was able to integrate into the moral theology of St. Thomas the best acquisitions of the Nominalists. This extraordinary group of theologians was led by Francis de Vitoria, a man who knew to perfection the major problems of his day and who was able to scrutinize the economic and political problems of the times in terms of Thomistic principles. He is known as the father of international law. Nevertheless, in these theologians Nominalism had deep roots which betrayed themselves by a tendency to concentrate on the *Secunda Pars,* the moral theology of St. Thomas, to the lessening of emphasis on the unity of the whole *Summa Theologica* and on speculative theology.

The sixteenth century saw the foundation of the Society

of Jesus and the emergence of the first Jesuit Doctors. Toletus, Gregory of Valencia, Gabriel Vasquez, and Suarez commented upon the *Summa Theologica.* Suarez in particular held to the direct knowledge of the singular and the importance of law. Accent upon the juridical is evident in the great work of Sanchez on marriage, important even in our own times; in the monumental work on justice and law by Molina, in which he studies the commercial and financial world of his day; in the work of Lessius on social and political economy. The same can be said of De Lugo's classical works on justice and penance.

Thomas, the Nominalists, Cajetan, the Doctors of Salamanca, and the early Jesuits taught in the universities. Their ideas influenced the times in which they lived. But the greater part of the Catholic clergy had a much simpler education, for the seminaries were established only after the Council of Trent. In their pastoral work they were guided by small works written for their use in reaction to the severe and mechanistic Penitentials of earlier times. These works were summaries for the usage of confessors, the *Summae Confessorum.* A great number of these appeared, the best of which was the *Summa Theologica* of St. Antoninus, although this work in size and scope far transcends the ordinary summary for confessors.

The *Summa Theologica* of St. Antoninus is arranged in four large volumes. The first considers the soul and its intellectual and volitional power, the causes of sins, and specifically the passions, sins, and law. The capital sins take up the second volume; the third considers states of life, the sacraments, and canonical penalties. The fourth volume develops the virtues and the gifts of the Holy Spirit.

Less pretentious and typical of the summaries is the *Summa Angelica* of Angelus de Clavasio. It is a volume of moderate size which treats in alphabetical order of the various problems that might be presented to a priest, e.g., abortion, absolution, *acceptio personarum* (human respect in distributing favors), adjuration, and so forth, from the moral, legal, liturgical, and pastoral points of view. At the end of the sixteenth century the Jesuits published this kind of small handbook for the use of confessors. But by the middle of the sixteenth century moral theology was ready for a new kind of development. It took the form of the *Institutiones Morales*, the form in which moral theology is presented today.

The Institutiones Morales. There was needed something more sophisticated than the summaries for confessors and less developed than the very long *Summae*, for solid and practical works which would at the same time do more than solve cases of conscience and which would satisfy the mind in search of principles while teaching the art of solving cases in terms of these principles.

The Reformation threw men back more on their individual consciences. The Counter-Reformation required of priests a more profound action on the soul in the Sacrament of Penance. Defining the quasi-matter of Penance as consisting in the three acts of the penitent—contrition or attrition with at least an implicit resolution not to commit sin again; confession; and satisfaction—the Council of Trent, in reaction to the ideas of the Reformers, defined that integral confession requires the accusation of all mortal sins in terms of number, species, and circumstances which change the species, insofar as after examination the penitent is aware of them. The same Council ordered the establishment of seminaries for the training of priests. Therefore, there was needed a methodical course of moral theology which could be completed during the course of seminary studies. The answer was the compilation of the *Institutiones Morales*.

The Jesuits filled this need. In the Jesuit system of seminary education all speculative questions are left to the professors of dogmatic theology. These supply the foundations for Christian living: the nature of God, God the Creator, the Trinity, sanctifying grace, the elevation and fall of the human race, the culmination of human life in the last things. To the professors of "cases of conscience" or moral theology are left the practical aspects of Christian living: human acts, conscience and law, sin, the virtues, all of which enter into every case, the Commandments, the sacraments, precepts of the Church for all, duties of particular states of life, and canonical censures. By this method the confessor was trained solidly for his work in the Sacrament of Penance and the priest for his duty of catechist and instructor on the duties of the Christian life.

The success of this method was universal and lasting. It was adopted by theologians from most of the religious orders and the secular clergy. Eminent among Jesuits were Azor, Castropalao, Coninck, Laymann, and especially Busenbaum. Busenbaum's chief title to fame, and great it is, was his book *Medulla Theologiae Moralis*, which ran to two hundred editions in various nations and languages within the space of 125 years (1645–1770). It provided the groundwork for St. Alphonsus Liguori in the eighteenth century and for Gury in the nineteenth, so that through these two authors it has influenced our own century.

The book is divided into seven parts: (1) The internal rule of morals which is conscience and the external rule which is law; (2) The precepts deriving from the theological virtues of faith, hope, and charity; (3) The precepts of the Decalogue and the Church; (4) The precepts proper to certain states of life; (5) Sin, which is a violation of these precepts; (6) The sacraments of the New Law; (7) Ecclesiastical censures and irregularities. Each chapter begins with a short, incisive explanation of the matter to be treated and its terminology, and then proceeds by topic in the form of an answer to a *Dubium*, i.e., a question.

The *Medulla* of Busenbaum and similar works of the period replaced the *Summae Confessorum* by completing them with fundamental principles and substituting the alphabetical by a methodical order. Empirical and self-contained, these works presupposed that the student knew philosophy, dogmatic and spiritual theology, and speculative moral theology. The *Institutiones Morales* were intended to supply sound principles for casuistry, the art of solving cases occurring in the life of the Christian, and as such they contained much of positive law. This explained their great success.

Controversies. The seventeenth and eighteenth centuries up to the time of St. Alphonsus were centuries of fervid controversy in moral theology. Since the schools which finally emerged from these controversies still exist and still uphold their positions, one must take into account the school to which the writer belongs who attempts to formulate the problem under controversy and his criticism of the other schools as well as his appreciation of his own.

The central problem can be summarized as follows. In the decision to perform a moral act there is quite frequently the alternative whether to follow the law (divine or human) or to follow liberty. When it is clear that the law binds, a man must obey the law if he wishes to serve God. When there is no law contrary to liberty, a man may act in the way he freely wishes without offense to God. His action might not be perfect or the better thing, but at least it does not offend God. But what should he do when he is not sure that the law binds him morally to a certain line of action, either because the very existence of the law is in doubt or because the extension of an existing law to this situation is in doubt? Is he bound to obey a doubtfully existing law? Is he bound to obey a law the extension of which to his case is doubtful? Or is he free to follow his liberty with the practical certitude that he is not thereby offending God?

Thus arose the long controversy about the theoretically probable but practically certain conscience. In the controversial discussions about this problem, the pendulum swung from laxism, which reduced obligation to an unreasonable minimum, back to rigorism, which laid intolerable burdens upon the conscience. Absolute rigorism was held by the Jansenist heretics. This system was condemned by Alexander VIII. Laxism was condemned by Innocent XI. Equilibrium was achieved by the development of the theories of probabiliorism, favored more by the Dominicans and one Jesuit Superior General, of probabilism, which originated with the Dominican Medina and was developed by the Jesuits and the Franciscans, and of equi-probabilism, which developed out of the writings of St. Alphonsus and is held by the Redemptorists. Today the field is held for the most part by the probabilists and equi-probabilists. Each of these schools holds to its own theory and expounds it in treatises on conscience.

St. Alphonsus Liguori. St. Alphonsus was moved to compile his moral theology for the benefit of the Redemptorist seminarians who, as priests and missionaries, were destined to direct the consciences of men by teaching and by hearing confessions. Therefore he sought to find a middle way between the rigorists and the laxists, and to compose a work that was small enough to be mastered and large enough to be complete. To achieve this goal he followed the method and division elaborated by Busenbaum, even to the extent of retaining the same chapter and sub-chapter headings. Without passion he reports each variant opinion on each subject with the supporting authors, gives his own opinion about the degree of probability each opinion merits, and modestly expresses his own opinion about which one should be followed. St. Alphonsus saved the Church from the extremes of laxism and rigorism and thus served her well. He was canonized by Gregory XVI and declared a Doctor of the Church by Pius IX.

The work of the casuists was completed by the large amount of spiritual writing during this era. The writings of Bérulle and Olier exerted a strong influence upon the Sulpician seminaries. Lallemant and Saint-Jure were highly appreciated. St. Alphonsus himself wrote spiritual works of high value and wide circulation. All of these spiritual writings completed the moral theology.

The Nineteenth Century. Coming to grips with the rationalism of the Enlightenment, Sailer and Hirscher opened the nineteenth century as moral theologians determined upon a renewal and reformulation of moral theology in terms of a discipline which would expose the ideal of the Christian life in its totality and its possibilities for growth. They would strip it of its juridical language, confine the juridical elements in it to Canon Law, and reintegrate moral into dogmatic theology.

Johann Michael Sailer (1751–1832) was a Jesuit up to the time of the suppression of the Society of Jesus. Thereafter he became a diocesan priest, a professor, and died as Bishop of Ratisbon. In 1817 he published his famous *Manual of Christian Morality*. This work was destined not only for the pastors of souls but also for educated Christians. It is not merely a pastoral treatise for the administration and use of the sacrament of penance, nor is it a collection of practical counsels for living a better life. It is a general study of the Christian life, formally presented as a conversion and a growth.

Johann Baptist von Hirscher (1788–1865), who taught at Tübingen for many years, developed his moral theology around the concept of the Kingdom of God. His thought is penetrating and at the same time practical, with reference to the problems of his times. He was followed by his student Moehler and the other theologians of Tübingen who placed the foundation of Christian morality on the gift of grace and its correlative call to the perfect life. The moral life is presented less in terms of static norms and more as a living struggle between grace, which calls men to higher things, and the world, which invites men to darkness and sin. They insist upon the liberty of the sons of God to which lies open a much larger field of action than a moral theology which is confined to the narrower limits of law. This liberty in the service of God inevitably approaches closer and closer to the life of the counsels.

The new interest in moral theology created by these theologians had a great influence in the pastoral and catechetical life of the German-speaking peoples, but beyond these frontiers the influence has been slight. At present, however, many of their ideas are being revived.

The Twentieth Century. Toward the end of the nineteenth century and continuing into our own times there has been a Thomistic renaissance in dogmatic theology, and at the same time, in moral theology, a reaffirmation of the value of the *Institutiones Morales* of the seventeenth century, especially as perfected and developed by St. Alphonsus Liguori. The manuals of moral theology used in the seminaries in the United States today were written mostly toward the end of the last century and the early part of the present century. New editions constantly appear in an attempt to keep them up to date.

All of these manuals basically have the same form and fundamentally teach the same doctrine. Roughly, they follow the general plan of the *Summa* of St. Thomas and the moral theology of St. Alphonsus: the end of man and how to attain it; it is attained by human acts; conscience is the subjective guide, and law the objective guide, for man in his human acts; sin is a deviation from the end. At this point a difference of development occurs. One group, more faithful to the plan of St. Thomas, develops the way to our end through the study of the theological and moral virtues. The other group, after a more cursory treatment of the theological and moral virtues, develops the way to our end through the study of the Commandments of God and the Church according to the plan of St. Alphonsus. Certain more important states of life induce special obligations. The administration and reception of the sacraments, although fundamentally they do enter into the Commandments and virtuous imperatives, are treated apart. Censures are impediments to life in the Church and are to be found at the end of the manuals.

Appreciation and Criticism of Our Present Moral Theology

These manuals have great value. Although the matter which they present is awesome, it is logically ordered, clearly presented, and easily mastered. Basic in their structure are solid principles that provide for a consistent and safe casuistry. In these manuals one finds the clear distinction between serious moral duties which cannot be ignored or violated and works of higher perfection to which man is called and invited by grace but not held to perform by strict obligation. Contained in the multiphasic exposition of duties are most of the moral, liturgical, rubrical, canonical, and pastoral precepts and problems which a priest is likely to meet in the pastoral and confessional ministry. Periodicals supplement every part of the manuals by presenting special writings on problems arising in psychology, medicine, law, business, marriage, education, politics, social order, and a host of other phases of human life. The manuals make these writings intelligible and usable, within the structure of moral theology. As it is taught today, moral theology leaves to ascetical and mystical theology, the literature of which is quantitatively enormous and qualitatively very good, the more detailed guidance of souls in the more perfect life. Moral theology is entirely consistent with the dogmatic theology which the seminarian studies during his four-year course of theology. Thanks to these manuals the priest upon leaving the seminary is able to enter without great difficulty upon his duties and to carry them out with a relatively high degree of effectiveness. Furthermore, he is open to whatever growth in pastoral perfection his experience might lead him.

But there are flaws. The moral theology of the manuals is far from perfect. Indeed, it is suffering a great amount of justified criticism. Before the last war there were initiatives toward reformulation. Since the war these efforts have redoubled and presage quite a change in the development and emphasis of moral theology. The following criticisms are, I think, justified.

(1) While moral theology in the choice of its subject matter does, indeed, depend upon revealed truth, it is, nevertheless, preponderantly a system of natural ethics in which reason takes the more important role in discovering moral truth revealed in nature rather than in seeking the moral truth contained in the Christian revelation as we have it in its sources, Scripture and tradition, partially left to us by the Fathers of the Church and taught us by the magisterium. It is true that the moral theologian reflects upon the doctrine taught by the magisterium and that some of the problems he works on arise from revelation and its sources, but in too many respects moral theology today is far from its sources as a theology.

(2) Moral theology today is more directly pointed toward a sound and principled casuistry than to the investigation into and the teaching of what is the Christian life to which we are called in Christ as individuals and as members of the Mystical Body. In one sense it is true that moral theology is the defender of human liberty because it will not lay intolerable burdens upon the human spirit but rather distinguishes carefully between strict obligation and evangelical counsel to more perfect acts. Nevertheless, moral theology appears to endorse and approve a minimalism in Christian living. It is true, also, that moral theology does express and explain many of the positive values—duties that are encumbent upon us—but these are most often not presented in their specifically Christian modality. To an inquirer about what Christian living is, one would hardly give a manual on moral theology. For that matter one would not give him a manual of dogmatic theology either.

(3) Moral theology devotes too much time and space to problems of positive canon law and rubrics. This is a problem of method and the syllabus of seminary studies. The priest has to know a certain amount of Canon Law, for this is the

law of the Church and is binding on the conscience. Sections of the Code of Canon Law give legislation on the priestly and religious states, on the administration and reception of the sacraments, and the celebration of Mass, on the care of the Holy Eucharist, on churches, on money and real property, on crimes and censures, privileges and dispensations, and other such materials. Since the matters contained in these laws are of immediate and conscientious concern to the priest in his pastoral duty they are usually taken up in moral theology while more general laws and matter more remote from his immediate concern are left to the courses in Canon Law. As a consequence, however, the sheer amount of this matter and its importance do distract the moral theologian from a more meaningful consideration, in terms of the Christian life, of the virtues and the sacraments. Hitherto he has felt justified in leaving this to other disciplines such as homiletics, catechetics, liturgy, and dogmatic and pastoral theology. The manuals, therefore, may appear to foster the thesis that living within the confines of restrictive law is all that should be said about Christian living.

(4) Moral theology today is a system of objective standards arrived at by analysis and arranged in very neat and complete categories. A moral theologian can be asked almost any question and he will immediately fit it into one of his categories. But this is to reduce Christian living to an abstract and static condition. Analysis always does this. Therefore, the study of moral theology does not bring about a dynamic inspiration to Christian living. The perceptive discovery of religious truth, the realization of what truth means in terms of living is inspirational and moving, and opens the way to growth. But the study and mastery of moral theology does not do this. This does not make it less true. It does make it incomplete and unsatisfying.

(5) Moral theology today is too separated from dogmatic theology. It is true that the best of the manuals attempt to give a substantial résumé of the pertinent dogmatic theology

at the beginning of each chapter. It is also true that the propositions of moral theology are consistent with dogmatic theology and that many of them flow by way of immediate consequence from dogmatic theology. But there is a separation. In the seminaries moral theology is a major discipline of a practical nature. Dogmatic theology is a major discipline of a more speculative character. These two are taught concurrently; the textbooks are worlds apart in content and in intent; the professors have time to relate the two disciplines in only the sketchiest manner. Thus the unity and integration which should exist is not immediately perceived. It is true that the able and serious student can think his own way to unity and integrate his moral theology with his dogmatic, ascetical, and mystical theology, and his Christian living. If he does this, the result is a complete and splendid person. It does require, however, the facile ability to study, to arrive at clear intelligence, and to relate the different aspects of total truth to one another. This is the fruit of meditation upon the matter taught in class and the reading which is recommended. The ability to do this depends upon the many variables which distinguish good students from better students.

Modern Trends and the Needs Which Must Be Met in the Reformulation

Moral theologians today might be divided into two groups according to the actual work they are doing in completing and perfecting moral theology. Both groups overlap considerably in the study of moral problems, and the work of both groups must somehow be integrated into any new approach to a reformulation of moral theology.

One group holds to the general framework of the classical moral theology and seeks to investigate more deeply into its propositions and to apply its principles more exactly to many modern problems. Representative theologians of this group on this continent are well known. The problems they are studying cover vast areas of life: medical ethics, alcoholism, adolescent chastity, mental illness, marital life, social problems, legal and business ethics, education. One key problem to which much thought is being devoted is the modification of the human act in terms of the consequent quality of responsibility for personal actions by the psychic structure of the personality and psychic pressures suffered by the individual. The field of useful research and writing in these areas is vast and most interesting.

The other group, chiefly centered in Germany, Belgium, and France, is searching for a revitalization in terms of a new formulation of moral theology which will retain the acquisitions and values of the classical moral theology and correct its defects. The moral theology of these theologians is seeking a clearer dependence upon and an enlightenment by theological sources, Scripture, the Fathers of the Church, and the great theologians of the past. They feel that moral theology needs to be integrated more closely with dogmatic theology in such a way that the unified Christian mystery can be perceived as sublime and attractive, as vital and dynamic, as richly and profoundly responsive to human needs on the level of the individual, of the social being, of the citizen of the world. Attention must be paid to the modern psychological, political, social, cultural, and economic environment and the needs created by it. Avoiding an excessively philosophical ethicism and a juridic extrinsicism, moral theology must be permeated by a theological spirit, informed by specifically Christian truth which will expose the Christian life, and provide constructive principles for its growth in the individual and in society in such a way that an interiorization of the obligation to live it will obtain. For this purpose this group is searching divine revelation and the great theological writers of the past for a unique principle fertile enough to inspire, practical enough to direct, and rich enough to sustain the efforts to construct a new edifice of moral theology and to live the Christian life which it is destined to serve.

We saw that in the last century Hirscher believed that he found such a principle in the theory of moral theology as the teaching of the realization of the kingdom of God among men on earth. In the past few years other theories have been advanced and several attempts have been made to develop them.

Current Attempts to Meet the Need of a Re-evaluation of Moral Theology

In his *Die Idee der Nachfolge Christi* and *Die Verwirklichung der Nachfolge Christi* (tomes three and four of the seven-volume *Handbuch der Katholischen Sittenlehre*), Fritz Tillmann has made one of the more felicitous attempts to reformulate moral theology.

He constructs his moral theology around the idea of the imitation of Christ, the unique and unequaled model. A tension exists, Christ drawing men to Himself by the attracting splendor of His Person and men being moved toward Him by a force within themselves. Imitation of Him existentially consists in living as the sons of God, which implies the acceptance of high moral obligations to make perfect the image of God. The imitation of Christ is looked upon from two perspectives. The first is that of the supernatural forces offered to man by God and by which man realizes his vocation. Here everything is the work of God. These gifts are developed as they appear in Sacred Scripture, as the new birth in God, the new creature, the spirit, being and life in Christ, divine sonship.

The second perspective is that of the human attitude or response to God, which expresses itself in religion and morality, which supposes the action of grace and the free consent of man, and which is centered on God. Moral duties are founded upon submission to God. By religion and morality a man resembles God more and more and lives out his religious and moral attitude by conversion, faith, love of God and of his neighbor, perfection and the observance of the counsels, and fulfilling his vocation. Nor can the Christian personality develop except within a community.

While religion and morality require on man's part humility, self-knowledge, asceticism, and divine sanctions, they, and consequently the imitation of Christ, are menaced by temptation and sin.

Man's duties are to God, to himself, and to his neighbor. To God he owes piety, the attitude toward God which orientates and informs his whole personal life and is always visible in his life. Affecting his piety are the time in which he lives, his environment, his sex, his character and temperament, and especially grace and Christ as model and source of his piety. The virtues of faith, hope, and charity, the virtue of religion with its duties of external worship and prayer are treated here.

Duties to himself are worked out in the perspective of the concrete unity of the human being. By use of his body a man works out his spiritual life, fulfills his goals, and executes his duties. In spite of original sin, the body is the work of God and should be used with respect in the service of God. Sex is treated in the same perspective. In this section he also takes up the education of the child, adult formation, and human culture. Culture is created by man subduing and reducing creation and its force for his own use. At this point he takes up the problem of popular culture, the Christian view of the world, vocations, work, and honor. He concludes man's duties to himself by the consideration of the different sacraments in his personal life.

The third group of duties are duties to one's neighbor. Here Tillmann considers the relations of individual to individual and then goes on to study social relationships in marriage, in the family, in the Church, and in the State. Throughout this section he stresses the notion of the solidarity or the common responsibility of the members of society in discussing duties to one's neighbor.

In 1954 appeared *Das Gesetz Christi*, a major work on moral theology in three volumes by the Redemptorist, Bernhard

Häring. The fourth edition of the work was translated into French and published under the title *La Loi du Christ*. The translation was carefully reviewed and corrected by Father Häring. An English translation is being prepared and two volumes already have appeared.

Häring has divided his moral theology into the usual two major parts: general moral theology and special moral theology. The special moral theology is also divided into two parts: Life in Communion with God, and Life in Fraternal Communion.

The author believes that he has found and developed a fundamental principle for a new formulation of moral theology, which he explains thoroughly at the beginning of his work as the *Idée Mère* of moral theology.

Religion is a dialogue between God and man. The Father speaks to man in the Word Incarnate, Christ Jesus, through the Holy Spirit Who interiorizes in man that which is said to him and by Whom man replies to God. The Word spoken by the Father is an invitation to respond and thus enter into communion with the Father in and with Christ through the Holy Spirit. By faith and hope resumed in charity man responds. Religion, therefore, is Word of God—response of man. By his religious response to God, man enters into communion with God and with all the sons of God, his brethren.

A moral life is possible insofar as man is responsible. The property of responsibility is the ability and the duty to give an answer to God for those things and persons who relate to Him. On the moral plane a man is responsible, i.e., must answer to God, for all created goods and for his brethren. Although the execution of these duties are acts of the moral virtues, nevertheless, man is influenced even here by the theological virtues of faith and hope resumed in charity. For this reason his response on the moral plane is religious too.

Other ideas have served as a basis for ethics and for moral theology. These are the seeking of one's last end or salvation, the Commandments and the law of God, the seeking of human perfection. Häring takes pains to show how his *Idée Mère* relates to these other ideas.

General moral theology is divided into two main parts: the call of Christ and the answer of man. The call of Christ takes up the nature of the man called and the human act, moral knowledge and conscience, the virtues. As forms which the call of Christ takes, Häring studies law and the object of the human act. Here he takes up the problem of motivation. The answer of man may be negative or affirmative. If he answers negatively, he sins. If affirmatively, he is converted. It is here that he studies the Sacrament of Penance.

Special moral theology begins with life in communion with God. It has two parts: theological life or life in communion with God through faith, hope, and charity; and religious life where he studies the life of worship, the liturgy, the sacraments in general, reverence for the name of God, consecration to God by vows, prayer and the Sunday observance. At the same time he takes up in the pertinent sections the faults against each one of these aspects of life in communion with God. In this way he carries out his general plan of the affirmative and negative answer of man to God's call.

Life in fraternal communion has two main sections: charity to our brethren and charity expressed in human relationships. Charity to our brethren takes up the commandment of brotherly love, its negative duty of avoiding scandal, and the positive duty of the apostolate and fraternal aid. Charity expressed in human relationships is presented under the form of fraternal exchanges: the exchange of truth and beauty, where he takes up the problems connected with the press, the cinema, radio, and television; corporal exchanges, where he considers problems of health, death, human sexuality and chastity, marriage and virginity; exchanges on the plane of material things, where he discusses material possessions, contracts, work and property, the socio-economic order; and finally, exchanges on the plane of society, that is the family, the State, the Church. Again in pertinent sections he takes up the faults against each one of these aspects of life in fraternal communion and so carries out his general plan of the affirmative and negative answer of man to God's call to live in communion with his brethren.

The work is heavily flavored with Sacred Scripture. Häring presents problems in terms of modern thought, and has introduced into moral theology many subjects not taken up by the manuals used in the seminaries.

At least a brief mention must be made of the important work *Le Primat de la Charité en Théologie Morale* by G. Gilleman, S.J. This book has been translated into English. Father Gilleman set himself the task of making a theological research into the means of applying the universal principle of St. Thomas, that charity is the form of all the virtues, to the formulation of moral theology. He wishes to establish the principles of a method which gives explicitly to charity, in the formulation of moral theology, the same vital function which it exercises in the reality of Christian life and in the revelation of Christ. This vital function is not one which merely parallels the other moral realities, but is a function of animation of the whole conscious and deliberate life exercised on a plane that is more profound than that of any determined act or other virtue.

The work has three parts. In the first part he intends to present explicitly the foundations of his further research. Therefore, he recalls the essentials of the doctrine of St. Thomas on the role of charity in virtuous and moral activity.

The second part establishes the basis of the method proposed by him. He does this by determining the mediation property of our moral tendency in relation to our fundamental supernatural tendency to charity, and the place of moral virtue in relation to our moral acts and fundamental tendency to charity.

The third part is a presentation of a tentative moral theology of charity in which his method is applied to different parts of moral theology. These parts are, among others: obligation, law, and sin; religion, fraternal charity; the body and suffering; chastity and justice.

Conclusion

When the Word became flesh in the Incarnation it was not only the human nature of Christ which was affected. In Jesus Christ the human race, all human activity and, indeed, all creation is assumed into a new and supernatural relationship with the Holy Trinity. Man, all of his activity, all of the things which he uses have been profoundly affected. A relationship that is religious enters into all of his living.

Therefore, the field of interest to the moral theologian has expanded to include all that a man does, for religion enters into everything that concerns man. The Church and her dogmatic and moral theology has lived through many ages. Some of them have been very complex, some relatively simple. In every age she holds to certain absolute values. Every epoch presents specific problems which call for an emphasis which is relative to their importance. Today the Church is faced with an explosive expansion of knowledge, a complicated change in traditional manners of life and work, an uncertain view of the future of mankind. Yet, the Father still calls the human race in His Son to live the Christian life by the Holy Spirit now unto eternal life. Theology must do its part to unfold the meaning of this vocation.

Chapter X

AMERICAN CATHOLIC THEORIES OF CHURCH-STATE RELATIONS[1]

by

Donald J. Wolf

The practical problems involved in the relationship between Church and State in the United States have in recent years become burning political issues. Church-State relations were a significant factor in the presidential campaign of 1960. They are a major issue in the dispute over federal aid to private and parochial schools. They were involved in the Supreme Court decisions in *Engel, et al.* v. *Vitale, et al.* (1962), where the recitation of a state-composed prayer in public schools was declared unconstitutional, and in the cases concerning compulsory Bible reading and recitation of the Lord's Prayer in public schools.

These practical problems and the many others that have arisen and will continue to arise in our country are worthy of consideration and discussion. But perhaps even more important than these practical problems are the theory and principles of the right relationship between Church and State. Principles, of themselves, do not solve practical problems. Yet practical questions can be solved only in the light of a correct idea of what the right relations between Church and State ought to be. Therefore, it is essential to have an understanding of the Catholic position on the proper relationship between Church and State.

There are several ways in which we could attempt to arrive at such an understanding. One way would be to make a historical study tracing Church-State relationships through the

[1] Part of this essay was published in *A Journal of Church and State*, May 1962. It is reprinted here with permission of the *Journal*.

early Church, the Constantinian era, the theory of the "two swords," the Gregorian reform, Pope Gelasius, modern absolutism, and the modern popes, especially Gregory XVI, Pius IX, Leo XIII, Pius XI, Pius XII, and John XXIII. Another approach would be to examine the thought of those theologians in the Church who have written on the question of Church-State relations.

Here we intend to follow a modification of the latter approach. We shall examine the thought of modern American Catholic theologians on the relationship between Church and State. We limit our study in this way both because of a limitation of space and because the thought of American theologians is most relevant to our own problems and experience.

In such a study the first thing to note is that the Church has as yet never made a dogmatic or *ex cathedra* statement on the right relationship of Church and State. The area is one in which there can be free theological opinion and discussion. And among contemporary European and American writers, there are two general positions with regard to this matter. We shall call these two theories the Disjunctive Theory and the Unitary Theory of Church-State relations.

For the Disjunctive Theory, we shall use primarily the analysis of Monsignor Joseph Fenton as representative of the group. For the Unitary Theory, we shall study the work of Father John Courtney Murray, concentrating on it primarily because we believe the Unitary Theory to be the substantially correct position, but also because the Disjunctive Theory is much easier and simpler to state and is more familiar to most Catholics. In fact, many Catholics and most Protestants think that the Disjunctive Theory is the *only* Catholic position.

The Disjunctive Theory

The Disjunctive Theory can be presented as a series of five

fundamental propositions from which certain conclusions can be drawn for American practice.[2]

(1) By the virtue of religion all rational creatures are bound to acknowledge God and pay homage to Him.

The first of these principles is an expression of the nature of religion itself. It is a statement of the fact that objectively religion is nothing more or less than the payment of the debt of acknowledgment which all rational creatures owe to God.

(2) Not only individual men, but all societies and groups must recognize God and pay homage to Him.

The next principle has to do with the extent of the obligation of religion or worship. Since man is totally dependent upon God, there is no realm or section of human life which can be exempted from this obligation of acknowledging God's supreme goodness. Thus, not only individual men, but also all societies or groups of men are bound to pay that debt of acknowledgment. If they fail to make that acknowledgment, their conduct is objectively lacking a good which it ought to include.

(3) In practice, a State, because of a difference of religious affiliation among its citizens, may be unable formally to pay homage to God. Though this may be historically inevitable it is in principle inadmissible.

Where the various citizens of a state have different religious persuasions, it is evident that the state itself is not in a position to exercise its own act of religion and pay its own debt of acknowledgment to God.

In such cases the non-performance of the religious act by the group or community may be morally excusable. . . . But, even under such circumstances, it is utterly incorrect to say that the condition of the community or group which does not offer social worship to God is, in the strictest sense of the term, a good thing. A state or any other community may not be in a position to pay

[2] The quotations which follow, unless otherwise indicated, are taken from Joseph Clifford Fenton, "Principles Underlying Traditional Church-State Doctrine," *The American Ecclesiastical Review,* CXXVI (June 1952), pp. 452–62.

this debt of acknowledgment or religion to God, but this failure to worship, despite its practical necessity, remains something objectively deplorable.

(4) In principle, civil society, and thus the State, must worship God according to the rites of the Catholic Church.

Still another principle . . . is the truth that God wills that the debt of religion should be paid to him in a definite and supernatural way. . . .

. . . the one acceptable and authorized social worship of God is to be found summed up in the eucharistic sacrifice of the Catholic Church. . . .

Hence it follows that religion and the Church are not in the best or the most desirable position in a land where, even for perfectly valid and acceptable reasons, the civil society itself does not worship God according to the rites of the Church. This holds true even where the Church shows a freedom and vitality greater than those it manifests in some of the countries where the civil society has offered the true and Catholic worship to God.

(5) Separation of Church and State in the United States is an acceptable policy based on expediency. Separation of Church and State in countries which at one time worshiped God according to the rites of the Catholic Church is morally wrong.

[Non-recognition of the Catholic Church] is allowable and expedient in America, as the only means by which the civil society can operate properly in the situation in which Americans profess many different religions or none at all. . . .

The *active* separation of the Church from the state in countries which previously were Catholic and which had previously, as civil societies, paid their real debt of religion to God according to the true worship of the Catholic Church . . . could be called neither legitimate nor expedient.

Thesis-Hypothesis

The Disjunctive Theory has been called historically the

theory of "thesis" and "hypothesis." The thesis states that, in principle, the State must recognize the Catholic Church as the true Church and worship God according to the rites of the Catholic Church. The hypothesis maintains that, in practice, the separation of Church and State may be tolerated where recognition of the Catholic Church is morally impossible. We call this position the Disjunctive Theory because it uses two different principles to solve the problem of Church-State relations. One principle demands recognition of the Church; another principle, that of tolerance or double effect, allows non-recognition in certain cases.

Disjunctive Theory and the First Amendment

Certain practical consequences follow from the Disjunctive Theory. One consequence is that *in principle* the State has the right and the duty to suppress the public expression of false religions.

> But it is fully within their [the civil rulers'] right to restrict and to prevent public functions and activities of false religions which are likely to be detrimental to the spiritual welfare of the Catholic citizens or insulting to the true religion of Christ. Nowadays, it is true greater evils would often follow such a governmental course of action than would ensue if complete tolerance were granted; but the principle is immutable.[3]

What is the consequence of this theory with regard to the American idea of non-establishment of religion as embodied in the First Amendment to the Constitution? That question is frequently put, especially by Protestants, in this form, "What will happen if and when Catholics become an over-

[3] Francis J. Connell, "Christ the King of Civil Rulers," *The American Ecclesiastical Review*, CXIX (October 1948), 250. It would be difficult to harmonize this statement with that of Pope John XXIII in *Pacem in Terris*: "Every human being has the right to honor God according to the dictates of an upright conscience, and therefore the right to worship God privately and publicly."

whelming majority?" It is only just to say that the American theologians who hold this view unanimously claim that Catholics do not intend or desire to modify the system prevailing under our Constitution; they insist they would allow all our citizens full liberty of conscience and complete equality of all religious denominations before the law. At the same time, it is correct to say that for these theologians the First Amendment is wrong in principle—*in thesi,* though it may be correct in practice—*in hypothesi.*

The Unitary Theory

The Unitary Theory of Church-State relations is defended most prominently in this country by Father John Courtney Murray, S.J. The theory is called "unitary" in contradistinction to "disjunctive" because it applies one single norm, the temporal common good of civil society, to the problem of Church-State relations.

The first place to begin the discussion of this theory of Church and State is with the very basic point of definitions. It is impossible to speak intelligently about the relations between two organizations or societies if the disputants are confused about the natures of the things which are to be identified, or separated, as the case may be. This is particularly important since an agreement on the meaning of the State would solve many of the problems which some Catholics find with Father Murray's position.

The first point of importance, then, is to have some concept of the nature of the Church. For the problem of the relations of Church and State involves a theological problem and a theological solution. The political problem cannot be solved except in the light of one's theological solution. The Church must be understood under three different aspects. First, it is a spiritual authority which derives its right from a direct commission of Jesus Christ without any dependence upon human institutions or any right of interference in its spiritual authority by any human being or institution other than its own constituted hierarchy. Second, the Church is a juridical institution with its own internal order of law and is competent, as are other juridical institutions, of solving and dealing with its own internal problems. Third, the Church is a community of the faithful, a visible society with a membership open to all under certain membership qualifications, as is true of any other visible society. Together with its spiritual authority goes the necessary consequence of universality both in authority and in intended membership, so that from her very being the Church is *for* all nations, and *in* all nations.

On the other side of the relationship is the State. And here there is need not only for definition but also for distinctions. Society is the total complex of all the social aspects of man's nature. Society in general is divided into two parts, civil and political. Civil society is the total complex of organized human relationships on the temporal plane. These arise either from nature or by free choice of man's will. They aim at the co-operative achievement of partial human goods by particular associations or institutions. Political society simply adds something to the notion of civil society. Political society is civil society formally organized for the common good. It is constituted by effective organization toward the political good, the good of the body as such. The terms political society, body politic, and people are synonyms.

To this society in its double aspect the State adds a particular "form," a method of activity. The State is not a person or even a group of persons as is society but rather a set of institutions organized in a certain way for a very definite and limited purpose. It is that particular subsidiary functional organization of the body politic, whose special function regards the good of the whole. Thus its purpose is not as broad as that of society and is circumscribed by the exigency of the common good. Government in turn is an even more limited organization. For government is the practical method whereby the ruler-subject and subject-ruler relationship is embodied in any particular State and society.

From these definitions and distinctions flow several important principles. The most immediate result is that governing society are two authorities and two societies. There is the authority and society of the Church and the authority and society which is generally termed the State, remembering the distinctions which have just been made. And both of these authorities have different spheres in which they are autonomous: the Church the spiritual, the State the temporal. This position rests upon a distinction between the natural and supernatural order. And if it claims the autonomy of the spiritual order, the Church is no less insistent upon the autonomy and validity of the natural order. The natural is adequate in its own order as long as it stays within the limits of its own purposes. Thus the State is also autonomous in its own sphere and for its own purposes within the natural law.

The problem becomes one of a relationship between the two societies, authorities, laws by which man is governed, in such fashion that it will preserve the correct position of both while allowing each to have its proper sway over the human persons under its authority. The difficulty is to determine the right relationship between the two. This right relationship is based on certain broad and general principles.

Principles of Right Relationship

The most important of the principles of right relationship is the freedom of the Church. The freedom of the Church is the single necessary end that the Church directly seeks in her relations with political society. This is based on the autonomy of the spiritual authority of the Church. For, once one admits the exclusive right of the Church over spiritual things both within the Church and within temporal society, it is a necessary conclusion that the Church must have freedom to exercise that authority. This is true not only of the immunities and empowerments of the Church as an authority but also of the Church as a community of the faithful. This community must have the right of access to the Church and the general rights within society of the Christian conscience. But this right of the Church in the temporal area is very general and its particular applications are in theory not specified. The extent of the actual specification will be seen later.

Another important principle is the freedom of the temporal people. The natural law demands human liberty as a basic principle. This human liberty consists primarily in man's right to submit his own choice to the moral law. The problem of religious liberty rests ultimately upon the freedom of the human person to seek God in the manner that God has determined. Thus on the natural level the most important principle is the human person and the powers and immunities which he enjoys under the two authorities, spiritual and temporal. Both of these authorities are co-ordinated in the human person by conscience. It is the problem of the human conscience which must harmonize faith and reason while preserving both. The demand which it makes of both State and Church is the freedom to perform this task.

The last major principle is that of concord and harmony. There must be harmony between the two authorities with regard to the place of the Church in the international community as it goes about its spiritual task. There must also be harmony between the two societies and the two laws in every society where the two authorities exist and therefore have mutual interests and contacts. Always there must be an attempt on the part of both State and Church to co-operate in all those areas where they come inevitably into contact.

Statement of the Problem

In the actual working out of these basic principles there have been a number of problems proper to certain specific historical periods. At one time or another the problem of Church and State has been approached from the point of view of the rights of the Church and the duty of the State, or again from the side of the rights of the State and the duty of the Church. At the present time the problem is that of the duties of the State in relationship to the Church. In the American context of constitutional disestablishment it is not so much the rights of the Church at stake because of the encroachment of the State. On the contrary, at present, the problem is the true field of action of the State and the obligations of the State with regard to the work of the Church.

This general problem in its modern context can be centered around two specific points: the legal establishment of the Catholic Church as the religion of the State and the consequent duty of the State of legal intolerance of heretical sects. Establishment of the Catholic Church would be a legal and constitutional act which by force of law makes it a duty on the part of the State to maintain the Catholic religion and to exclude all other religions from public existence and activity. The question can be formed on these grounds:

> The primarily crucial question is simply put: Does the dogmatic concept, "the freedom of the Church," entail by necessary consequence the constitutional concept, "the religion of the state," in such wise that, where the latter concept does not obtain, an inherent right of the Church is violated and the constitutional situation can therefore be the object only of toleration, on the grounds of factual necessity, the lesser evil, etc? Or on the contrary, is this constitutional concept as applied in the nation-state, simply a particular and contingent, historically and politically conditioned realization of the dogmatic concept, "the freedom of the Church," in such wise that, even where it does not obtain, all the inherent exigencies of the freedom of the Church may still be adequately realized and the constitutional situation may be the object of approval in principle as good in itself?[4]

The Unitary Theory chooses the second position.

[4] John Courtney Murray, "On Religious Freedom," *Theological Studies,* X (September 1949), pp. 422–23.

Suppression of Evil

The Unitary Theory maintains certain theological and philosophical premises. The theological premises are a consequence first of the nature of the Church as instituted by Christ and, second, of the historically limiting factors of the Church in societies as they are now constituted. The major theological premise is that religious and moral unity in the world are the Will of God. The Catholic Church is the single religious and moral authority to which all men are obliged to belong. This is evident enough from the nature of the Church which has already been explained. But alongside this goes the fact of religious and moral divisions. This latter is more than just a fact. It is also a part of the divine economy and to that extent also a theological premise and a "good" of a certain kind. For Christ himself predicted that His doctrine would meet opposition and result in division. Furthermore, this division was permitted by God and this permission is good. For, in God's wisdom, this division works ultimately to the service of good.

From these premises the Unitary Theory draws certain conclusions. Granting the preceding argument, it follows that suppression of evil is not always good. And if it is not always good there is no universal obligation to suppress evil under all circumstances and wherever it may appear. In certain cases other principles must be consulted to determine the matter of the suppression of evil. On the other side of the coin, toleration of evil is not always an evil. Toleration does not need to be justified simply on the grounds that suppression under certain circumstances is impossible. Toleration of evil, when put into the total complex of a situation of fact, may in itself be a positive good. Again, the deciding factor is some other principle which is brought to bear in these circumstances.

This simply means that suppression of evil is not the ultimate goal within society. For it is possible that under certain circumstances there is no right whatsoever to suppress evil. And without a right there certainly cannot be any duty. Thus, under certain circumstances toleration may be obligatory and thus good. The ultimate principle to be used here in the case of evil within society is the principle of wisdom and prudence. And wisdom and prudence on the part of public authority means the common good. The common good is the criterion of the suppression of evil within society. Thus, on the practical level in which authority must deal with the question of the suppression of evil, the problem becomes the path which authority is to take granting the human fact of moral and religious division.

Law, Truth, and the Public Advantage

In order to solve the problem of the relationships of Church and State with regard to this problem of evil, the initial principles of the distinction between the two authorities must be remembered. The two authorities have different ends in view. Thus they look on the problem of evil and its suppression from different standpoints. The Church has as its single norm the unity of truth and faith in obedience to Christ; therefore evil regardless of where it exists is the only enemy of the Church, and it is everywhere her enemy. The prime concern of the Church is truth and morality. What is not true and what is not moral should not exist in either word or action.

But the same cannot be said for that reality which is the State. For the State has a different end consonant with its nature as already explained and defined. The end of the State is the unity of the social body. The State's purpose is to ordain what the common good and the exigencies of a humanly virtuous life in common demand. It is this unity in peace of the body politic that the State attempts to secure. For the existence of society arises from an association of human beings for a common purpose, the joint temporal advantage.

And the State is only that set of institutions which has as its specific purpose the care of the common good.

For the State this problem of the suppression of evil with relation to the common good has its effect in law. For law is the general mode of action on the part of the State. First, it must decide whether a particular legal action is in conformity with truth and the principles of morality. And second, the State must determine whether this legal action is in the public interest. Both determinations must be made and they are not identical. Of great importance is the fact that the second norm is the more important for the State and the first must be ordered to it. For the prime end of the law is the common advantage, and in certain cases this may demand a subordination of the criterion of the abstract demands of truth.

This does not, of course, mean that truth does not matter in the legal order or that the State is not concerned with truth. The State is neither irreligious nor immoral. The State has a moral function in that the common good which is its special province contains the common moral good as well as the common material good. Therefore in its activity it may not positively act against religious or moral truth. This is a negative norm preventing the State from obliging the human person to evil. In a more positive vein, the State may not act from the premise that good and evil are irrelevant in the order of law. On this point the State cannot be neutral. It must take a positive interest in the moral bases of society. The function of the State is moral, it is a limited function. It is confined within the limits set both by its own origins, which are from nature and from the consent of the people, and by its own finality, which is the common good.

This brings the question back again to the norm of the public advantage. This is the norm to which appeal must be made. The moral norm is not enough, the norm of prudence is necessary. In fact the norm of prudence and the common good is itself a moral norm. It is not just an appeal to expedience in a pejorative sense. Of course, in practice this does not really solve the problem since the contents of the common good are at any particular time and place unspecified. The public advantage is the norm, but just what is to the public advantage at any particular time is not easy to determine.

Even here, though, certain negative actions can be excluded from the action of the State in legislating for the common good. The first prohibition is that the State has no part in the proper sphere of the Church, the care of souls. The State has only a political end and only indirect effects upon the spiritual. As has been pointed out, the State has no obligation legally to enact the whole of the moral law and thus to repress all social aberrations. This will, of necessity, exclude legislation on the opinions of the members of society. In the case of coercion, it will be evident to the State that coercion is a doubtful tool in dealing with truth and error. Only in case of a significant public disturbance can these areas come under the immediate jurisdiction of the State.

Tolerance : Intolerance : : Separation : Union

Now all these principles have immediate application to the problems of toleration and separation of Church and State. It should be clear that tolerance or intolerance depend upon the determination of the public advantage, the common good. The one unitary norm to be used in this problem is the norm of the common good—the effect of tolerance or intolerance upon the body politic. This is a norm which depends upon the determination of facts by the prudence and wisdom of the legislature of the State. Depending on the effects upon a given society at any particular time, either tolerance or intolerance may be good law. If it is a good law, whichever policy is accepted is morally obligatory upon the State. Furthermore, since this is a determination of facts in the temporal order of the State, it must be made not by the Church but by the authorities of the State. The legal determination of such a matter comes within the function and competence of that natural set of institutions which is the State.

Intolerance is itself merely a consequence of the juridical recognition of a religion of the State. Therefore, the question of the legal institution of a religion of the State is a parallel problem to that of tolerance or intolerance. Legal institution, too, is to be decided by the unitary norm of the public advantage. Establishment or nonestablishment depends upon the test of every good law, the effect upon the body politic. Thus it is that establishment or nonestablishment is simply a means to the attainment of religious freedom, civic equality, and social peace. They are political, not religious determinations.

Establishment and nonestablishment generally are cast in terms of "union" and "separation." Frequently in Catholic circles separation comes to mean an active policy which is anti-Catholic and antireligious. But generally, and it is taken here in this sense, separation means the nonestablishment of religion. Separation in this sense, and its opposite, union, are themselves matters of human law to be judged by the norms of human law. As such, separation and union are different applications of one and the same principle. Union, since it is an application to a complex factual situation, does not represent a permanent and unalterable conclusion of Catholic principles. Union is not a product of the ideal but of the real. It is not part of principle but a contingent application of principles to facts, which application must change if the facts concerned are altered. The difficult task at all times is to make the necessary adaptation of principles to contingent situations. In the Unitary Theory there can be no "ideal" realization in historical circumstances. Neither union nor separation can be considered the "ideal."

Civis Idem et Christianus

Though union or establishment is not a principle of the Catholic position on Church and State, yet there is a principle of their contact and mutual co-operation. For it will be remembered that concord and harmony between Church and State is one of the original foundations from which the Unitary Theory proceeds. If the legal establishment of the Church is not the answer, what is the method of achieving fruitful contact between the two authorities? For the Catholic, just as for every other member of society, the human person must have an effect upon the temporal order that is the State. In this contact he cannot jettison his Catholicism; quite the reverse, since there is a positive obligation on the Christian to have a Christian influence upon the society of which he is a member and upon the State and government of that society. This is true of the Christian in every society but particularly so in any democratic society. There is a special duty incumbent upon every Christian in a democratic society to be a constructive member of that society.

This is an important point. Since the rise of democracies the methods of contact between Church and State have changed. The problem today falls upon the civic person who, through the medium of the democratic institutions, is in a new and legitimate sense self-governing. The time when the social order was created from the top down has passed. If the modern democracies are to be affected, the influence must come from the bottom up. It must come by men of the world who are capable of bringing the two societies, Church and State, into harmony with respect for freedom.

The reconciliation of the two distinct societies takes place where the obligation to both societies begins, in the individual. The harmony takes place in him who is *civis idem et christianus*, the man who is both a citizen and a Christian. Thus, the solution comes from the dualism that exists, not in some abstract realm of the ideal, but in a human person who is at one and the same time a member of the Church and a citizen of the State. In both societies the human person is the object and end of consideration. It is for the same human person that a harmony between Church and State is necessary. And it is the same human person who by his action as Christian and citizen ought to establish this harmony in actual fact. Harmony comes about through the exercise of citizenship governed by the Christian principles to which the human person is obligated. In fulfilling the twofold obligation of citizen and Christian there is accomplished the harmonization of the two societies.

Thus, the problem of whether the Church has a direct or indirect power is solved by putting the entire power of the Church's authority in the temporal order in the hands of a single individual, *civis idem et christianus*. There is no doubt that the Church will in many areas bump up against the State, and vice versa. But in such cases the implications of Christianity are mediated to the State through the individual citizen in a democratic society. In this fashion the entire problem returns to its starting point, the freedom of the Church and the individual human person in society.

The First Amendment

The similarity between the discussion immediately preceding and American practice should be evident. For the First Amendment, in making nonestablishment a legal requirement, puts the question of harmony upon the individual. It will be remembered that it has already been determined that establishment cannot be considered the ideal relationship between Church and State. Therefore, the problem with regard to the First Amendment is to determine whether or not a Catholic can accept the American practice as a valid application of principles to factual circumstances. The problem is whether or not the First Amendment is good law and therefore acceptable to all citizens, Catholics included.

The first point to be noted is that America started with a previously existing diversity of religions and a need for a working social harmony. In achieving this harmony the Constitution was based on certain principles. Among these are the recognition of God and the natural law, a consensus on the aims of government, the necessity for the consent of the governed, the requirement of a Bill of Rights. Implicit in these is the recognition that government is limited and that certain areas are not within the immediate concern of government. One of these areas is the individual conscience. And on the same level is the personal religious freedom of the human person. The American consensus recognizes here a definite distinction between the purposes of Church and State and in consequence a definite difference in their authority. It is from this realization that the religious clause of the First Amendment arises.

This clause in itself has no religious content. It was never meant to decide the question of man's religious allegiance, the importance of religion to man and society, the nature of religious truth, the importance of one religious sect over another, or questions of similar import. The First Amendment is not an answer to theological problems. It is not a dogma of Catholic ecclesiology. It is not a dogma of Protestant ecclesiology. It does not mean that all churches are voluntary and of equal value; it does not mean that Catholicism is an alien religion because it insists on its own uniqueness and universality. These problems are irrelevant to the First Amendment. The First Amendment very simply recognizes the limitation of the State in the realm of the human conscience and religion. It recognizes the distinction between Church and State. In this manner it relegates theological questions to the human conscience where they belong. By decreeing the nonestablishment of religion, the First Amendment does not establish a particular religious viewpoint.

Therefore, the First Amendment must be looked at not as religious dogma but as law. A rather long quote from Father Murray can set the Amendment in its proper framework:

We should, therefore, make some advance toward clarity if we could all agree to take the First Amendment exactly for what it is —not a theological, but a political document. It does not define a concept of the Church but a concept of the State. Fundamentally, the First Amendment asserts that political sovereignty is limited by the rights of conscience inherent in man. It has simply an ethical and a political content. Its ethical content is the doctrine that religious conscience is immune from governmental coercion. And its political content is the assertion that the rights of conscience will be most securely protected and the political ends of the American State most effectively furthered by guaranteeing the equality of all religious consciences (and, by implication, of all religious bodies) before the law. It cannot be too much emphasized that the religious liberty proclaimed by the First Amendment is not a piece of religious mysticism, but a practical political principle, ethically grounded on the obligations of the State to the consensus of its citizens and its own end—social harmony, prosperity and peace.[5]

As a political and legal document the only criterion upon which the First Amendment is to be judged is the criterion of a good law.

The First Amendment, as has already been noted, was the result of social necessity. For at the time of the formulation of the Constitution and the Bill of Rights the facts of the American scene would allow nothing less if there was to be social peace. America on the religious plane exhibited several limiting characteristics. There was a large mass of people who claimed no particular religion and owed allegiance to no particular Church. On the level of organized religion, there was a multiplicity of various religious denominations and the

[5] Murray, John Courtney, "Separation of Church and State", *America*, LXXVI, December 7, 1946, p. 261. (Reprinted with permission of *America*, The National Catholic Weekly Review, 920 Broadway, New York, N. Y. 10010.)

majority of the people making up the society of the Colonies had experienced reasonably widespread religious freedom on both sides of the Atlantic. Under these circumstances public peace could only be attained by the nonestablishment of religion.

The result of this denial of establishment for the United States has been most beneficial. On the side of the religious sects, there has been a legal freedom and stability which has been unknown in any other country in the world. As for the Catholic Church, it has enjoyed a greater measure of freedom than in any other country. On the practical level the First Amendment has proved that political unity is possible without religious uniformity. Not only that, but experience in the United States has shown that the exclusion of religious differences from the domain of the State has increased, not lessened, the stability of political unity. Thus, on the political level, the level upon which the First Amendment exists, the Amendment fulfills the criterion of the public advantage. The First Amendment is a good law. It is founded on social necessity. It contains a valid expression of the distinction between Church and State. Experience proves that the Amendment is eminently formulated to lead to the attainment of social harmony and peace.

Being a legal enactment or principle meant to be applied to changing circumstances, the First Amendment is subject, as are all parts of the Constitution, to a certain amount of development and interpretation. It is not always simple to tell in practical cases just what does or does not constitute establishment of religion. The interpretation of the Amendment must keep up with the sociological changes and the new alignment of forces which has taken place since the eighteenth century in the United States. Each case that arises must be decided upon its own merits as a legal case, only keeping in mind the norms of the real meaning of the nonestablishment clause.

To say that the First Amendment is good law is not to say

that it is the ideal arrangement. Remember that it is a practical response to a social situation. But it is a good response. It does not mean that the American state is perfect in its treatment of the relations of Church and State. This in itself is an impossibility. Yet, it does mean that the statement of the contemporary problem is substantially the same statement of the problem that is now accepted by the Church. As good law the First Amendment is entirely acceptable to American Catholics. American Catholics have always accepted the basic American consensus; they have given full allegiance to the religious clauses of the First Amendment; they have entirely accepted the policy of nonestablishment as one of the most important of their principles and completely compatible with their religious position.

On these grounds it is easy to see why the Catholic conscience has always consented to the religion clauses of the Constitution. They conform to the highest criterion for all legal rulings in this delicate matter. The criterion is moral; therefore the law that meets it is good, because it is for the common good. Therefore consent given to the law is given on grounds of moral principle. To speak of expediency here is altogether to misunderstand the moral nature of the community and its collective moral obligation toward its own common good. The origins of our fundamental law are in moral principle; the obligations it imposes are moral obligations, binding in conscience. One may not, without moral fault, act against these articles of peace.[6]

Conclusion

These, then, are the two general theories held by American Catholic theologians on Church-State relations. It would be incorrect to give the impression that every theologian who holds one or the other theory would agree with every point attributed to these positions in this analysis. But all the the-

[6] John Courtney Murray, "The Problem of Pluralism in America," *Thought*, XXIX (Summer 1954).

ologians who have developed a position in this area agree substantially with one or the other theory.

As was mentioned earlier, it is not within our purpose to apply these theories to the practical problems of Church-State relations as experienced in the United States. These theories do not solve the current questions dealing with education, censorship, marriage, divorce, birth control, or the general question of what constitutes an "establishment" of religion under the First Amendment. It should be clear enough, though, that the theories themselves are in opposition to each other. As a result, one's approach to any practical question will depend upon which theory is judged to be correct.

In a certain sense, the Disjunctive Theory makes it easier to solve practical questions. This is true because this approach is clear-cut in its assertion of the duty of the State toward the Catholic Church and of the authority which the Church exercises over the State. On the other hand, the Unitary Theory makes the solution of practical problems more complicated because the Church is not given a direct power over the State. Rather, in this approach the Church acts upon the State primarily through the citizen and recognizes the autonomy of the State in its determination of the temporal common good. It does not claim that the Church does not directly influence the State. It does claim that the Church, as such, does not have a direct or indirect authority over the State, and that the State does not have an obligation to recognize the Catholic Church. The judgment as to which approach one takes depends upon the intellectual conviction of the individual. And that judgment will have serious consequences upon the future of the Church in this country, and upon the country itself.

Chapter XI

THE SOCIAL MISSION OF CHRISTIANITY

by

James V. Schall

Every man spends a certain amount of time on earth. During his allotted days, man is engaged in some kind of earthly task. It may be political, industrial, commercial, educational, or agricultural. But whatever it is, it constitutes the major part of his life. Since these worldly affairs occupy so much of his time, it is legitimate to inquire about their ultimate significance. Are they merely more or less unimportant incidents calculated to keep man busy, or do they form a network of spiritual responses which help determine man's very meaning? Clearly modern man believes that his public, human work is of great spiritual value. Indeed, this concern for the temporal fate of all men, perhaps even more than the definition of God, has been the distinctive mark of modern times. Disbelief in God has almost always been related to concepts of God which allow no free or significant activity on the part of man. Consequently, the effort to inquire about the meaning of man's temporal life on earth is a real issue of contemporary life, one that especially concerns the Church.

Since 1870 the Catholic Church has, in her official statements, been quite conscious of the importance attached to man's temporal life on earth. There has been an intelligent and profound recognition of the validity of St. Thomas's notion that man cannot be expected to practice virtue if the material conditions of his life are not adequate. Since 1870 some four major steps in social doctrine have been taken: the encyclicals *Rerum Novarum* of Leo XIII in 1891, *Quadragesimo Anno* of Pius XI in 1931, several speeches and letters of Pius XII in the 1940s, and 1950s, and finally *Mater et Magistra* of John XXIII in 1961 and *Pacem in Terris* in 1963. The record of the Church in this area has in general been quite excellent.

These four series of social documents reveal a development of doctrine and an expanding scope of social concern. *Rerum Novarum* dealt principally with "rights," the rights of labor, the rights of owners, the rights of property, the rights of the state. A greater or lesser balance of these rights, it was felt, would serve to guarantee the rights of all. *Quadragesimo Anno,* profiting by the experience of World War I, industrialization, and the Depression, recognized that the social order itself, its organization and smooth functioning, was of prime importance if people were to live in adequate prosperity.

Pius XII was concerned with avoiding totalitarian experiments in managing the social economy; thus, he emphasized the rights of the individual, the economy, the state, and of property. John XXIII was, by contrast, "duty-oriented" in his conception of the social structure, with a great stress on experiment and flexibility. He emphasized the need of economic development and political maturity both in the nation and in the world. He insisted on the duty of all men to aid those in need, but in a socially productive manner. The system itself must be such that it will provide for the material needs of man. All ownership and social organization should tend to this end. *Pacem in Terris* insists on the acceptance by Christians of social and political wisdom and experience wherever it is found among men. Finally, various sessions of Vatican II are in great part concerned with the relation between man's social life and his religious life.

Freedom and Purpose

What is common to all current papal thought, as well as to all Christian thought, is the centrality of the free human person in economic, political, and cultural life. Every economic, political, and social form must be built on and show marked signs of the primacy of the free human person. And, conversely, the free human person is not the isolated god of individualism, but the rich, varied person whose conscious life is in fact bound up with all men.

The primacy of freedom in man, the very idea of a free human person, implies a necessity to determine the direction and purpose of this freedom. Freedom in its highest essence is not primarily the ability to avoid evil, but the possibility of accepting and embracing the good, the real. Men, however, cannot even talk about personal freedom without, in principle, asking what they have to do as men.

The consciousness of freedom is a primary human datum, something at the very root of man's personal being. This freedom implies personal responsibility. And responsibility takes a man outside of himself into the world of man, history, and nature. Man's responsible connection with others and with the world outside of himself is so basic that he can never free himself from the suspicion that *what the world will be* depends somehow on himself. This is his destiny and his dignity.

There is, however, a respectable tradition in Christianity which seems to imply the opposite. This tradition is best characterized by Thomas a Kempis' dictum that "I had rather feel compunction than know how to define it," and John Wesley's "I am sick of opinions; am weary to bear them, my soul loathes this frothy food. Give me solid and substantial religion, give me a humble and gentle lover of God and man." It is a tradition that is quite true when properly understood, but which tends to derogate ideas in favor of emotions and simplicity. Somehow in the history of Christianity, whenever piety has lost its roots in dogma, it has been inclined to confuse man about his proper task in this life. Invariably this has cut Christians off from the true problems of their eras. And this has been tragic in its consequences.

Worldly and Otherworldly Christians

The most frequent charges leveled against Christians can, in essence, be paraphrased in two almost contradictory accusations. One says that Christians are too worldly. The other suggests that Christians are too otherworldly. Of these two statements, the first is the more mild. After all, to intimate that Christians are worldly is equivalent to a reaffirmation that Christians are, in the end, just like other men. Little sophistication is required to understand how Christians are basically like everyone else, neither more dedicated nor more virtuous. Actually, such a similarity is exactly what the non-Christian would expect. He would presume that Christianity, barring any obvious proof to the contrary, would leave men pretty much the same. This is why worldly Christians do not surprise or even disedify the rest of the world too much. Worldly Christians merely confirm the initial suspicion that men are pretty much the same all over.

Otherworldly Christians, however, present a very different problem. All Christians obviously are "otherworldly" in the sense that they recognize that man's ultimate meaning and happiness do not come about in this life. This belief is, no doubt, a real and profound judgment of this world. It prevents man from finding his ultimate meaning in the social and political movements belonging primarily to the order of time. The otherworldly Christians that are of concern here, however, are those who carry this reasoning a step farther to conclude that because the next life is all-important, which indeed it is, *therefore* the tasks of this life *are not important at all* or, at least, of minimal importance.

Such stress on personal salvation, if extreme, easily results in a serious neglect of the conditions and requirements of men. Christian life and spirituality will, as a result, pursue a neo-Platonic or gnostic path. Matter and all that is connected with it will become an impediment, if not a positive evil.[1] From such a context evolved that spirituality of withdrawal from the world and from the tasks of the world which is found so disturbing in many passages of such a book as *The Imitation of Christ*. Perfection became merely self-perfection, a goal to be achieved away from the cares of this life since such concerns only hindered man in the attainment of his mission. Thus, in this view, any institution that would compromise man's quest for self-perfection was to be shunned and restricted. Man must not be soiled by the worldly tasks lest he miss his end.

Whenever this otherworldly attitude touches the heart and mind of the men of modern times, it never fails to strike a kind of terror in their souls for, with disarming subtlety, it appears to undermine the very foundations of human life. Men today recognize, as if by instinct, that man's temporal existence does place definite and all-embracing responsibilities on their shoulders.

Two Presuppositions

In discussing the value of man's life on earth, two presuppositions with which most people would agree seem to be in order. The first is that life and the world are not illusions. The peoples of a Western tradition are not as tempted by this view as are those who have grown up in a more Oriental tradition. But the suspicion of illusion is not altogether absent. The most obvious proof that illusion is an inadequate theory is pain and suffering, though, paradoxically, the experience of intense pain, more than anything else that enters human life, makes the world seem unreal and alien. The more intense pain is the more man loses contact with the

[1] Cf. Jacques Leclercq, "Holiness and the Temporal," *Cross Currents,* IV (Winter 1954), pp. 92–108; Godfrey Diekmann, *Come, Let Us Worship* (Baltimore: Helicon Press, 1961), p. 8 ff.; Charles Davis, "The Danger of Irrelevance," *The Downside Review* (Spring 1961), pp. 93–104.

ordinary world of everyday life. Perhaps this is why the central event of Christianity centers on the cross, in the reminder that suffering and death really happen to men in the world.

The second presupposition is that divine transcendence and human finiteness are, in themselves, irreconcilable as far as can be humanly judged. Danielou, in one of his books, remarks that "it is not necessary to be a Christian to suppose that God is God and man is man. But to believe that God is man and man is God, that is the very essence of Christianity."[2] In other words, the Incarnation, the Word becoming flesh, casts its spell over everything. With the Incarnation, it is not only false to proclaim that the world is an illusion, it is equally false to maintain that the transient world is only the transient world. The Incarnation and the Resurrection make the world and those who dwell in it not just finitely real as contrasted to illusion, but in some sense permanently real as contrasted to perishability, to the fleeting passing away of the leaves and the grass. The reality of our world and of our lives has become, because of the Incarnation, something of transcendent significance. The question of what remains for man to do in the world, therefore, has ramifications far beyond the cycle of birth and death to which our senses accustom us.

Hebrew and Greek Origins

In looking at Western history, the origins of Western thought are Hebrew and Greek. Practically all Western peoples are what they are because the Hebrews and the Greeks were what they were. The West has received a living tradition. From the Hebrews comes the transcendence of God, His governance of the earth and the skies, the presence of Yahweh in every finite activity. For the Hebrews, the Almighty is a person. He creates out of love and mercy. He expects His crea-

[2] Jean Danielou, *Christ and Us,* trans. Walter Roberts (New York: Sheed & Ward, 1961), p. 202.

tures to adore Him and to live up to the promises He has made to them and those they have made to Him. The Hebrew God is the Lord of history, of the history of which creation itself is a part. He guides all events to His loving end. The task of man is to respond to this God by keeping His commands and covenants. The Hebrew law is the loving response of man to God. Moreover, while the Hebrew God did choose a particular people in whom He was to accomplish His purpose among men, still He extended His concern to all the nations, as the Books of Jona and Jeremia, and Deutero-Isaia especially teach. The mission of the men who loved the Hebrew God somehow involved all the nations.

The intellectual foundation of the relation between the transcendent and the finite by the Greeks was, and in many ways still is, definitive. The Greeks were, much more than the Hebrews, man-centered. The highest human virtue for the Greek concerned human perfection and happiness. "Who is the best man?" was the abiding problem that continually bothered the Greeks in all aspects of their lives.

The Hebrews were accustomed to attribute all activity to God; the Greeks were much more inclined to stress the proper activity of man. In this latter Greek tradition there is a kernel of truth hidden, which it is worth while to examine closer. The Hebrew tradition of attributing all to God and the Greek tradition of stressing the activity of man are not necessarily contradictory. But there is definite difference of attitude which produces a different mode of looking at the world. Perhaps the best way of understanding this difference is to look at the way the Greeks, especially Aristotle, looked at the city. The proper activity of man was the public life of the city. This life distinguished man from all other creatures. Man was mortal. His public life was his effort as a mortal being to overcome the encroachments of time and decay. For this reason, man built monuments which would last beyond his lifetime. He wrote poems that future generations would read. He carved out statues which depicted what he did while on earth. But, above all, he built cities in which he and his followers could live in peace and dignity. The total effect of these efforts was to establish man's visibility, to show what he was and where he dwelled.

While this Greek emphasis on the visible worldly life of man was of primary concern and, indeed, distinguished man from other creatures, still man's highest activity was contemplation, which indicated that he was something more than a mere city-builder. This contemplative activity enabled him to pass beyond the limits of time and, as it were, reach the source of reality itself. This activity was the highest thing man could do. But while he dwelled on earth, his life in the city defined for him what he was.

The Christian Outlook

The world into which Christianity was born was one in which man was very confused about his proper life. The practical life of the public order seemed to be confused and chaotic in spite of the superficial orderliness imposed on it by the conquests of Alexander and Rome. The contemplative life also showed the effects of so much contact with the Eastern and African worlds.

Christianity contained within itself the key to the solution of the ancient problem about how to balance the contemplative and the political life. Christians believed in the Resurrection of the body and life everlasting. These doctrines meant that man is open to God, that man can abide permanently with the eternal being, but after this life. Man's highest desires of permanence and love can be fulfilled. But this also proves that man's life on earth, his proper task here will not, as such, fulfill those desires of men which arise from contemplation. Earthly life is temporary in its very essence, and therefore it is incapable of being elevated into the completion of man's deepest desires. Christianity in theory frees the political and practical order from the perennial threat of itself becoming a religion, for it establishes that this life and its proper tasks are important but temporal. Political life can now be the construction of the city of man, the home of the being who would die.

There is a strange paradox about the effect of Christianity on public life. On the one hand, Christian tradition accepts the exaltation of God as the primary being and the cause of reality. On the other, it also accepts the centrality of man in the world and exalts him as the primary reason for the rest of creation. A reading of the Epistle to the Romans will suffice to show this. Man is, in a very real sense, the center of the cosmos for the Christian. Indeed, man is not for the cosmos, the cosmos is for man. Man's mission really is to humanize nature, to put the stamp of man on the cosmos. Genesis, along with Psalm 8, in effect already said this same thing when it commissioned man to dominate the earth. The Epistles to the Ephesians, Colossians, and Romans re-emphasized and extended this function of man in the universe. In principle, at least, the atheist humanist, the Marxist, and the Christian do meet in a common task; namely, in the effort to humanize and transform the world. Paradoxically, the humanization and socialization of the world, to use Marx's phrases, are most Christian attitudes. For this, in the final analysis, is the task that is left to be done by the Christian—he does have a vocation to humanize the world. The Christian analysis of why and how the world is to be humanized, however, stands on its own ground. All Christians accept Calvin's dictum of *soli Deo gloria*, glory to God alone. The task of the humanization and socialization of the world is itself ordered to a return of the world to God by a free principle within the cosmos itself; that is, by man's personal freedom.

The Trinitarian Background of Christian Social Life

What must be seen, consequently, is how the task of humanizing the world is properly a human social task and, at the same time, an endeavor that gives glory to God alone. What exactly is it about the human effort that makes it simultaneously human and divine? The starting point of this consideration is the doctrine of the internal life and reality of God, of the Trinity, a doctrine too little appreciated and realized.

In essence, the Trinity means that God is not alone, that loneliness is not at the heart of the Almighty, that God is life and fullness of life, that community is the very being of God, that to give of oneself is the very nature of the spiritual life and the only possible way for remaining oneself. The life of the Trinity is complete in itself, so that none of its activity can proceed from need, but only from love. It is an ordered life; the relations of the Persons to one another are definite and irreversible. The Father begets the Son in His image of creation. The Father and the Son produce the Spirit through an act of mutual love. The Spirit is God as the terminus of the internal life of God; all that He is and has, He has received. The personal name of the Spirit is love and gift. This terminus of God's interior life is the beginning of His free activity outside of Himself. Thus, God creates out of love, not out of need. That is why any intellectual analysis of created reality will always terminate in mystery, in the mystery of a free love since it is God's choice that makes everything what it is, that sets the limits and direction of the reality of things.

This trinitarian God is the Lord of Creation and of history. His essential purpose in creation was to associate in His communitarian life other beings who would freely be able to know and love the divine Persons and who would be loved by Them. The mysteries of Creation, Incarnation, Redemption, Resurrection, and Parousia all flow from God's adhering to His original purpose in creation. His abiding promise never changed. As Paul insisted in his First Epistle to Timothy, He willed all men to be saved and to come to a knowledge of the truth (I Tim. 2:4). The trinitarian life means the communication of and sharing of a common divine nature. The divine activity always bears this mark of mission. The Father sends the Son, the Son sends the Spirit. The Son chooses disciples and sends them into the world to do the Father's mission. The Son sends the Spirit to give life and to guarantee the reality of the divine mission. The divine concern descends from the Father to the Son to the Spirit to the Apostles to the Church to all ages and to all men. There is this constant commissioning of men to do the Father's will. Christianity is forever mission-oriented.

In creating other beings in His own image, God created them capable of sharing, in some manner, His power of causality and activity. The physical universe was established as a place for man, the physical universe was the object of man's distinguishing power, his intellect. Relative to this power, the whole universe is a "word," a communication, the image of the eternal Word. Thus, the universe was to return to God through man. Therefore, there was a principle in the universe which summed up the universe itself and which could personally reach out to God. But for the Christian, as for the Greeks, man was still the mortal. He had a proper earthly task which was his to accomplish in this life.

The Christian Earthly Task

The distinguishing addition of Christianity to this whole development, as we can see especially in the First Epistle of St. John, is that the locus, as it were, of man's relation to God lies in his relation to his neighbor. "And this commandment we have from him, that he who loves God should love his brother also" (I John 4:21). The earthly task is a humanizing one. The whole quality and fabric of human life are involved. All men are included. Moreover, as much of modern philosophy is rapidly coming to recognize, all human things are likewise social. Man's relation to others constitutes his very structure. And, as St. John teaches, man's relation to his brother has been divinized. John Wesley put it well when he observed, "The Gospel of Christ knows of no religion but social, no holiness but social holiness."

Man cannot exercise his proper causality and efficiency to improve God. If God be not already complete, He is not. Any form of Hegelian becoming in God Himself sets aside His very being. Man can, however, be actively creative, he can actually imitate God by assisting and aiding those whom God loves. And if man is really to provide for all men today, he must transform the world, the stamp of man must be everywhere to create a social communication and distribution that reaches all. Christian charity and concern, as St. James implied, must be productive and effective (Jas. 2:14–26).

What remains to be done, therefore, by Christian man is the real and effective creation of the human city in response to God's covenant with us to love our neighbors as He has loved them. This will be a human city with a maximum of diversity and order. Indeed, we cannot have the maximum of order without the greatest of diversity among men. This is the fallacy of all movements that seek to unite men by abolishing their differences.

The over-all earthly task of the human race is to provide a visible life for mortal men who will soon die. But the crux of this death, the issue at stake in dying, is whether the man who dies had lived a life of effective concern for his brothers. This does not just imply aiding in the community of Christ, but in the productive development of all instruments and techniques that can assist man in his earthly effort. The modern Christian view clearly insists on the spiritual necessity for men to participate in this endeavor. This, for the Christian, is a work of love according to which he shall be judged. "'Lord, when did we see thee hungry, and feed thee . . . ?' 'Amen I say to you, as long as you did it for one of these, the least of my brethren, you did it for me'" (Matt. 25:37–40). The world for the Christian is a gift as are his brothers. "What hast thou that thou hast not received?" (I Cor. 4:7). And, as in the exemplary case of gift in the Trinity, in the Holy

Spirit, the proper response of one who has received all he has is to give back all that he has received as an expression of a love that is open to the other person.

The Limits of This Life

How does the Christian outlook really distinguish itself from that of the humanist or the Communist, who also wish to form an earthly city suitable for men? The issue is joined at the problem of death. Man's ultimate desires are not and cannot be fulfilled in this life. Every attempt to do so ends up by destroying the distinctive features of the temporal life itself. The Christian sees that if the earthly life is to remain itself—i.e., a period of trial and transition—it cannot, as such, be made the center of reality. Man is not at the center of the cosmos unless he is the man-God.

Death, personal death, forces us to ask ultimate questions. One may perhaps decide to conclude with Ernest Hemingway that "We just don't know," or that this is "our one and only life." But, in any case, the politics and economics, the literature and art, the many tasks proper to mortals, the numerous tools by which they achieve their earthly goals, all of these, to remain the human tasks that they are, cannot be transformed to substitute for religion, from which man first discovers what he is. But man, to live at peace in the earthly city, must be willing to accept the essential order of reality, the basic relation between himself and God, as something "given," as something he does not make. He must do this before he can rest content to accept the earthly task for what it is. Yet, this suggests that the problem of death, as it stands for men without the vision of personal resurrection, almost of necessity involves them in a futile effort to create a temporal order of this life which would seek to establish for men some form of this-world immortality.

But death and resurrection are not our own efforts. They are pure gifts of God, who has created the cosmos itself to enable men to share in His trinitarian life. The Christian is able to face the truth that this world will pass away; he can live in his very perishability. The Redemption includes the redemption of mortality, pain, sickness, and death. Their reality, which remains ever real to man, is transformed. The man who is to be saved, and for whom we are to be responsible while he is in this life, is a mortal man, and he is subject to all the tragedies of our earthly lot. This is the man to whom human concern must be extended. Man cannot change these truths of his being, nor does he wish to do so. "Oh death, where is thy victory? Oh death, where is thy sting?" (I Cor. 15:55). The *felix culpa* remains a central belief of Christianity.

Conclusion

The social mission of Christianity, therefore, suggests that what remains for man to do in the world is to exercise his proper activity and freedom under God by showing forth his love of God in an effective love of his neighbor. Indeed, the love of God and the love of neighbor are the same love. Man cannot really aid the human race without transforming the world, without humanizing nature so that the dictates of charity can become capable of universal achievement. The Christian sees that this whole effort is, at the same time, possible only because of the prior justifying act of God, who first gave man the possibility of sharing His life as a pure gift. The work of returning the world to God, then, the worshipful setting aside of all things for His purpose in creation, is wholly God's work and wholly man's work. What remains to be done, therefore, is that work by which simultaneously the universe returns to God, by which man transforms the earth, and by this very process, by which mankind escapes the shadow of death. All of these result in the Christian view: "And this is his commandment, that we should believe in the name of his Son Jesus Christ, and love one another" (I John 3:23).

Chapter XII

THE CATHOLIC CHURCH AND PROTESTANT CHRISTIANITY

by

Joseph Wall

The beginning of this discussion must be a brief account of the nature of Luther's challenge to the historic Catholic Church. The heart of the Lutheran protest is in the dogmatic theology that is behind the expression, "justification by faith alone." The use of the word "justification" supposes that man feels himself in some need of being made right; that is, he feels himself somehow wrong. The question is, how does man right his wrongness? How does man escape that nagging feeling that the best of men have—that what he has to offer God is not worthy of God? How is he justified?

Luther insists that it is God who makes man right. There is nothing a man can do of himself, such as gain an indulgence or go on a pilgrimage, or say prayers or develop penitential practices; and much less is there anything that another can do for him. It is God and God alone who can make up for the unrighteousness of man. The expression "by faith alone" is meant to indicate that the process is not one whereby man makes himself righteous, but whereby man is righted by God. The attitude of man is the acceptance of this righteousness offered by God in Christ, which means the giving up of his own futile attempts by ascetic discipline or use of the sacraments or mortification or pilgrimage and other practices to make himself, by some activity of his own, righteous. So it involves on man's part the humble acceptance of the fact that his state is such that he needs God to make him right. And there does not arise in his spiritual history the moment when this need is no longer felt. After his being made righteous, after his baptism, after his coming into grace, he still is a man whose actions are imperfect—who needs constantly the forgiveness of God. Judged by some other standard, yes, man may do things that are deserving of human praise. But no one, not the best of us, does something that is worthy of God. In our best actions we stand in constant need of forgiveness. So the "faith" in the expression "justification by faith alone" is chosen to show that the attitude of man is acceptance; not the doing of the right thing, but the allowing, the accepting of what is being done to him.

Luther's Basic Message

As Luther read the New Testament, this is the core of what it has to tell us—that God has been merciful to us in Christ, and what we must do is not some new activity on our part, but the acceptance of what God has done for us, what he is doing for us in Christ. If my righteousness, therefore, is going to come from my acceptance of God's Word that I am righteous, if my righteousness is to come from faith, then God must announce His mercy to me; He does not owe this to me, I cannot infer it, and so He must give His Word that He stands ready to make me righteous. This message of forgiveness is the core of the Christian Gospel. And this is the meaning of the Gospels as the Word of God (not the elaboration that is a later development of Fundamentalism, as though the Scriptures were written as a personal letter to the individual reader, and a key to the understanding of physics and chemistry and geography), that the Scriptures contain, and contain in a way that the simple reader can grasp, the essential Word of God that He stands ready to forgive in Christ those who will accept that forgiveness in a humble faith. And so, the Christian truth comes to man from the Word of God which is Scripture.

So the first Lutheran principle is the "justification by faith alone." The second Lutheran principle which re-enforces this is "The Word of God understood in Scripture alone." Luther had no desire to destroy Christian unity. He had no desire to challenge Church authority. He wanted to recall Christendom to Christianity as he understood it, and he understood it as expressed in the two formulas above. But because the authority seemed to him to place itself against the "justification by faith alone," which was the essential Christian Gospel, and to place itself against the Scriptures as the sole source of this Christian message of forgiveness, he felt it incumbent upon himself to challenge the authority and to break the unity of Christendom that existed at his own time. So the third theological challenge raised by Lutherans was a challenge to the unity of the Church and to the authority by which that unity is preserved.

Followers of Luther

In the generation after Luther, his immediate successors set for themselves the task of organizing his religious insights. Luther was not a systemizer. He was a forest of religious intuitions. But the next generation of Lutheran theologians developed this series of religious insights into a connected system, into a series of logically concatenated propositions, each of them with its proof and rejection of contrary opinions in much the fashion of the medieval Scholastics. And so, this second generation of theologians is called in the history of Protestant thought, "Protestant Scholasticism." Now, from the point of view that interests us here, one of the byproducts of this Protestant Scholasticism was to focus in clear, definitive theses on the points where Lutheran theology opposed itself to the Catholic statement on the same subject. Thus, there was a sharpening of opposition. There was a like sharpening of the opposition on the Catholic side. The Council of Trent was long delayed. By the time it was called, European Christendom was already divided into two subcultures, one Protestant and one Catholic. There was a feeling of "our crowd" and "their crowd"—a feeling that looked for division, looked for a point of argument. The section on Justification in the Council of Trent was drawn up with the Lutheran and Calvinist theologies in mind, so as to focus Catholic teaching in a way that would explicitly challenge and contradict Lutheran and Calvinist teaching. Thus, in the generation after Luther and Calvin, there grew up a Catholic way of expressing the truths that Luther had challenged the Church to pronounce on, and a Lutheran way of pronouncing on those same truths, both of which "styles" became sharper and sharper until they reached the point where the men of the two camps could no longer easily talk to one another. Little by little, the men of the rival traditions no longer thought of the same thing when they used the word "faith." And that example could be multiplied a thousandfold. The extent to which that division was a real parting of minds and souls, and not simply a choosing of alternate formulas, is a debatable point. My own personal opinion is that, to a larger extent than has been realized, it was a question of words. For four hundred years there went along a parallel development of Lutheran and Calvinist theology on the one hand, and of Catholic theology on the other, the extent of the cleavage being very difficult to determine because the men of the two camps could no longer easily talk with one another on the same subject.

Liberal Protestantism

At the opening of this century the Catholic and Protestant theologies were farther apart (and this time, indubitably, a real separation and not merely a verbal one) than they had ever been in all the last four hundred years of their history. The dominant school among Protestant theologies at the opening of the century was liberal Protestant theology. Now, theologically, liberalism is an insistence on the powers of man, on the goodness of man. The liberal theologians frequently talked in terms of the inevitable progress toward the deeper religiousness of mankind. Man was essentially good. There was a spark of the divine in him that needed only a further human history to burst into the great flame of the Christianity of the future. The liberal theology denied or accepted only verbally the notion of original sin. And having done this, it denied the reality of grace as Luther understood it because God's grace is God's merciful answer to the plight of man which is original sin. If there is no meaning to original sin, then there is no meaning to grace. In general, liberal theology was a denial of the supernatural, a denial that there is any more to man's relationship with God than comes from man's essential constitution—that there is any question of God's gracious condescension to treat man in a manner more liberal than the constitution of man indicates. And so, liberalism is far from the viewpoint of the original point of Protestant departure, "justification by faith alone." Man was now to be justified by the optimum use of his own inherent talents; the other theological truths that are grouped around "justification by faith," grace and original sin, are just discarded. But this discarding of the original Protestant position does not bring the liberal Protestantism closer to the Catholic Church than the reformers were—quite the contrary. The Catholic Church, to a liberal theologian of fifty or sixty years ago who knew anything about it, must have seemed altogether too Lutheran and Calvinistic for his tastes because that which the liberal theology had discarded, while it was Lutheran or Calvinist, was precisely that element in which Luther and Calvin were at one with the whole of Catholic tradition.

Moreover, liberalism was connected with a new attitude toward the Scriptures. The human element of the Scriptures became more and more evident as man came to know more about the literatures of societies contemporaneous with the Jewish people and Apostolic Church that produced our Scriptures. The character of the Scriptures as documents written by men, and men of their time, became more apparent; and, in the first flush of that discovery, the temptation to treat the Scriptures as just another human document was widely yielded to. Liberal Protestant theology normally looked upon the Scriptures, and particularly the Synoptic Gospels, as containing as their core some ethical sayings of Our Lord that were the discovery of his own religious spirit, and which constitute the real contribution of Christ to the world. And all the further development, the divinity of Christ, the miracles of Christ, the centrality of Christ to human history, was looked upon only as so much wrapping given to this basic ethical message. The denial of the Scripture as the unique place of the announcement of God's word, and the identification of Scripture as just one more expression of greatness of the human spirit, is another departure from Luther and Calvin; but, again, it is not a departure that brings Protestantism closer to the Church, because that which they have discarded is precisely what Luther and Calvin had in common with the body of Catholic tradition.

Lastly, the third question raised by the Reformation, that of authority and unity, was given an un-Calvinist and un-Lutheran, but still more un-Catholic, answer by regarding the plurality of denominations as an ideal. The liberal was inclined to judge it a tribute to the profundity of Christianity that it spawned sects of so many varieties. There is a Christianity to every man's taste, and that shows its marvelous adaptability. And so, unity and authority were discarded even as an ideal. Luther and Calvin felt compelled, against their instincts, to go against authority and to break up unity for what they thought was a necessary move to save "justification by faith alone," and "the Word of God understood in Scripture alone." What they did reluctantly, the liberal Protestant theologians did gladly. Visible, organic, this-world unity was no essential part of Christianity.

On the Catholic side, at the opening of this century there was a sharpening of Catholic opposition to liberal Christianity. In its condemnation of Modernism, the Church condemned what there was of liberalism within the Church because Modernism was, like liberalism, a relying on the experience of man rather than on the Word of God, declared in the Bible, as the ultimate source of religious truth; it was, like liberalism, a denial of the radically different character of the supernatural. Modernism, the interior parallel of Protestant liberalism, was expunged from the Church. On the third point that the Reformation originally raised, that of unity and authority, the Church had solemnly defined (in Vatican Council I) the authority of the Church at the point where Protestants found it most poignantly distressing, in the universal jurisdiction and the infallibility of the pope.

So, in the questions raised by the Reformation, justification by faith alone, the Word of God understood in Scripture alone, and the unity and authority of the Church, the two camps which had been divided for almost four hundred years were farther apart at the beginning of this century than they had ever been in all their long history.

Reactions to Liberal Theology

What happened to make the present situation some sixty years later so radically different? The change took place between the First and Second World War. What is the first single element of change? A name—Karl Barth. Right after the close of World War I he wrote a challenge to the liberal theologians on the Christian character of what they called Christianity. In a series of books, and primarily in his commentary on the Epistle to the Romans, he pointed out that whatever it was, whatever good or evil there might be in the thing they were preaching, it simply was not Christianity. And he returned to the central affirmation of the Protestant heritage, justification by faith, not intending it in opposition to the Catholic Church, but using it now in opposition to liberal theologians. And further, he did not return to Luther alone, but to Luther as an expositor of a whole body of Christian tradition, of Luther as an avenue of insight into St. Augustine and St. Paul, of Luther as a guide to the essential meaning of Christianity. And so the first issue of the Reformation was raised again, but now not containing the acrimony against Catholics with which it was first raised.

The second thing I would mention is the progress in Scriptural scholarship. After the exaggerations of the new Biblical scholarship of the nineteenth century in the first flush of the historical understanding of the New and the Old Testaments, a saner, sounder, Biblical scholarship grew up. Unlike the liberals, Barth and those influenced by him are finding in the Scriptures not just another example of what might be found in different dress in any number of non-Christian religions, non-Christian sacred books, but they are finding the distinctive Word of God announced in the Scripture. Moreover, this new Scripture scholarship has highlighted something of importance to ecumenical discussion, the relation of Churchly tradition with the Scriptures. The men who have studied the process whereby the Christian traditions, oral and written, grew into the unities we now have as the books of the New Testament, understand the Gospels, not simply as history, but as a testimony of faith of the Apostolic Church. They are community documents. They were formed by tradition. They are an expression of tradition. It is tradition that has singled out certain books and insisted on the sacred character of these and only these. And it is tradition that has distinguished the core of Scriptural teaching as distinct from relatively superficial and unimportant side remarks. And so, modern Protestantism is returning to the second principle of the Reformation, the Word of God as found in Scripture, and again returning with a difference, returning with a realization of the interconnection between Scripture and tradition, returning with a "Catholic" twist.

The third thing I would point out is the Protestant ecumenical movement, which is the result of their missionary activity. There has always been missionary activity in the

Protestant churches, but, until the middle of the last century, there was never anything in the history of Protestantism like the modern Protestant zeal for the missions. So, the problems raised by an extensive missionary effort are relatively new to Protestants. The problems raised by bringing Christianity to cultures where it has not been before are complicated a thousandfold by the divisions within Protestantism itself. The proliferation of sects, which the liberals at home were inclined to look upon as a good thing in itself, seemed, when they turned to the mission field, an impediment to Christianity. What sense does it make that I ask a man in Canton to be a Southern Baptist? Does that mean the people in Shanghai are Northern Baptists? It makes sense to ask him to be a Christian; but what sense does it make to ask him to be a Christian of a particular denomination whose history is determined and whose character is formed by conditions in America or Europe which have no parallel in the place where he is about to become a Christian? In realization of this, the Protestants set out to find what unity they could among themselves. The great instigators of the modern Protestant ecumenical movement were missionary-minded Protestants. In their World Councils (the first were in the 1920s and 1930s) they were forced to ask what kinds of unity and authority are proper to the Christian Church. And so, the third question of the Reformation was raised again.

Thus, Protestantism returned to the three crucial issues of the Reformation, but with consideration given to the Catholic position.

Changes in Catholic Attitudes

At the same time there has been a modification of the Catholic attitude toward these issues that makes it easier to talk to Protestants. In the first place, the Church, in addressing a secular-minded world or her own people who are influenced by the secularism, finds it necessary to emphasize original sin and grace, and the radical, supernatural character of Christianity; thus, she finds it necessary to insist on the same religious points as did Luther at the beginning of the Reformation. Secondly, the Council of Trent found it expedient to insist that the Christian truth is approached both directly according to Scripture and through tradition, because Luther had laid the emphasis he did on Scripture. But this two-ness, in the course of time, became in Catholic theology books a very separate kind of two-ness and so the Catholic formula was announced that there are two sources of revelation—Scripture and, conceived independently as another way of getting at the truth of God, tradition. But now Scripture and tradition are coming to be conceived not as two isolated sources of God's Word, but as a single source of it with two aspects. And so, tradition is not so thought of as an altogether independent way by which God's truth comes to us, but as the source, protector, and interpreter of Scripture. Scripture is the unique and privileged announcement of tradition because it is the expression for future generations of the Church's teaching in Apostolic times, the privileged time, of Church history. Lastly, Catholics are approaching the third question raised by the Reformation with a different nuance of attitude. At the first Vatican Council the Church developed in detail the function of the pope in the life of the Church. But the Council broke up before there was time to balance this announcement of papal prerogatives and papal duties with a definition of the status of bishops in the Church, or to balance the statement on the hierarchy with complementary statements on the role of the laity in the Church. Thus, the authority of bishops other than the pope, the rights and sacral status of the members of the Church who are not in authority, and (what belongs in any balanced treatment of authority) the right of individual consciences, are questions that occupy currently a prominent place in Catholic theologizing.

And so, in the twenties and thirties the Protestants returned to a serious concern about what were their own historical starting points—the nature of justification, the role of Scripture, and the role of authority. And they returned to these questions with an attitude of mind that might be called an openness to the Catholic aspect of these questions. There were at the same time many reasons why Catholic theologians should be open to the Protestant side of the same questions. Thus, we see a gradual lessening of tensions on both sides along with many opportunities for common agreement.

Chapter XIII

THE CATHOLIC CHURCH AND ORTHODOX CHRISTIANITY

by

Terrence R. O'Connor

The greatest scandal in the history of the Church has not been that Christendom was divided. It has been that Christians, for the most part, came to take that division for granted, to accept it as part of the ordinary scheme of things. Some even saw it as a good thing, or perhaps worse, regarded it with a serene indifference born of ignorance. In our own times, however, those tragic attitudes are becoming more and more a thing of the past; and this encouraging phenomenon permits us to entertain a note of optimism which fifty years ago would have sounded like sheer wishful thinking.

Yet we can not close our eyes to the fact that only the first steps have been taken—essential and heartening steps, it is true. Yet the road to union stretches long before us, tortuous and obscure. For the division, as we know it today, remains profound, with its roots stretching back even to the very beginnings of the Christian era; and each new century has compounded the misunderstandings of the old. There must be some attempt, then, to sketch the history of the problem, however real the risk of oversimplification.

One Christian Commonwealth

The decree of liberation issued by Emperor Constantine in 313 not only terminated the age of persecutions but made Christianity more or less the established religion of the empire. Constantine referred to himself as a "bishop among bishops," charged with the task of protecting the Church and fostering its growth. In 325, he convoked and presided over the first ecumenical council, at Nicaea, to cope with the Arian heresy which threatened the unity not only of Christians but of the empire. Despite its failure to restore peace immediately, the council served as a conspicuous symbol of the "unitarian ideal." The Church was no longer a sect within the empire; rather, there was now one Christian commonwealth, with civil and ecclesiastical hierarchies joined together for the salvation of men. This was seen as the earthly triumph of the Kingdom of Christ which, according to St. Paul, was to draw both parties, that is, the Judaeo-Christian and the Graeco-Roman, into one (Eph. 2:11–21). Christian literature would compare Constantine and his successors to the royal line of Old Testament theocracy.

It is not too difficult to see why this unitarian ideal, despite the persistence of strife and dissension of various kinds, was embraced with enthusiasm and came, in time, to belong to men's instinctive attitudes.

In 395, Theodosius the Great divided the empire between his two sons, Arcadius, ruler in the East, and Honorius, ruler in the West. The dividing line ran roughly south from Singidunum, modern Belgrade, down through Dalmatia and Macedonia to Cyrene in Libya. This was regarded simply as a division, for administrative purposes, of an empire still regarded very much as one. But even at this time, Greek had supplanted Latin as the official language of the Eastern court; and in general, it could be said that Greek influence prevailed to the east of the line, and Latin influence to the west. Difference of language was only one external manifestation of a cultural divergence that was deeper, perhaps, than was generally realized.

The Council of Nicaea had sanctioned the principle that areas of episcopal and metropolitan jurisdiction should adapt themselves to the areas of civil jurisdiction. The principle would seem to recommend itself by a certain simplicity. However, even though it was not always strictly applied, one can easily see how it could become a significant factor in involving the Church in this cultural divergence and in straining relations between the various sees.

The Twenty-Eighth Canon

It was not long before a classic conflict arose. In 451, the Council of Chalcedon was convoked. Its main work was the condemnation of Monophysitism; but more pertinent to our subject was its Twenty-eighth Canon, which reads as follows:

> The fathers rightly attribute to old Rome privileges which correspond to its political importance. And it is by a similar sentiment that the five hundred bishops have accorded to new Rome [Constantinople] equal privileges, rightly judging that, having both the emperor and his senate, it ought to enjoy the same advantages, to have the same importance in ecclesiastical order, and to keep in all things the second rank after old Rome.

Pope St. Leo I's legates protested against the decree, and neither Leo nor any of his successors ever acknowledged its validity. The decree itself bore only eighty-four signatures, having been proposed after the regular sessions of the council when most of the 630 members had already departed for home.

The resultant controversy has often been presented by both Orthodox and Catholic authors as a power struggle between "Old Rome" and "New Rome." In this connection, two things call for mention. First, neither Pope Leo nor the advocates of the decree regarded it as an attack on Rome's traditional rank. Second—and more significant—Chalcedon's condemnation of Monophysitism was a heavy blow to the prestige of Alexandria, to its school of exegesis, and to Egypt in general. Alexandria ranked traditionally as the second see after Rome, and its prestige had been greatly heightened just twenty years before, when the teaching of Cyril of Alexandria had carried the day at the Council of Ephesus with the condemnation of Nestorius, bishop of Constantinople. Now the tables were suddenly turned. Alexandria finds not only its doctrine condemned by Chalcedon, but its rank claimed by Constantinople. This latter was salt in the wounds. Whatever be said about the validity of Constantinople's claim, and whatever the motives of Pope Leo in resisting it, the fact remains that the Twenty-eighth Canon could not have been proposed at a more tragically inopportune time. Nor did it help to continue to press for Leo's acknowledgment of the decree when the main task of the Church was to prevent Alexandria from falling away. In any event, negotiations with Alexandria broke down, Egypt broke away, and the split has lasted to this day.

It may be that Alexandria would have adhered stubbornly to its Monophysitism even had the Twenty-eighth Canon never been proposed. History is a precarious field for second-guessing. But what is clear is that much more was at stake here than a bilateral rivalry between the old and new capitals of the empire.

At any rate, despite the failure of negotiations for papal approval, the Eastern sees, Alexandria of course excepted, came to regard the Canon as valid. Rome has never done so, though in the thirteenth century it recognized Constantinople as a patriarchate.

When controversial writings became the order of the day, Orthodox theologians referred back to the Canon as proof that the only basis for Rome's first rank was that it was the capital city. The papal claim, however, derives from the succession of the Roman bishops from Peter, the Rock, who had received from Christ the power of the keys. The popes defended their primacy, then, as instituted by Christ, and consequently as a prerogative quite independent of whichever city might happen to be the center of civil administration. This issue, of course, is very much alive today.

The Filioque

Toward the end of the eighth century, another point of controversy developed. Eastern clerics noticed that Western monks, on pilgrimage, had inserted a new word in chanting the Creed during the liturgy. The Creed used practically throughout the whole Church had professed faith in the Holy Ghost as proceeding "from the Father." The Easterners were scandalized to hear the Western monks professing that the Holy Ghost proceeds "from the Son also" (*filioque*).

The doctrine of the *filioque*, it should be noted, was of Eastern origin. St. Augustine borrowed it from the School of Alexandria, where it had been in use as early as the time of Origen, around 250. From Augustine, the formula traveled to Spain, and it was there that it first was inserted into the Creed in the liturgy. The practice spread to Gaul in the fifth century, and then throughout the Germanic regions to the north.

Understandably, then, the East did not object at the outset to the doctrine of the *filioque*. They resented it rather as an unwarranted tampering with the formal pronouncement of an ecumenical council. This too, is readily understandable. Moreover, it closely parallels the attitude which prevailed in Rome for well over two centuries. When Pope St. Leo III, in 809, was asked by the Synod of Aquisgradensis to introduce the practice into the Roman liturgy, he refused, not on doctrinal grounds but because he feared to make an addition to a traditional, official formula of faith. It was not until the eleventh century that Pope Benedict VIII, at the urging of the Emperor St. Henry II, adopted the *filioque* in Rome.

The Crowning of Charlemagne

In the latter years of the eighth century, wars in both West and East were setting the stage for another decisive event.

Italy, struggling to push back the onslaught of the Lombards from the north, had appealed in vain to Constantinople for aid. But the imperial city itself was threatened by attacks from Bulgars, Slavs, and Moslems. At this point, Charlemagne stepped into the breach and stopped the Lombard advance. Then on Christmas day, 800, Leo III crowned Charlemagne Emperor of the West.

This action staggered eastern Christendom. It appeared as a political stab in the back, with all the lack of sensitivity of blunt opportunism. It was no palliative to hear that Charlemagne had proved himself an effective "defender of the faith," or that he was not really a usurper inasmuch as the imperial throne at Constantinople was, at the time, vacant. The Christians of the East felt that they had been simply written off the books and were shocked at the idea of the traditional glories of the empire being precipitously committed to an uncultured leader of barbarian hordes. The crowning of Charlemagne meant either the end of the Byzantine throne, which was unthinkable, or the existence of two independent emperors, which would mean the destruction of that unitarian ideal which was fundamental to the conception of Christian society. Antipathies deepened.

Perhaps it was inevitable that sooner or later time should produce the men and the circumstances to bring all these divisive factors to a peak. The first great swell of the gathering wave was the Photian schism in the late ninth century.

The Photian Affair

Photius has been depicted as an ambitious usurper who wrested the patriarchal throne from the saintly Ignatius, was deposed by Pope St. Nicholas, connived his way back into power only to be deposed by a council of eastern clergy, and who composed a series of rancorous attacks against the papal primacy and, in general, against the teaching and practice of

Latin Christianity. He has been called the cause of the schism of the Churches.[1]

A quite different evaluation emerges from more recent scholarship. The following are some of the more significant findings.

Photius did not usurp the throne. He was duly elected after Ignatius had abdicated in the interests of peace.

His attacks against Pope Nicholas were more than a matter of rancor. Nicholas had turned against him when the Ignatian party (independently of Ignatius) had promised to Rome jurisdiction over Illyricum (roughly, modern Yugoslavia). With the passage of the years, the East-West frontier established by Theodosius had become a somewhat vague and vacillating border, with both sides attempting to extend their own sphere of influence. But these regions had been evangelized for the most part by the great Greek missionaries Cyril and Methodius. To Photius, the attempt by the West to introduce Latin usages among peoples recently baptized in the Byzantine rite seemed a pointless source of confusion. Photius' common-sense view has been vindicated by subsequent history. However, for all his vehement condemnation of the policies of Pope Nicholas, he never attacked the notion of the primacy as such.

His polemic against Latin practices listed such things as the use of unleavened bread in the Eucharist, suppression of the Alleluia in the lenten liturgy, allowing milk and cheese during the lenten fast, and the celibacy of the clergy—who, moreover, shaved off their beards! Paltry matters, it may seem, at a time when unity between East and West was so much in jeopardy. But they must be seen in proper context. Here again, Photius was concerned about the confusion these Western practices were causing among the newly evangelized Christians of the Balkan regions.

[1] This distorted view long prevailed in the West, but it is not exclusively western in origin. In the Middle Ages the Greek reunion party represented Photius as the cause of the schism.

It is correct that Photius wrote lengthy attacks against the *filioque*, both as an unwarranted insertion into the Creed and as an erroneous doctrinal formula. But he had grounds for believing that his position had Roman approval. Up to this time, Rome had been consistent in its refusal to adopt the *filioque* into the liturgy. Photius, in a letter to Nicholas in 860, had written of the procession of the Holy Spirit as "from the Father," with no mention of the Son; Nicholas in his reply had stated that Photius' doctrine was perfectly orthodox.

Patriarch Michael Caerularius

But it was a successor of Photius, Patriarch Michael Caerularius, who in 1054 brought all the ancient grievances to a climax. He borrowed from the polemical works of Photius and expanded them into a broadside attack on Latin Christianity. He then closed all the Latin churches in Constantinople. Pope St. Leo IX sent Cardinal Humbert and Cardinal Frederick to negotiate. Patriarch Michael kept them waiting day after day, until finally the two cardinals laid on the altar of the Church of Hagia Sophia a papal Bull excommunicating Michael. This meant schism, though many felt that, as in past crises, all would blow over. But this time it lasted. The year 1054 is as convenient a date as any for marking the definite break between East and West—but the break is more properly described as a gradual process of estrangement that cannot be pinpointed in time.

The Conversion of Russia

Meanwhile, an event of profound significance took place. Vladimir of Kiev was ruler of a vast area bounded by the Gulf of Finland, the Volga River, and the Carpathian Mountains. In return for forming a military alliance with Emperor Basil II, he was granted the hand of the Emperor's sister, the Princess Anne. The princess came to Kiev accompanied by a brilliant entourage, among them a number of the Greek clergy. In 989 Vladimir received baptism and undertook the obligation of spreading the faith throughout his realm. This action of the "Clovis of the East" was the real beginning of what was to become the great Church of Russia.

Two remarks are pertinent here. Russia received the faith from Constantinople and, except for the fact that the liturgy was translated into the Slavic tongue, her rite and traditions were Byzantine. She regarded Constantinople as her Mother Church. All this occurred at a time when, as we have seen, Greek antipathy toward the West was approaching its climax. In her subsequent relations with Western Christendom, Russia's actions and attitudes would, on the whole, run parallel to those of the Greek Church.

Secondly, the Russians had a long memory of frequent attacks by Western tribes attempting to occupy the warm, fertile lands of the Ukraine region. As a result of these two factors, the Russian Church started off with a native suspicion of "the West" in general, and an acquired suspicion of Western Christianity in particular.

The Sack of Constantinople

We turn now to the most tragic event in this whole, sorry chronicle. At the turn of the thirteenth century, when the Fourth Crusade was moving east across the Balkans, the son of the deposed Emperor Isaac II made offers of financial and military aid as well as of religious reunion, on condition that the Crusaders help restore his father to the throne. The Crusaders were driven back in their first attack on Constantinople, but their second attack succeeded. Once within the gates, they thoroughly sacked the imperial city. They then established a Latin Empire of the East, and divided lands, as feudal estates, among the Western nobles. Half of Constantinople was awarded to Venice, which had played the major role in financing the crusade. This anomalous empire lasted for over fifty years, until destroyed by Emperor Michael Palaeologus.

In subsequent years, when alliance with the West was suggested to meet the menace of Moslem invasion, the cry of the people was: "Better the turban than the tiara." The shameful sack of Constantinople, along with the avaricious and incredibly tactless establishment of a Latin Empire in the East, probably constitutes the greatest single factor in the development of the schism. And the memory of it remains even today as one of the greatest obstacles to reunion.

The Reunion Movement: Lyons and Florence

What is remarkable in the light of this whole series of corrosive events is that an active reunion movement quickly grew up in the East. It is perhaps more remarkable that one of its prime movers was the same Michael Palaeologus who had evicted the Latin Empire from the East. Unquestionably, military and commercial considerations played a very large role here. The Moslem threat was constant. Even so, the movement could hardly have gotten under way at all except for the stubborn persistence of the century-old "unitarian ideal" of Christ's Kingdom on Earth based on a common faith.

The movement resulted in two councils of reunion. The first convened in 1274, at Lyons, and seemed to get off to a good start. The ambassadors of the Empire, Michael Palaeologus and the Patriarch Germanus, presented a document signed by 550 Eastern bishops and archbishops, in which they acknowledged the primacy of Rome and accepted the *filioque* into the Creed.

The agreement, however, never really took hold. After his return to Constantinople, Michael was unable, despite persistent efforts, to gain general acceptance of the union.

The second reunion council was that of Florence, which arrived at a formula of agreement in 1439. Seven hundred

Greeks attended, including the Emperor and the Patriarch of Constantinople. Agreement was reached on the controverted doctrines (including papal primacy, the *filioque*, and purgatory). But again the union was brought to naught by the Byzantine clergy and laity, who met with reproaches the bishops returning from the council.

It is true that some of the Eastern bishops claimed that they had not acted freely at these councils, because of political pressure. This claim has often been repeated in an attempt to show that the signed professions of faith were only paper agreements and in no real sense the voice of the Orthodox episcopate. Certainly, history has known clerics who placed expediency or personal security above the truths of faith. But to group in such an unenviable category so many hundreds of Byzantine bishops is a rather sweeping indictment of the Eastern episcopate of that era. Moreover, the action of Bishop Mark of Ephesus alone seems sufficient to discredit the claim; for before, during, and after the Council of Florence, he attacked the policy of reunion persistently, openly, and with impunity.

Since the Council of Florence, both sides have tended to withdraw to more or less fixed theological positions. Yet the gap between the lines imperceptibly grew ever wider, until neither side knew accurately what positions the other really held, so that sporadic verbal barrages fell far short of the mark. In time, few realized that their obsolete ammunition had little effect—except, perhaps, that it made an impressive noise to reassure the troops.

Difference of Language

We have already seen some of the historical events that contributed to this progressive estrangement. There are two other factors. One, of course, was the difference of language. Even those who share the same mother tongue frequently have difficulty in communicating on complex issues. Difference of language compounds the difficulty, particularly in any attempt at verbal expression concerning the ineffable mysteries of the incomprehensible God and His eternal providence. During the centuries of controversy between East and West, the language barrier contributed more than a little to the confusion.

Orthodox theologians rightly object to misunderstandings of the same kind in our own day. *Theosis* and *kenosis*, for example, are key words in the ascetical vocabulary of the East. The former can be translated by "deification," the latter by "utter self-renouncement." But these dictionary renderings miss the rich, traditional nuances connoted by the terms. Failure to realize this has led to sweeping misrepresentations of Orthodox spirituality. Similarly, "harmony" hardly catches the implications of *harmonia* as a radically operative concept in Orthodox teaching on Church and State.

From the other direction, Catholics have been disturbed, for example, by the words used to translate infallibility: *anamartētos* in Greek, *Nepogresimyi* in Russian—both of which connote the idea of impeccability. I have known Orthodox who were sincerely puzzled (understandably enough!) to understand how Catholics can believe the popes are incapable of sin.

Difference in Theological Approach

A further complication was the emergence of divergent emphases in theological method. This difference became evident particularly at the Council of Florence and has persisted as a significant barrier to communication. In discussing a controverted aspect of revealed truth, the Eastern theologian will tend to appeal to the authority of the Councils and the Fathers of the Church, whereas the Western theologian will tend to stress the demonstrations elaborated by Scholastic theology, a systematic treatment of Christian truth deriving in large part from the influence on medieval Europe of Platonism and Aristotelianism.

As is usual with such sweeping comparisons, this one has been exaggerated, even caricatured—as though the mystic Easterner were incapable of precise speculation or a grasp on the here and now, and the rationalistic Westerner were deaf to the voice of tradition and insensitive to the meaning of mystery.

Yet, the distortion does not lack foundation in fact. Some Latin theology manuals, with their near-Euclidian demonstrations and terse, precise answers to proposed objections, convey the impression that theological knowledge has been wrapped up in a neat, self-sufficient package, secure from any element of opposition from without since all difficulties have already been resolved. Certainly, theology must aim at clarity; but it must at the same time acknowledge frankly its own inherent mystery—without which, incidentally, it loses its fascination. St. Thomas and the other great Scholastics were fully aware of this and took it for granted that the theologian should be well versed in Scripture and tradition. But Scholastic theology, as represented by some of its lesser proponents, can lead one to ask whether logic has supplanted the *Logos*, the Word.

If to Eastern eyes it appears that Latin theology has left tradition behind, the Westerner is apt to feel that the pace of time has, in certain respects, left the Orthodox behind. In the West, Catholicism faced attack from Protestantism, Modernism, secularism, and scientism. There was no choice except active engagement in an intellectual arena demanding proofs both sacred and secular. In the East, however, the conflict had been less a matter of the syllogism than of the sword. Orthodoxy fought for its life against Saracens, Mongols, and Turks in a desperate struggle to hang on to a traditional way of life. Conservatism—even a certain fixism in religious thought and external patterns—was an understandable consequent. And it was able to persist because the West left relatively untouched intellectually the vast majority of the Orthodox faithful. But events in our own times have drastically changed the scene. All the traditional areas of Byzantine influence have been shaken by political and social upheavals—particularly the Russian Revolution of 1917—which have scattered Orthodox faithful by the thousands throughout the world. Meanwhile, the world rapidly has grown smaller; and if this were not enough, the grim fact of modern warfare has shocked all mankind into an awareness of the complex challenges of the twentieth century. The relative seclusion of Orthodoxy under the old regimes, whether Slav or Greek, has suddenly been supplanted by a day-by-day confrontation with a new environment. Here Orthodoxy finds its own imbalance. Orthodox theologians have acknowledged frankly that their traditionalism, which could flourish in an earlier age, does not of itself supply a sufficient range of concepts for the diversified dialogue of today.

The Classical Theological Issues

Although these two factors, difference of language and difference of theological approach, have been a long-standing obstacle to any real meeting of minds, in time there was clarity at least about what the major points of debate were. If for no other reason than that they have become the classical doctrinal issues, they should be recalled here.

The Orthodox Churches do not accept the Catholic teaching on the *filioque*, purgatory, the Immaculate Conception of Mary, and papal primacy. Catholicism teaches that, for valid confection of the Eucharist, the celebrant need pronounce only the words of consecration as used by Christ at the Last Supper. Orthodoxy requires in addition an invocation (*epiclēsis*) petitioning the action of the Holy Spirit. A vast literature on each of these points has accumulated over the years. Except for the question of papal primacy, these questions today are of less significance than might appear. Though the other four issues have loomed very large in theological debates, they have not been the radical, operative factors in causing the schism nor in its continuance; nor, I think, should their theological resolution be regarded as the major means for resolving the schism. For it would be a historical distortion to think that, first, certain doctrinal issues arose, leading successively to polemic controversy, mutual misunderstanding, deepening antipathy, and finally schism. It was rather the other way around. Non-doctrinal differences, some of which we have described, created a prior climate of misunderstanding and antipathy. In this increasingly hostile atmosphere, theology was all too often used on both sides, not as a quest for truth but as a prop for partisanship. It was a repetition of the sorry human tragedy of Arianism so accurately diagnosed by St. Basil. Few perceived better than he the doctrinal issues at stake, yet he repeatedly warned, paraphrasing St. Matthew, that the real cause of the division was that charity had grown cold (Matt. 24:12). Provincial pride, political ambition, commercial avarice, rivalry between sees, nurtured prejudice—in a word, manifold self-seeking—such is the breeding ground of schism.

This implies no denial of the pertinence of doctrinal issues to the present problem of reunion. They remain as factors of disunion and merit the best efforts of competent scholarship. But even the most objective, thorough research, if directed toward debate rather than discussion, toward dispute rather than dialogue between brothers in Christ, will accomplish little. The experience of nine hundred years makes this all too clear. The basic ailment has been self-interest. The main ingredient for its antidote is not doctrinal clarity but active charity. Pope John XXIII insisted on this frequently, and it receives daily confirmation in the fruits of the contemporary dialogue. It is a heartening thing to see it stated by prominent participants on both sides that none of these four classical issues stands today as a sign of basic doctrinal incompatibility. The ponderous proofs marshaled in the past are becoming a matter of academic rather than practical interest.

Papal Primacy

However, the fifth classical issue, papal primacy, cannot be handled so summarily. The primacy of the pope, according to Catholic teaching, involves power of rule over the universal Church and, under certain fixed conditions, infallibility in matters of faith and morals. There is little reason to review here the arguments pertinent to this claim. These have been presented often, and are easily available. In relation to the current stage of discussion, it seems more important to emphasize two things: First, the question of papal primacy is not an isolated theological issue, but must be viewed in relation to the whole problem of the nature and structure of the Church of Christ, the problem which more than any other engages the attention of Christian theologians today. Second, the whole problem has become more complex and obscure by reason of historical contingencies which properly are not theological, but have profoundly influenced theological attitudes. There is a need of sifting here if any approach to a solution is to be found.

We can make a beginning by asking what elements of agreement have a solid basis in the tradition of both East and West. It seems to me beyond question, from documentation of the early centuries, that in both East and West there was clear consciousness of the existence of a real authority to rule and to teach in the Church as a visible society. This authority had been conferred by Christ on the Apostles, and handed on to their successors, the bishops (Matt. 18:18; 28:19; John 20:21–23). There was, moreover, a consciousness of at least some degree of monarchical direction in the Church. The various sees differed in rank, and the highest rank, acknowledged universally, was that of Rome. Here, of course, Orthodox and Catholics read the documents differently. Catholics see a vindication of real primacy perpetuating the prerogatives conferred on Peter (Matt. 16:15–19). The Orthodox will acknowledge only a primacy of honor—a priority of respect, involving perhaps a certain organizational direction but no universal jurisdiction or doctrinal infallibility. The bishop of Rome was *primus inter pares*, first among his peers. If Catholicism stresses the "first," and Orthodoxy stresses the "peers," both do nonetheless acknowledge the "first," though they understand it differently.

This should be seen in the light of the unitarian ideal which captivated Christendom after Constantine's decree of liberation in 313. That this spiritual commonwealth should be monarchical in structure was taken for granted in both East and West. But here we must consider the history of each separately.

Factors of Divergence: The East

In the East, the unitarian ideal led to the advantage of the emperor. He came to be regarded as the anointed of God, and was likened to David and Solomon. He bore the charge of protecting the Church and fostering its works—and not rarely he interfered in the spiritual affairs pertaining to the hierarchy. But the emperor was not the only figure of the monarchical structure. As time passed, the power and prestige of the patriarchs of Constantinople grew, and they assumed the title of "ecumenical patriarch." More often than is perhaps realized, they resisted imperial encroachment into the ecclesiastical sphere. But the direction of external affairs of the Church fell in large part to the state authority. This was true of the East in general, for the Churches there were for the most part within the imperial frontiers, in areas long civilized and accustomed to law and order. In this Christian commonwealth, then, external affairs of the Church could be regarded as pertaining more to the Christian emperor and his regional functionaries than to the bishops of the various sees.

In the late sixteenth century, the idea of the "Third Rome" began to take hold in Russia. Constantinople, as the seat of both emperor and ecumenical patriarch, had long been regarded in the East as the center of Christendom; for not only was "old Rome" no longer the capital city, but it was in schism. But in 1453, Constantinople, the "new Rome," had fallen to the Turks. A little more than a century later, Moscow was the center of a vast empire, complete with a Czar (*Caesar*) and a patriarch. It seemed only logical that Moscow should now be regarded as the "Third Rome," the center of Christendom. The patriarchate lasted about a century, until its suppression by Peter the Great.[2] During that period one patriarch resisted the principle of subordination to the Czar —the Patriarch Nikhon, who likened himself to the sun and the Czar to the moon. But Nikhon went too far. In a trial presided over by the patriarchs of Alexandria and Antioch he was deposed, and the patriarch was declared subordinate to the Czar. The same principle generally prevailed in the autocephalous national churches of Byzantine rite.

The Classic Theory and the Sobornost

Yet, in the classic Orthodox teaching on the Church, the consciousness of the power of "binding and loosing" (Matt. 18:17) committed to the bishops is clearly expressed. It embraces both jurisdictional and doctrinal authority, manifested authentically in ecumenical councils. Conciliar decrees are of themselves infallible, but acceptance by the whole Church is an external norm of the council's ecumenicity.

The difficulty with this theory was that Orthodoxy maintained that as long as there was schism between East and West, an ecumenical council could not take place. Hence there was no ultimate, infallible organ of doctrine. This need contributed to the formulation of the *sobornost* theory, pro-

[2] This suppression of the patriarchate lasted until a patriarch was elected at the synod of Moscow after the Revolution of 1917.

posed in the middle of the last century by the great Russian lay theologian Alexis Khomiakov, and elaborated by Sergius Bulgakov (d. 1944). *Sobornost* is weakly translated by "community" or "togetherness"; but the idea is that the ultimate repository of infallibility is the community of all the faithful, the Mystical Body of Christ. The bishops, even in council, act only as witnesses to the faith of their flocks, and their decrees are the infallible voice of the teaching Church only insofar as they are accepted by the faithful at large. In the teaching of P. Florovsky, the bishop is controlled by his flock and can be deposed by them.

The *sobornost* theory is generally held by Slavic Orthodox theologians, and is gaining wide acceptance among the Greeks, among whom the classic theory prevailed until around the turn of the last century. But there are still those who feel that the *sobornost* belies Byzantine tradition by making the Church a loosely knit democracy, deprived of authority and of a truly discernible organ of infallibility.

Factors of Divergence: The West

In the West, historical circumstances caused a quite different development, although, during roughly the first millennium, the situation had much in common with that in the East. The unitarian idea was strong—to the extent that, as we have seen, when the West felt it had been deserted by the emperor, Pope Leo filled the vacancy by crowning Charlemagne. There was also, of course, a clear awareness of the jurisdictional power of local bishops, and of their power to pronounce authoritatively and infallibly for the Church universal when they acted as a body, *collegialiter*.

As regards papal primacy, Catholic scholars maintain that documentary evidence shows that the primacy in its essentials was both claimed and exercised by popes during this period. But no one can claim that the see of Rome possessed then the degree of influence and power which it was to acquire in later centuries. Though there is evidence that the popes maintained a right of sanction even when the bishops acted *collegialiter*, local bishops had greater autonomy in the administration of their own dioceses, and there was less centralization of jurisdiction in the Roman jurisdiction. The change begins to occur with the beginning of the second millennium. This point is significant, and some of the major factors of the change should be recalled here.

First, Christendom in the West, unlike the Eastern church, had a task both of converting and of civilizing. In the vast barbarian regions to the north there was but little tradition of established law and order, and scarcely literacy, let alone education. The machinery of imperial administration could not keep pace, and the organization of society fell in large part to the clergy—often the only ones in a whole region with any education. This association with external affairs inevitably had an effect on the jurisdictional position of Rome, the hub of what was at times the only consistently functioning administrative organization in the West.

Second, Constantinople seemed far away from Spain, Gaul, or Britain, but Rome retained at least something of the magic of her name even for the hordes who had battled against her. Moreover, the Eastern capital was often forced by its own troubles to leave the Western areas to shift for themselves. When Constantinople fell to the Turks, it was still Rome, now the seat of the new line of Western emperors, which was thought of as the center of things in the West.

Third, the pope became temporal ruler of the Papal States, an area comprising most of central Italy. The Papal States and their army are gone, but the court ceremonial remains as a symbol of centralization of ecclesiastical jurisdiction.

Fourth, the Protestant Reformation of the sixteenth century attacked not only papal primacy but also the very notion of the Church as a visible society with juridical authority. The Catholic response resulted in new emphasis on centralized jurisdiction in the structure of the Church.

Fifth, the First Vatican Council, after defining the universal jurisdiction and infallibility of the pope, broke up before the rest of the agenda concerning the Church, which were to deal with the episcopacy and the laity, could be treated. Consequently the acts of the Council give a topheavy impression of the nature and structure of the Church. Catholic defense against the attacks on the defined papal prerogatives gave added stress to that impression both within and without the Catholic fold. Most significant, perhaps, was the diminished awareness of the collegial function of the bishops. The local bishop was seen by some as something like a viceroy: simply a local extension of the plenitude of jurisdiction held by the Supreme Pontiff. Prior to the convocation of Vatican II, some Catholics even felt that the definitions of Vatican I had rendered superfluous any subsequent ecumenical councils. In this whole framework the laity could too easily be thought of as a passive element whose function was merely to listen and obey, and "the Church" too often connoted simply officialdom—the clergy in its various grades.

Divergences between West and East

It is in this period that the divergent developments in East and West reach their climax. Ecumenically, the profound significance of this phenomenon lies in this: Just at the period when this topheavy conception of the structure of Roman Catholicism was most conspicuous (the late nineteenth and early twentieth centuries) the *sobornost* theory was gaining wide acceptance in both Slav and Greek Orthodoxy. Nothing could have served to highlight more starkly the differences wrought by this evolving divergence, and to obscure the elements which both traditions held in common. To Catholic eyes it could appear that in Orthodoxy the traditional office of the hierarchy as leaders and teachers of the faithful had been supplanted by a vague, inarticulate democracy. To the Orthodox, Catholicism could seem an awesome juridical juggernaut, a totalitarianism crushing all freedom and initiative. Unfortunately, there were spokesmen on both sides who lent credibility to these distortions.

But, even when the exaggerated distortions are taken into account, there remains a divergence that is real. The next step, then, I believe, is to recognize how greatly this divergence has been fashioned by the widely disparate *historical* contingencies we have just discussed, transient factors which, of themselves, are quite extrinsic to the perennial factors of genuine theological tradition.

This is no denial of a true development of Christian doctrine, of insights which deepen with time. Such development has place particularly, perhaps, in the dogmas concerning the Church, an institution existing in time, even to the consummation of the world. But time can cast shadow as well as light. One such shadow can be thrown by an obscurantist tendency to view the current status quo, with all its prevalent emphases and varied historical accretions, as an adequate and accurate reflection of traditional doctrine as such.

This calls for a clearing of the air by a deeper self-knowledge as a prerequisite for mutual understanding. A Catholic, for example, who hears an Orthodox maintain that infallibility rests with the mass of the faithful, may see only an inversion of proper order, a threat to his belief in infallibility as a prerogative of the hierarchy. But, before he condemns, he should recall from his own tradition the practical theological implications of the dictum: *Vox populi vox Dei* (The voice of the people is the voice of God).[3]

Similarly, an Orthodox may feel that the universal jurisdiction centered in the Bishop of Rome cannot be reconciled with the collegial and individual authority of the bishops. But some clarity may be gained by viewing the problem ac-

[3] A recent example of this is the definition of the doctrine of the Assumption of the Virgin Mary. Catholic bishops were asked before the definition to give not only their own theological opinion on the doctrine, but also the *sensus fidelium*, the "mind of the faithful" in their own dioceses.

cording to the Orthodox principle of harmony, as it was applied in reference to the jurisdiction in ecclesiastical matters exercised by the emperors.[4] The above two examples do not constitute any "proofs" one way or the other. They are simply instances of an approach whereby the apparently "alien" can be seen in a more familiar light.

Divergence Yielding to Convergence

The divergence, however, has passed its climax and is giving place to a marked convergence. This could be documented by countless books and articles by Orthodox and Catholic bishops and theologians. But the point can be made more briefly and authoritatively by juxtaposing certain aspects of the 1962 Pan-Orthodox Synod at Rhodes and the current Vatican Council.

In reading the agenda proposed for consideration at Rhodes, one is struck by the stress on juridical matters and uniformity. Suggested recodification of Church laws would treat matters such as: uniformity of procedure in ecclesiastical tribunals; method of electing primates and bishops in closer conformity to earlier canons; reorganization of administrative distinctions (patriarchs, metropolitans, and so forth); uniform legislation on marriage impediments; subordination of training of clergy to immediate surveillance of the Church. Also suggested were the publication of a unique Orthodox profession of faith and of uniform liturgical texts, and discussion on the infallibility proper to ecumenical councils.

The general principles on the liturgy passed by Vatican Council II contain much that has direct bearing on the nature of the Church. As Christ is the basic, first-born sacra-

[4] It should be noted, however, that the imperial power was less legislative (except in the hands of some high-handed emperors) than executive and judicial. Decrees of an ecumenical council became part of imperial law, and the emperor was to see to their enforcement. This arrangement was in effect long before the schism, and cannot be regarded as exclusively Eastern.

ment, so the whole Church is born of Him as a sacrament to carry on His redemptive work. This it does primarily through the liturgy, "always, as with Christ Himself, in an incarnate and sacramental structure." A significant indication of decentralization is the stipulation that the Holy See no longer reserves to itself exclusive judgment on liturgical changes, but commits matters of local adaptation to regional episcopal synods. In this connection, wider use of the vernacular receives particular mention. The over-all emphasis is on the laity, as participants in corporate worship and as objects of sanctification through the liturgy.

Where now the easy, sweeping generalizations contrasting Orient and Occident? What has become of that mystic East with head in the clouds and a reluctant foot on earth? What has happened to the practical West with an eye only for juridical order and external efficiency? If they ever did exist, the most authoritative assemblies of Orthodoxy and Catholicism have made it clear that they exist no more. But if we wish nonetheless to retain these easy generalizations, then Rhodes has spoken to the West, and Vatican II has spoken to the East.

What I have said thus far does not add up to a vindication of papal prerogatives. It has been an attempt to climb to the top of the dividing wall for a look in both directions to see both sides as we really are. From this vantage point, I hope we have seen that external, juridical uniformity—even with a real kind of centralization—is not alien to authentic Orthodox tradition. Perhaps we have also seen that authentic Catholic tradition excludes neither the collegial function of the bishops nor a conception of the Church as a dynamic, interior union of all its members in a mysterious, sacramental reality. If we can catch this panorama, then the top of the wall seems at least a favorable spot—possibly the only profitable spot—for Orthodox and Catholic to sit down and discuss the primacy, even though both know the wall is still there. But this done, much will have been gained.

A final word to Catholics, for I write as a Catholic. It is not enough for us merely to climb the wall; we must climb it as Christians, in penance and humility. Earlier, I related how Catholics of the West contributed to the origin and continuance of the schism. If we cannot bring ourselves to acknowledge these offenses, our converse with our Orthodox brothers will lack the ring of sincerity. It is gratifying to see this point made publicly and forcefully by Cardinal Cushing of Boston. Speaking of the need to seek forgiveness, he listed our neglect to send aid against the Moslems, the pride and ruthlessness of the Crusaders, the sack of Constantinople, the assumption that Latin customs and outlooks were superior, and the hostile spirit of not a few Western controversialists—even in comparatively recent times.

We come back to the basic thing, charity in Christ. If the schism occurred because our charity grew cold, it cannot be mended without sincere mutual love and esteem. Within the span of our own memories, this has already accomplished the apparently impossible. But it demands more than that we meet each other halfway. We must be ready to go the extra mile (Matt. 5:41).

Chapter XIV

CONCLUDING REFLECTIONS

by

Daniel J. O'Hanlon

Now that we have ranged over the whole field of contemporary Catholic theological work and seen its variety and multiplicity, it is time to stand back and try to acquire some perspective. What common patterns emerge from all this diversity? What general characteristics are discernible in all the different areas of Catholic theology as it confronts the future?

The *first* of the traits which even a casual observer cannot help noticing in Catholic theology today is a sense of *movement*, which is another name for a sense of *history*. This sense of movement is closely allied to the growing awareness of theology's ecclesial dimension. If theology is a function of the life of the Church, and if the Church is a historical community, vivified by the indwelling presence of her risen Lord and pressing forward toward the day of His final manifestation, living "between the times" of Christ's first and final coming, then theology quite naturally catches this sense of movement which is inseparable from the life of the Church.

Indeed, the progress which is going on in theological understanding is itself one aspect of the larger forward movement which is the life of the Church. In the nineteenth century and the first part of the twentieth, Catholic theologians, with a few exceptions such as Moehler and Newman, took a dim view of development and movement. It was perfectly all right for the Church to grow in width and breadth by drawing more men into her orbit; in fact, missionary expansion was one of the glories of Christianity in the last century. But growth in depth was another matter. To allow or encourage such movement seemed to some like calling into doubt the permanent validity of Christian truth. Catholic theologians see more clearly today that it is their task not only to preserve the deposit of faith undamaged and make it available to more and more people, but to enrich the Church with clearer and deeper and fuller insights into the inexhaustible object of Christian faith and to purify that faith of merely human accretions.

This sense of movement and history is closely allied to the *second* characteristic of contemporary Catholic theology, a strong sense of *confidence*. No one will move very far or very fast into uncharted areas unless armed with the assurance that the path ahead is safe. If the theologian feels that movement into unexplored areas is not part of his task, if he conceives his work as mere repetition of what has already been said, any movement or development will be regarded with distrust. The only approved movements will be those of marking time, or of circling around or crisscrossing a well-defined and clearly charted area. But mere repetitious crisscrossing or marking time are not characteristic of Catholic theology today. One senses among theologians a confidence that the spirit which is leading them beyond their present understanding is the Holy Spirit Himself, who "will teach you all the truth" and "the things that are to come he will declare to you" (John 16:13). This sense of confidence is heightened by the restoration of the mystery of the Resurrection to the center of Christian life and theology. Not so long ago, the Resurrection figured very insignificantly in the theological curriculum. Apart from the time given to it in the apologetics course, where it was presented as a proof of Christ's claims about Himself, the Resurrection was almost completely absent from the normal theology curriculum. That is no longer true. It is increasingly evident to theologians that the Resurrection is far more than a clinching argument to prove that Christianity is true; it is itself the central mystery of Christianity. This rediscovery of the Resurrection, if we may give it so bold a name, carries with it a spirit of confident assurance which spills over into every area of Christian life, not the least of which is theology itself.

The cautious theologian may be tempted to regard this exuberant confidence with suspicion. What is the difference between this bold assurance and the outdated optimism of the nineteenth-century theological liberal? The first response which must be made to this question is that the progress myth would have been inconceivable apart from the Christian soil out of which it grew. Modern progress myths, whether Hegelian, Darwinian, Marxist, or other, are all distortions of the Christian sense of history. Had Christians not allowed their own heritage to go by default and tried to escape into a non-historical system of timeless truths, falsely labeled as Christianity, then the "Communist" revolution might have been a thoroughly Christian thing.

Yet there is something inherent in the mood of the nineteenth-century theological liberal about which a Christian has a right to feel uneasy. He was tempted to feel that man would soon master the whole of theology with clear and distinct ideas. Is not the confidence of the Catholic theologian today just another form of that distortion? The simple answer to such misgivings is that the spirit of rationalism and the spirit of Catholic theology today are poles apart, and the element which makes the difference is a sense of *mystery*, the *third* trait of Catholic theology today. It is not out of any conviction that man is about to write the final sentence in the book of theology that the theologian moves ahead confidently in his work; indeed, precisely the opposite is true. He is driven on by an awareness of his inadequacy, and of the inexhaustibility of God's manifestation in Christ. Even in the field of secular inquiry, men are drawn to further investigation by this sense of mystery. The physicist, for instance, who tries to understand the subatomic world, falls far short of complete intellectual satisfaction. The more he comes to know about the world of matter, the more he realizes that his knowledge is a mere fraction of what remains to be learned. This experience is compounded for the theologian, since he sets out to understand nothing less than God Himself and His ways with man. Whatever confidence, then, is felt by the theologian stems from his assurance that the risen Lord, to whom he has committed his life and work, is master of that infinite uncharted area beyond the frontiers of his present fragmentary understanding, and that his tentative explorations into the Christian mysteries are guided by the Holy Spirit, whose direction is promised to individual Christians. Their theologizing, in turn, is safeguarded by the presence of the same Spirit in the community in which they live and work, the Church.

Confident movement forward, then, is a characteristic trait of contemporary Catholic theology. Paradoxically, however, this forward movement is accompanied by an equally vigorous movement backward, by a *return to the sources,* which is the *fourth* characteristic of Catholic theology today. Perhaps it would be more accurate to speak of reaching backward rather than of moving backward, since there is nothing of retrogression or romantic primitivism about current theology. The word which expresses it best is renewal. It is a *re*newal, because it is a return to and a restoration of something out of the past; but it is also a re*newal,* because these decisive events of the past are made to live afresh today. The primary source is the Bible, the inspired record of God's intervention in human history, and the place where these decisive events are really made new and altogether contemporary is in the liturgy, whose very essence is the making new again of the central Christian mysteries. It is no accident that the pope who said that the work of the Second Vatican Council is really directed entirely toward giving back to the face of the Church of Jesus the splendor and the pure and simple lines of its birth is the same pope who chose the liturgy as the first subject for the Council's deliberations.

The *fifth* characteristic of contemporary Catholic theology, which also is reflected in the work of the Council, is a *widening of horizons*. During the Middle Ages, practically all the "known world" was Christian, and the problem of relating Christianity to the non-Christian world was practically nonexistent. The breakdown of medieval unity was followed by successive hardening of the siege mentality—first Catholics throwing up protective walls against Protestants, then Protestants and Catholics together, weakened by their quarrels and divisions, finding themselves increasingly isolated from the rest of the world. But the fantastic development of communications within recent decades makes ghetto life an utter impossibility. Catholic theology is beginning to take seriously its claim that Christianity is for *all* men, and it is trying to see more clearly what relation Catholic theology bears to other Christian theologies, to modern technology, to the new cultures where Christians are still a tiny fraction of the population. It is a question of discovering how all the positive values of every religion, science, and culture find a place in Catholic Christianity, which more than ever before experiences the need of being truly catholic. Nothing which is conceived in any terms smaller than the whole human family has any real future in the world which is now taking shape.

This expansive spirit also finds expression in the movement away from religious individualism toward a sense of *community*, which is the *sixth* feature of Catholic theology today. The most decisive place where this is happening is in the life of worship. The theology of worship and worship itself are becoming more and more consciously communal. One development, which is both a sign of the movement toward worship as a community and a means of making that community more real, is the increase in the use of the vernacular in worship. Without communication, community is impossible, and without the use of a language understood by the participants, meaningful communication is inconceivable. The more extensive use of the vernacular in public worship, accepted in principle by the Second Vatican Council, has grown out of a recovered awareness that Christians are the people of God, and that they go to Him not merely as separate individuals but also as a community.

This sense of community is beginning to show in the teaching of theology. Very few institutions responsible for theological education are unaffected by the trend toward education through group dynamics. The increase of small seminars and discussion groups is evidence that theology is thought to be learned best when ideas are shared and clarified by free give and take in a group. Theology faculties too are forced willy-nilly to work as a team. The vast flood of information and research in all branches of theology is beyond the physical powers of any single man, no matter how intelligent or robust, so that a theology faculty today which does not work together as a team is doomed to mediocrity or worse.

The growth of community is also a striking feature of apostolic work in the Church. Such developments as the Cursillo movement and the specialized movements of Catholic Action derive their effectiveness, in large part, from their commitment to working together as a team.

A *seventh* tendency of Catholic theology in our time is the return to real *theologizing,* as contrasted with mere learning or talking *about* theology. This fact is so closely related to what has already been said about the sense of movement and confidence, the return to the sources, and the widening of horizons, that little more is needed than to advert to it here. By theologizing, we mean actually carrying on the work of theology, i.e., consciously employing a method which is understood and making use of materials and tools in a fresh way. Theologizing is still done somewhat hesitantly and tentatively in America, but as theologians come to a fuller possession of the sources, a clearer consciousness of theological method, and a real facility in handling the tools of the trade, we may expect greater assurance and livelier creativity from American theologians to match the lead given by Europeans like Rahner, Congar, and Küng.

An *eighth* feature of contemporary Catholic theology is the shift of emphasis from proof to *understanding*. More and more the theologian conceives his task as one of grasping more adequately the meaning of what is given to him in Christian faith. He is less concerned with apologetics and defense and more absorbed in positive exposition of the data of revelation. Frank Sheed, the eminent lay theologian who has given hundreds, perhaps thousands of street-corner lectures on theology, tells us that, even from the viewpoint of apologetics, nothing turns out to be so effective as a simple exposition of what it *means* to say, for instance, that God exists. Apologetic effectiveness is a less than adequate reason for adopting a certain theological method; yet, theologians who for better reasons have turned their attention more to understanding than to proof may be pleased to know that this approach in no way weakens the apologetic usefulness of their work.

The *ninth* of the features which stand out as we survey the work of Catholic theology in the sixties is a movement away from fragmenting analysis toward *unifying synthesis*. This does not mean that a synthesis is now completely ripe; indeed, it is more accurate to speak of the present period of theology as one of *quaestiones disputatae* rather than of *summae theologicae*. Still, the movement is toward synthesis, and if the promise which is given by what we now see developing is fulfilled, we may look forward to a theological synthesis richer than anything yet seen in the two millennia of Christian history. History takes many strange and unpredictable turns, but I doubt whether anyone who knows the history of Christian theology and who has been watching what is happening in the Catholic Church and in Catholic theology would consider this an extravagant hope.

SUGGESTED READING

Each of the chapters of this book is designed to give an introduction to a specific phase and area of Christian theology. These essays are designed to provide the reader with enough background to enable him to do some further reading in each of the areas of theology discussed. The following reading lists, then, are brief, yet broad enough in scope to enable the reader to realize and understand the broad movements of theology in our day.

Chapter I: Catholic Theology: A Brief History

1. Joseph Ratzinger, "The Changeable and the Unchangeable in Theology." *Theology Digest*, September 1962, pp. 71–76.
2. Piet Fransen, "Three Ways of Dogmatic Thought." *Cross Currents*, September 1963, pp. 129–48.
3. Charles Davis, "The Danger of Irrelevance" in *Theology for Today*. New York: Sheed & Ward, 1962, pp. 13–26.
4. J. H. Nicolas, "One Theology or Many?" *Theology Digest*, Fall 1962, pp. 209–14.
5. Philip Hughes, *The Church in Crisis*. Garden City, New York: Doubleday & Company, 1961.

Chapter II: Modern Trends in Theological Method

1. M. D. Chenu, *Is Theology a Science?* Vol. II of Twentieth Century Encyclopedia of Catholicism, H. Daniel-Rops, ed. New York: Hawthorne Books, 1959 ff.
2. Michael Brown, "The Method of Theology." *The American Ecclesiastical Review*, December 1954, pp. 362–75.

3. Peter de Letter, "Trends and Fashions in Theology." *Clergy Monthly*, October 1959, pp. 298–308.
4. E. Quinn, "Renewal of Theology." *The Downside Review*, October 1956, pp. 289–301.
5. Ignatius O'Brien, "Nature and Method of Sacred Theology." *Australasian Catholic Record*, January 1958, pp. 74–81.

Chapter III: Rediscovery of the Bible

1. Alexander Jones, *Unless Some Man Show Me*. New York: Sheed & Ward, 1960 (Stagbooks), Chapters 4–6.
2. H. Daniel-Rops, *What Is the Bible?* New York: Hawthorne Books, 1958.
3. W. F. Albright, *From the Stone Age to Christianity*. Garden City, New York: Doubleday & Company, 1957, Anchor.
4. John L. McKenzie, *The Two-Edged Sword*. Milwaukee: Bruce Publishing Co., 1956.
5. Pius XII, "Divino Afflante Spiritu", *Biblical Studies*. London: Catholic Truth Society, 1943. (Available in several editions.)

Chapter IV: Covenant in the Ancient World

1. Joshua 24; Exodus 24; Deuteronomy 6:10–19.
2. C. Charlier, "The Bible's Converging Themes," in *A Christian Approach to the Bible*. Westminster, Md.: The Newman Press, 1958, pp. 161–84.
3. George Mendenhall, *Law and Covenant in Israel in the Ancient Near East*. Pittsburgh: Biblical Colloquium, 1955.
4. John Bright, *A History of Israel*. Philadelphia: Westminster Press, 1959, pp. 132–42.
5. G. Ernest Wright, *The Old Testament Against Its Environment*. Naperville, Ill.: Allenson, 1955, pp. 54–76.

Chapter V: Contemporary Liturgical Revival

1. H. A. Reinhold, *The Dynamics of the Liturgy*. New York: The Macmillan Company, 1961.
2. Charles Davis, *Liturgy and Doctrine*. New York: Sheed & Ward, 1961.

3. Cypriano Vagaggini, *The Theological Dimensions of the Liturgy*. Collegeville, Minn.: Liturgical Press, 1959.
4. J. A. Jungmann, *The Early Liturgy to the Time of Gregory the Great*. Notre Dame, Ind.: University of Notre Dame Press, 1959.
5. *Constitution on the Sacred Liturgy*, decree of Vatican II. London: Catholic Truth Society, 1964.

Chapter VI: The Layman in the Church

1. Yves Congar, *Lay People in the Church*. Westminster, Md.: The Newman Press, 1957.
2. Daniel J. Callahan, *The Mind of the Catholic Layman*. New York: Charles Scribner's Sons, 1963.
3. James O'Gara, *Layman in the Church*. New York: Herder & Herder, 1963.
4. I. Sangerle, "The Laity in the Parish" in *The Parish: From Theology to Practice*, Hugo Rahner, ed. Westminster, Md.: The Newman Press, 1958, pp. 84–94.
5. E. H. Schillebeeckx, *The Layman in the Church, and Other Essays*. Staten Island, N.Y.: Alha House, St. Paul Publications, 1963.

Chapter VII: Salvation–A Sacramental Encounter

1. E. H. Schillebeeckx, *Christ The Sacrament of the Encounter with God*. New York: Sheed & Ward, 1963.
2. Karl Rahner, *The Church and the Sacraments*. New York: Herder & Herder, 1963.
3. A. M. Roguet, "What Is a Sacrament?" in *Christ Acts through the Sacraments*. Collegeville, Minn.: Liturgical Press, 1958, pp. 11–39.
4. M. O'Connell, "The Sacraments in Theology." *Thought*, Spring 1961, pp. 40–58.
5. Henri de Lubac, *The Splendour of the Church*. New York: Sheed & Ward, 1956, Chapters 1 and 6.

Chapter VIII: Authority in the Church

1. Romano Guardini, *Power and Responsibility*. Chicago: Henry Regnery Co., 1961.

2. John M. Todd, ed., *Problems of Authority*. Baltimore: Helicon Press, 1962.
3. Karl Rahner, *Free Speech in the Church*. New York: Sheed & Ward, 1960.
4. Hans Küng, "The Church and Freedom." *The Commonweal*, June 21, 1963, pp. 343–53.
5. P. A. Liégé, *The Historical and Mystical Christ*, A. M. Henry, ed. Chicago: Fides, 1955, Vol. 5, Chapter 5, pp. 336–69.

Chapter IX: New Approaches to Moral Theology

1. Gérard Gilleman, *The Primacy of Charity in Moral Theology*. Westminster, Md.: The Newman Press, 1959.
2. Fritz Tillmann, *The Master Calls*. Baltimore: Helicon Press, 1961.
3. Bernhard Häring, *The Law of Christ*. Westminster, Md.: The Newman Press, 1961.
4. Gustave Ermecke, "Catholic Moral Theology Today." *Theology Digest*, Vol. 2, 1954, pp. 19–22.
5. Gérard Gilleman, "Moral Theology and Charity." *Theology Digest*, Vol. 2, 1954, pp. 13–18.

Chapter X: American Catholic Theories of Church-State Relations

1. John Courtney Murray, "Freedom of Religion." *Theological Studies*, June 1945, pp. 229–86.
2. Francis J. Connell, "The Theory of the 'Lay State.'" *The American Ecclesiastical Review*, July 1951, pp. 7–18.
3. Donald Wolf, "The Unitary Theory of Church-State Relations." *A Journal of Church and State*, May 1962, pp. 47–65.
4. John Courtney Murray, *We Hold These Truths*. New York: Sheed & Ward, 1960.
5. Sidney Z. Ehler, *Twenty Centuries of Church and State*. Westminster, Md.: The Newman Press, 1957.

Chapter XI: The Social Mission of Christianity

1. E. E. Y. Hales, *The Catholic Church in the Modern World*. Garden City, New York: Doubleday & Company, 1960; Preface, Chapters 16 and 23.

2. John F. Cronin, *The Catholic as Citizen.* Baltimore: Helicon Press, 1963.
3. Jacques Maritain, *Scholasticism and Politics.* Garden City, New York: Doubleday & Company, 1960, Chapter 9.
4. James V. Schall, "The Responsibility of Christians to the World." *Social Order*, October 1962, pp. 367–75.
5. John XXIII, *Mater et Magistra* and *Pacem in Terris.* Several editions.

Chapter XII: The Catholic Church and Protestant Christianity

1. Robert McAfee Brown, "The Issues Which Divide Us," Chapter III of *American Catholics: A Protestant-Jewish View*, Philip Scharper, ed. New York: Sheed & Ward, 1959.
2. Bernard Leeming, *The Churches and the Church.* Westminster, Md.: The Newman Press, 1960.
3. Louis Bouyer, *The Spirit and Forms of Protestantism.* New York: William Collins Sons & Co., Ltd., 1963.
4. D. J. Callahan, *Christianity Divided.* New York: Sheed & Ward, 1961.
5. Roger Schutz, "Our Serene Hope." *Cross Currents*, Spring 1962, pp. 239–43.

Chapter XIII: The Catholic Church and Orthodox Christianity

1. Yves Congar, *After Nine Hundred Years.* New York: Fordham University Press, 1959.
2. Francis Dvornik, *The Idea of Apostolicity in Byzantium.* Cambridge, Mass.: Harvard University Press, 1958.
3. J. Meyendorff, "Orthodoxy and the Council." *Cross Currents*, Spring 1962, pp. 212–18.
4. J. Gill, *The Council of Florence.* London: Cambridge University Press, 1959.
5. S. Runciman, *The Eastern Schism.* New York: Oxford University Press, 1955.

Chapter XIV: Concluding Reflections

1. Hugo Rahner et al., *The Church, Readings in Theology.* New York, P. J. Kennedy, 1963.

2. Bernhard Häring, *The Johannine Council.* New York: Herder & Herder, 1963.
3. Robert Kaiser, *Pope, Council, and World.* New York: The Macmillan Company, 1963.
4. Leonard Swidler, *Dialogue for Reunion.* New York: Herder & Herder, 1962.
5. Karl Rahner, *The Christian Commitment.* New York: Sheed & Ward, 1963.

GENERAL SUPPLEMENTARY SOURCES

In addition to the books and articles mentioned after the chapters, the following three sources will provide much information on current theology:

1. *Theology Digest,* 1015 Central, Kansas City, Missouri 64105. This is a digest of major articles published throughout the world. Several of these yearly collections have been bound into paperback form.
2. *Cross Currents,* 103 van Houten Fields, West Nyack, New York. This is a quarterly journal containing many important articles in current theology.
3. *The Twentieth Century Encyclopedia of Catholicism,* H. Daniel-Rops, ed. New York: Hawthorne Books, 1959 ff.

Each volume is written in easy to read style and gives a good summary of current theological problems as well as the history of theology.

THE AUTHORS

Rev. Robert H. Dailey, S.J.: Professor of Moral and Pastoral Theology, Alma College. J.C.D. in Canon Law, Gregorian University. Author of *The Primary Effects of the Union "Pleno Jure" of Parishes with Religious Communities*. Published in *Theological Studies, University of Detroit Law Journal, Bulletin of the Guild of Catholic Psychiatrists*. Contributor to *The New Catholic Encyclopedia.*

Rev. John E. Huesman, S.J.: Professor of Old Testament, Alma College. Ph.D. in Scripture, Johns Hopkins, S.S.L. in Scripture, Pontifical Biblical Institute. Author of a commentary on *Isaia* (2 vols.), *A Commentary on the Book of Exodus, A Commentary on the Book of Judges*. Published in *Biblica, Perspectives, Worship, Bible, Life and Worship*. Contributor to *The New Catholic Encyclopedia.*

Rev. James A. Mara, S.J.: Professor of Dogmatic Theology, Alma College. S.T.L. in Theology, Weston College.

Rev. Frank Norris, S.S.: Professor of Dogmatic Theology and Religious Education, St. Patrick's Seminary. S.T.D. in Theology, Angelicum. Author of *God's Own People: An Introductory Study of the Church*. Regular contributor to *Worship*. Published in liturgical and catechetical journals. Contributor to *The New Catholic Encyclopedia.*

Rev. Terrence R. O'Connor, S.J.: Professor of Patrology and Liturgy, Alma College. S.T.D. in Theology, Gregorian University. Author of *The "Communio" as Revealed in the Writings of St. Basil the Great*. Published in *Theological Studies, Catholic Mind, Review for Religious.*

Rev. Daniel J. O'Hanlon, S.J.: Professor of Fundamental Theology, Alma College. Ph.D. in Theology, University of Tübingen and Gregorian University. Co-editor (with Hans Küng and Yves Congar) of *Council Speeches of Vatican II*. Visiting Professor at Stanford University. Co-editor of *Christianity Divided*. Published in *Theological Studies, Cross Currents, America, Com-*

monweal, Worship. Associate Editor of *America* for the Second Vatican Council.

Rev. Paul Palmer, S.J.: Professor of Sacramental Theology, Woodstock College. S.T.D. in Theology, Woodstock College. Author of *Sacraments and Worship, Sacraments and Forgiveness, Sacraments of Healing and Vocation, Mary in the Documents of the Church, Mary and Modern Man*. Published in *Theological Studies, Collier's*. Contributor to *Junior Catholic Encyclopedia, Encyclopædia Britannica, The New Catholic Encyclopedia*.

Rev. Joseph Powers, S.J.: Professor of Sacramental Theology, Alma College. S.T.D. in Theology, Gregorian University. Author of *Symbolic-Instrumental Causality of the Sacraments in the Theology of E. H. Schillebeeckx, O.P.*

Rev. James V. Schall, S.J.: Ph.D. in Political Theory, Georgetown University. Co-author of *American Society and Politics*. Published in *Social Order, Commonweal, The Thomist, New Scholasticism, America, The Month, Thought, Catholic World, Modern Age, Review of Politics, Cithara, The American Ecclesiastical Review, World Justice*. Contributor to *The New Catholic Encyclopedia*.

Rev. Joseph Wall, S.J.: Professor of Dogmatic and Ascetical Theology, Alma College. S.T.D. in Theology, Gregorian University. Author of *The Providence of God in the Letters of St. Ignatius*. Contributor to *The New Catholic Encyclopedia*.

Rev. Donald Wolf, S.J.: Ph.D. in Political Theory, Georgetown University. Co-author of *American Society and Politics*. Published in *America, Social Order, The Catholic Educator, Cithara, A Journal of Church and State, The Review of Politics*. Contributor to *The New Catholic Encyclopedia*.

Rev. John H. Wright, S.J.: Professor of Dogmatic Theology, Alma College. S.T.D. in Theology, Gregorian University. Author of *The Order of the Universe in the Theology of St. Thomas Aquinas*. Published in *Gregorianum, The Way*. Contributor to *The New Catholic Encyclopedia*.

Rev. Albert J. Zabala, S.J.: Professor of Old and New Testament Studies and Chairman of the Department of Theology, University of San Francisco. S.T.D. in Theology, Catholic University of Paris.

THE AUTHORS

[illegible]

[illegible]

[illegible] of Sacramento. [illegible]

[illegible]

[illegible]

[illegible]

[illegible]

[illegible]